PRAISE FOR UNRAV

BY SONDRA U......

M000087488

Book 1 ROBBED-Innocence Stolen
Book 2 RIPPED-Lies Exposed
Book 3 RESTORED-Truth Unfolds

A triumphant story based on shocking true events, on how an innocent child, a determined woman, and a Christian counselor, journey for the truth to overcome unimaginable abuse. **Couldn't put the books down**. ~*M.J. Turner, Retired Christian Counselor*

A captivating novel based on actual events. Determined and combating evil with faith-based principles, confrontations ignite, and spiritual weapons discharge, leading to victory! A story of sexual addiction that exposes the hidden lies of many. **Offers hope and restoration**. ~*Jean Christine*

When all feels lost, discover hope, healing, and redemption—**a page-turner**. ~*Genevra Bonati, Author of series: Forgiven and Free: A Halted Heart*

The author of Unraveled-Rewoven pens an excellent trilogy that unmasks the inconceivable abuse and anguish of the brokenhearted. A novel based on true events—a faith-igniting story of perseverance and victory **leaving your eyes wide-open.** ~*Catherine Scholz M.Ed., M.S., LPC*

This riveting novel takes you into the depths of an evil realm swirling with lies, abuse, and sheer terror. Yet faith rises-and light battles against the darkness, finding perseverance, promises, and power. **Based on a true story—A MUST READ. ~***Anna Wise, Author of Mercy Me www.Anna-Wise.com*

As a retired sergeant major, a police officer, and a public servant, I have seen abuse, violence, and dysfunction on many levels. These novels, inspired by real events, expose subjects that need to be brought to the light while showing healing and redemption that come through faith. A spiritual story of perseverance and purpose. **Eye-opening and captivating**. ~*R.L. Richards* SGM Ret

Unraveled–Rewoven is a trilogy inspired by real events. This story exposes a broken world of unthinkable abuse and trauma. Determined and combating evil with faith-based principles, a spiritual battle erupts, leading to victory! **A wonderful story of hope and restoration**. ~*Healing Heart Ministry, Inc.*

As a victor and overcomer of childhood abuse involving parental dysfunction and addiction, I was able to relate to this compelling trilogy. Unraveled-Rewoven exposes the silent violence of trauma. These books **offer hope, encouragement, and freedom** that comes by unlocking long-buried thoughts and fears. I would **highly recommend** these books. ~*Nicole Zurcher*

The Unraveled – Rewoven Trilogy is a **MUST READ**! In her debut novels, Sondra Umberger grips the reader with the style of a veteran author. Sondra takes us into the dark, dark world where Satan rules. The evil, the abuse, the cruelty she reveals, most of us would prefer not to see. We need not only to see, but we need to take action to stop evil. I pray readers will recognize the truth and act. At the end of this trilogy, Sondra invites you to the greatest remedy of all. One caution: Once you start reading, you won't want to put the book down. This trilogy will cause missed meals, sleeping, and total schedule destruction.~*J.C. Richards, Author of Shattered Trust www.jchrisrichards.com*

UNRAVELED·REWOVEN

BOOK 1 ❖ A NOVEL BASED ON TRUE EVENTS

ROBBED

SONDRA UMBERGER

Check out the latest about Sondra Umberger www.ConnectingToChrist.com

Unraveled-Rewoven, Book One: Robbed-Innocence Stolen

Cover artwork by Keno McCloskey kenomccloskey@gmail.com

Edited by Debbie Maxwell Allen dallenco@gmail.com

Published by Connecting to Christ www.connectingtochrist.com,

Disclaimers:

For mature audiences. Discretion is advised.

This book deals with child abuse, satanic ritual abuse, sexual assault, domestic violence, pornography addiction, and other forms of abuse and violence. While the author has taken great lengths to ensure the subject matter is dealt with in a compassionate and respectful manner, it may be troubling for some readers.

This book is inspired by real events therefore names, dates, locations, and identifying details have been changed to protect the privacy and safety of individuals.

This book is for informational purposes only. While every precaution has been taken in the preparation of the book, neither the author nor the publisher shall have any liability to any person or entity with respect to any loss or damage caused or alleged to be caused directly or indirectly by the instructions contained in this book.

The information provided in this book is not intended as a substitute for the medical advice of physicians, psychologist, or any other professional. [v5]

ISBN 978-1-953202-00-0

Printed in the United States of America.

In loving memory of my dear friend
and sister in the Lord,
Maria

Maria knew all too well that the unspoken—screams havoc. Because Maria
was unable to use her voice or tell of her abusive story before her passing:

~I am speaking out on her behalf.

~I am speaking out for the countless victims of untold abuse.

~I am speaking out for those who still suffer silently.

Victory and triumph, then and now,
are in our Lord, Jesus Christ.

Maria, I know you are in the presence of God,
embraced in his love. My heart sings with joy,
knowing this truth,
knowing you have freedom,
and knowing we will be together again.

Unraveled-Rewoven is dedicated to those in need!

I have written this series of books to encourage anyone who desires hope and healing to become a truth-seeker, striving for answers that will set you free. After reading this trilogy, I hope the story will inspire and equip you to fight the battles that rage in your life.

Stand firm, each moment, each day, each week, until the passing of time is merely a reminder that you are an overcomer in Christ.

I encourage you to study and apply the holy scriptures into your life with the intent of building intimacy with the Lord. I pray your truth journey will take you from victims to victors, Unraveled-Rewoven!

ROBBED

Sondra Umberger

Marion
Christian Counselor
January 2000

C atherine and I met in 1992. She was a keeper of secrets. Secrets she kept hidden for decades—too long for anyone to carry such toxic burdens. She sought me for counseling and became one of my favorite clients, and thus far, my most challenging.

Continuing to hide from her *lost years* was no longer an option for Catherine. Even while she slept, her mind incessantly labored to unearth the hidden secrets of her past, when her family called her "Catie." Fragments of images would creep out of her subconscious and merge into one recurring nightmare.

I had no idea what would be unlocked within the broken heart of this thirty-something, stylish, confident, and beautiful college student. Entering into her hidden world of torment and terror would change both our lives—forever.

CHAPTER ONE

Catherine
Switzerland 1992

The full moon reflects off the Vierwaldstättersee, meaning the lake, in the Swiss town of Luzern. I inhale the autumn leaves' fresh earthy scents as we stroll around the lake, just having finished a late dinner. I love being out with good friends, and my evening is as full as my stomach loaded down with rich raclette cheese and white wine.

"That was so delicious, but I ate too much." I pat my bloated belly and let out a satisfied giggle. Not wanting to go home and face the inevitable, I wonder, should I tell them? No, why open a can of worms? Instead, I ask, "Do you guys want to stop by at the Pickwick Pub for a nightcap before we call it a night?"

"Sorry, Catherine, but I'm going to have to pass. I have to

work in the morning." Faye says, wrinkling her nose with disappointment. Her auburn-red bangs wisp slightly to the side from a soft breeze.

Maureen joins in. "Yeah, I should head home as well. I don't have to work, but I've been burning the candle at both ends for most of the week. Sorry, but I'm beat."

She stretches her back and neck side to side, releasing an ache, a familiar feeling to Faye and myself, being we are all dental hygienists working abroad.

At times I want to pinch myself at my good fortune of living in the Swiss Alps.

We continue toward the Kapellbrücke, a wooden covered bridge, before stopping to hug and say our goodbyes.

My heels echo off the cobblestone streets as I climb the steep hill leading to my flat in the old Stadt or old part of the village where only foot traffic is allowed. Flashing lights blink in the distance from the radio tower perched on top of Mount Pilatus.

Tomorrow is my day off, and I hope to sleep through the clock bell tower bonging at 6 am. Nervous butterflies twitch in my stomach. Is it the cheese I had for dinner, or my fears? I suspect anxiety from not knowing what the night will bring?

I jerk awake. My hands clench. My pulse races. My breathing is heavy and labored. I struggle to sit, fighting with the sheets tangled around my legs.

From out of the corner of my eye, something flickers across the room. A shape? A shadow? Is it real? Or is it the dream?

Again, the dream. Always the dream. The same recurring, unrelenting nightmare, tormenting and haunting me, as far back as I can remember.

I wipe my brow against the edge of my pillowcase. Rubbing my eyes is a futile attempt to erase the horrific images that appear every time the dream pays me a visit. As if tattooed to my eyelids, the vivid pictures refuse to leave. I lie back against the damp sheets, ordering my adrenaline-flooded body and mind to relax.

My mind won't have it. My thoughts rush back, attempting to arrange and rearrange the details, piecing together any particulars. Over the years I've memorized the clues, yet have failed to unlock their mysteries. I'm always left searching for answers to the same question. What is this dream trying to tell me? My nerves ramp up. I suspect…it holds the truth, connecting me to the real nightmare of my past.

I hate it. I hate not understanding what the nightmare means. I only know I'm frightened for my life—talons of fear grip my mind. It's impossible to shake. I try to hide, but the fear seeks me out.

I rub my temples to ease the tension. This morning is no different. There's no going back to sleep. I've learned from bitter experience that the nightmare will start over—with more intensity.

What triggers it? Lack of sleep? Something I ate? A movie or a conversation? I don't know. No answers. For decades this dream has kept me on edge, wondering, when will it return?

Soft early morning light illuminates my entire Swiss one room flat. My windows back up to a lush private garden with high bushes, so there is no need for drapes. The opportunity to bask in the blush of the morning teases me in the twilight of waking. My tired body longs to stay in bed, but my exhausted mind knows I must get up.

My eyelids weigh heavy, begging to close and then *slam*—like a flashback of a homemade movie, a new memory pops into my mind. It's me, as a kid, when my family called me Catie. I'm at Teenage Granny's house. She's my dad's mother. He calls her Mama, but we call her Teenage Granny because she's as fun and feisty as any teenager. She likes to dance and sing the blues.

Catie
Summer 1965

It's Saturday afternoon. My baby brother, Charley, and me are rompin' around in Granny's dirt backyard. We take turns pickin' out what we're gonna play. Sometimes we play Barbies. Other times GI Joe. Then, we play Barbies and GI Joe together. I love playin' army with my brother. Daddy and Granny say I'm a natural at boy games, 'cuz I'm a little tomboy. Charley says he loves havin' a sister who plays like a boy. I'm almost nine, but Teenage Granny thinks I'll grow out of my rowdy years by the time I'm twelve.

It's hot and sticky today, the kind of thick heat that makes me tired. Teenage Granny calls it "damn humidity." I've had enough of this mugginess. I wipe the sweat off my face with my navy-blue shirt. I like the color navy, 'cuz it doesn't show dirt. I brush off my matchin' knee-knocker britches, trimmed in white, and shuffle inside to cool off in front of the window fan.

This breeze against my hot skin feels almost as good as rubbin' myself with ice cubes, till Granny snaps at me, "Quit blocking the cool air, Missy. You're not the only one burning up with this heat. Move your butt before I pop you one!"

Sometimes she gets ornery, 'specially with me, 'cuz she says, I have a habit of not givin' her enough privacy. In my mind, I can hear her, rantin' and ravin', as she would call it. "You just like being up my butt, wanting to make sure you don't miss out on anything."

Yeah, Granny's right 'bout that. But I just love bein' near her. Needin' to get on Granny's better side, I show her my loose tooth, the one on the bottom. I've been wigglin' it, hopin' it will fall out. My two front teeth are huge—'specially now, 'cuz the teeth next to them are missin'.

My second and third older sisters, Claudia and Carolyn, say I look like a rabbit. Granny says their favorite pastime is pesterin' me, and they should know better 'cuz they're older. We're all about two years apart. I don't like their teasin'. Or losin' teeth. Not one darn bit. But I like the money the fairy leaves. To hear my friends talk, they say their fairy leaves way more money than ours. Our tooth fairy must be fussier 'cuz she only leaves a nickel for front teeth, a dime for back molars, and nothin' if your tooth has a rotten spot.

Granny's couch is squishy comfortable and big enough that I can stretch out from the top of my head to the tips of my toes. It's perfect for nappin' on moments like this.

After bein' on the battlefield with Charley, I'm tired and worn out, so I snuggle on the sofa. It's only seconds before I'm dozin' off into dreamland.

I'm hot, sweaty, and feel heavy—too heavy. It's as if I'm bein' held down or covered with a ton of dirt. My head's bein' squeezed —tight, like it's stuck. I'm afraid. I can't see, but somethin' awful is comin'. It's bad, really bad.

Scary pictures flash through my head. I want them to stop, but they won't.

I moan and try to call out. I can't breathe. My eyes pop open. Granny looks over at me from the dinin' room table. She's playin' her usual quiet game of Solitaire.

"Are you okay, Catie?"

"I don't know...umm..." I bolt up—my back is as straight as a broomstick. "I'm really scared. I was in danger. Somethin' big and bad was after me, tryin' to kill me...I think."

I scoot my fanny to the edge of the couch, and lean forward with my hands on the cushions, ready to run, hide, or...well, I'm not sure. I cock my head and try to remember.

Granny looks at me, with worry on her face. "Catherine Kay, I think you might've had a night terror."

"What's that, Granny?"

7

"Same as a bad dream. Makes you wake up feeling sweaty with your heart pounding hard like you've been running a race. You're so afraid you could plum jump out of your own skin. It can be pretty scary stuff, having you afraid for some time. I'm thinking maybe you and Charley might want to play some cards with me, to take your mind off that bad dream."

"I know all 'bout bad dreams. But...I'm still afraid." I clasp my hands to stop my shakin'. "Do you think you can hold me?"

She nods. I hurry over and jump into Granny's chubby arms. She hugs me tight.

"And can you call me Catie, Granny? I don't like Catherine Kay. That's what Daddy calls me when I've done somethin' wrong."

I cuddle close, puttin' my cheek next to hers. "But you're right, I think, I did have one of those night terrors."

CHAPTER TWO

Catherine
Switzerland 1992

Startled by this new revelation, dream, or whatever it was—I jump out of bed, making myself dizzy. Stumbling to my desk, I tug on the drawer handle. The wood, swollen and warped from humidity, refuses to budge. I push, shove, wiggle, and just when I'm about to lift my leg to give the drawer a kick, it finally gives way.

I grab my journal. Gripping the pen, as if holding on to each word, I write—only pausing to stretch my cramping fingers. Can it be? Am I finally remembering?

I gasp. Unbelievable! I saw myself as a child, as Catie. It's the same nightmare! After all these decades, years of yearning to understand, to have a clue, any glimpse into the mystery of my past—and now? Finally—a memory returns!

I piece the fragments together. I scribble bullet points: there's heaviness, a paralyzing hold. I can't move, can't see. Panic. Pitch blackness. The haunting feelings are all too familiar. The nightmare started at Teenage Granny's house. Judging by my teeth, I'm about eight, maybe nine years old. I do the math. It would've been in the late summer of 1965 after everything changed.

My eyes widen. I choke on my saliva. Grabbing a tissue, I wipe my mouth. Oh my gosh, the dates coincide with the same time as *my lost years*. Ages six to almost nine. My heart races. My breathing is labored. My skin peppered with raised goosebumps.

Could it be that my recent dream and the recurring nightmare have something to do with my three lost years?

Not sure how I know, or why I know, but I know. They're connected. And the timing makes sense. It becomes apparent that I haven't forgotten everything, only the hidden secrets.

My thoughts, emotions, and questions are scribbled and strewn across the pages like disconnected clues of a mystery novel. With the last entry, I'm finally done writing—for now. Just the act of recording my glimpses of memory on paper brings me a bit of solace.

I spring up, shove back the chair, and race to the bathroom, having waited too long. Relief. Washing my hands, I stare at my reflection. Searching my face, a thirty-five-year-old woman stares back at me. My golden-brown hair lays limp well below my shoulders, unlike my typical soft curls that bounce with fullness. My bed-head hair looks as fatigued as my bloodshot teal eyes. I pat a cold washcloth to my face.

Do I *sincerely* want to solve the mystery? Unlock my forgotten years? I'm not sure. Do I have the courage and weapons to battle this nightmare and uncloak the conundrum? An argument erupts within my mind. Feeling fragmented, I wrangle with the child inside of me.

Child: Yes, Yes…for sure, yes. Go for it!
Adult: You know it will open a can of worms. Everything we've tried to forget.
Child: Yes, you must. You can do this. It's time.
Adult: Why…why now?
Child: Because there are others. Suffering, like me. You need to remember 'cuz someone has to tell.
Adult: But I'm afraid.

I shut down the debate with the slam of the bathroom door and head toward the kitchenette, craving strong coffee. The fresh, steaming espresso fills my favorite mug, and I add a hint of honey and lots of pure Swiss crème. Yum. Perfect. My first sip sends a calming warmth to my empty stomach.

Turning, I gaze into the main room. The morning sun radiates through the window as I breathe in the fresh, crisp air of the Swiss Alps. My eyes follow the shafts to where they shine onto my open journal. A beam of light rests on the new blank piece of paper as if awaiting my return. I gently lower my coffee cup onto the table. My mind is as full as my mug with thoughts threatening to spill over.

With eagerness, I entitle the page, Spring-1992. I'm careful to describe my experiences and the goals I've fulfilled since moving abroad in 1988. I've been on a quest for inner healing. After all, wasn't that the reason I moved to Switzerland?

Some would say, I'd run away. However, being an optimist, my motto was and is, if you're going to run away—do it right—move to Europe. After all, Switzerland is definitely God's creation. His fingerprints are all over its beauty.

I gulp a mouthful of the rich coffee, then settle on the couch and think back to a time, a time of beauty, similar to the Swiss Alps. A time before my lost years. A treasured time with my mother, a moment in my early childhood. I savor every detail, like a coveted drip of water in the desert, a taste of honey, and a sweetness that had passed on. I was about three and a half years old.

Catie
1959 3.5 years old

M ommy and me stand in front of the refrigerator. The door is open, and the light shines out into the kitchen. The fridge's air makes my toes cold.

"But Mommy, I don't wanna swallow that oil. It's icky and tastes yuckier than a stinky dead fish. Please, no."

I tug away as she holds me tight in her arms. I whirl my head from side to side tryin' to avoid the spoon.

"Catie, Cod-liver oil is good for you. Come on, Sweetie, open up for Mommy." She places the spoon in front of my mouth. I keep fussin'. "Catherine Kay. Open!"

I whine. "But I don't wanna."

"Catie, the words are *want to* not wanna."

Mommy tickles me, since it makes me giggle. "Catie, I have a riddle for you. Want to hear it?"

I love riddles. Grandpa always comes over with new riddles for us kids to figure out.

I smile, "Yeah, what is it?"

"What do bees make?"

"That one's easy, Mommy. Honey."

Then with a big smile, pretendin' to be ever so shy, Mommy says, "Oh, don't be so fresh!"

"I know what fresh means. I get it. I get it. I called you honey like Daddy does when he's flirtin' with you."

I giggle and smile at her as she tickles my tummy again. She pinches the end of my nose, and then kisses me.

"Catie." She cuddles me close and softly speaks into my ear, like it's a secret. "The real reason I want you to take this oil is because it will make your hair shiny and beautiful."

I pull back to look into her face. "Shiny and beautiful like Charlotte's, Claudia's, and Carolyn's? Will it also make me a *toe-head*, like them?"

"No, Sweetie, your older sisters are blondes, but you're my special brunette."

"What color is your hair, Mommy? It's different all the time. Do you have a special kind of hair that changes colors, like magic?"

Mommy laughs. "Oh Catie, you and your questions. I do something to change my hair color, but my natural color is a brown, but not as pretty as yours. You're my *only* daughter with rich brown hair making you even more outstanding."

"Even more than baby Charley?"

"Charley isn't a blonde or a brunette. He has sandy brown hair." Mommy presses her nose on my nose. "And…this oil will make your hair *even prettier.*"

I don't know what outstandin' means, but I know it's good. My sisters have beautiful hair and big blue eyes. Everyone tells Mommy how pretty they are, so if I swallow this stinky oil, maybe people will notice me and my new shiny hair. I smile big at the thought.

"Okay, Mommy."

I open wide and shut my eyes. She puts the spoon in my mouth. I gulp it down, just like she said.

It's horrible! I gag.

"Yuck…yuck!" I wipe my tongue off on my shirt-sleeve.

Mommy puts a glass of orange juice to my lips, tips it up, and I chug it all tryin' to erase the yucky dead fish taste. She follows it with a teaspoon of honey. Mommy is the best.

I skip into the bathroom and crawl up on the step stool to look in the mirror. Even when I squint hard—I don't see any changes. I crawl down and run back into the kitchen.

"Mommy, when will it start to work? And why do you call the girls 'toe-heads'? Their heads don't look like toes. Is that why you put peroxide in their shampoo and not mine? Do their heads smell like toes, and does that keep the stink down? *I'd never noticed before.* Sometimes Charley's head stinks but not like toes…"

"Slow down, Catie. Remember to ask one question at a time, and then wait for the answer before you ask another question. That is what polite young ladies do." She tickles me. "Okay, Missy?"

I bob my head up and down, and a giggle escapes.

"Now it sounds like 'toe-head,' but it's spelled differently. You'll understand when you learn to read. It means a very light white kind of blonde hair. It's only a saying. And the peroxide keeps their hair bright and shiny, just like this oil will keep your hair pretty and shiny *over time.* Understand?"

"Yep."

The doorbell rings.

"That must be your Grandpa."

I run to the door as fast as I can. After two big tugs, the front door pops open.

"Grandpa…Grandpa!" I jump into his arms.

"Catie-girl, give your grandpa some sugar."

I give him a million kisses all over his face. Mommy comes over and gives Grandpa a hug and kiss.

"Hi, Dad. Is Mom with you?" She peeks around his shoulder.

"No, not today. She's busy with laundry, but sends her love."

I jump up and down in excitement. "Did you bring the stuff to make my sandbox?"

"I sure did, Catie-girl. You want to come help me carry the supplies into the back yard?" He winks at Mommy and then takes my hand. We head toward the front door.

Charley, who's still a baby—not a big girl like me—starts cryin'.

"Catie, have fun with Grandpa. Dad, it sounds like Charley needs his diaper changed or is hungry—again."

I look back. Mommy rubs her head.

"You got a headache, Mommy?"

Grandpa chimes in. "Belle, are you all right? His forehead wrinkles. "Do you have these headaches often?"

"No, I'm fine." She shakes her head. "Just busy."

"Are ya sure, Mommy? When we're done buildin' our sandbox, you wanna come out and play with Grandpa and me?" I tug on her blouse.

"Catie, Sweetie, remember, it is better to say, do you *want to…*"

"Okay, Mommy. Sorry. I hope you *want to* come play."

I flash a big smile then run out the door. Mommy and Grandpa laugh behind me.

I climb my way into Grandpa's truck bed before he comes out. I wiggle under the brown tarp, and see a bunch of lumber and big heavy bags. I squat and wait.

The front screen door slams and Grandpa's footsteps shuffle across the dirt driveway, gettin' closer. He stops. I guess he's lookin' around for me. I try extra hard not to giggle. I throw the brown burlap back and spring out.

"Surprise!"

Grandpa jumps. He burst out into a chuckle. "How did you get up in the back of my truck by yourself?"

"I'm part monkey." I round my elbows, knees, and hands, then move around in a circle, makin' monkey sounds, "eeh, eeh, eeh."

Grandpa shimmies out four pieces of lumber. They're all the same length. I count 'em as he puts two pieces under each arm. He's so strong. I like to squeeze his big muscles and play with his hair; it's the same color as yummy chocolate. I'm excited 'cuz I get to carry the brown paper sack of nails and the hammer. I scurry behind.

I love my grandpa. He's my only one. Daddy's father died a long time ago, and he only has Teenage Granny left. Daddy must miss his daddy. I think I'd be forever sad if Daddy, Mommy, or Grandpa were gone. But I'm the lucky one 'cuz my grandpa is funnier than all the grandpas in the whole wide world.

After the sandbox is finished, he rests it up against the house. We scan the back yard for a place where there's no grass. Grandpa says our yard needs some help, but I'm thinkin' we have lots of no-grass-places to pick from.

He sets the box ever so easy on the ground next to the swing set, close to the fence.

"Why'd you put my seats on the ground, Grandpa, and where's the bottom?"

Scratchin' his head, "What seats, Sweetie?"

I point to the small pieces of wood nailed onto the corners.

"Those, Catie-girl, are what you call braces. That's what holds the boards tight so that the sandbox won't wiggle."

"But, uh…I thought those would be my seats. I can get into the sandbox with play clothes, but if I've got on my good clothes, I can use the seats."

"Well, aren't you a pretty smart fellow, or is that a pretty fart smeller?"

I'm in stitches, gigglin'. "You've got to tell Mommy! My face hurts, Grandpa, 'cuz you make me laugh…bunches. Is that one of your riddles?"

"No, just a funny."

I love the way his belly jiggles like Santa when we laugh together. Mommy says that grandparents are supposed to make you giggle. Grandpa flips the sandbox over, so my seats are on top. Then he pours in the bags of sand.

I reach up and hug him around the neck and sing, "I love you, a bushel and a peck, I love you, a hug around the neck." I kiss his cheek. "You are the funniest Grandpa and the very best storyteller in the whole wide world."

He sits me on the ground, and I look up. "Are you gonna be here for supper? And can you stay till bedtime? Will you tell me one of your stories?"

I forgot Mommy's rule, one question at a time, but Grandpa din't seem to mind. I can't wait to play in my brand-new sandbox. It feels like there's a smile in my heart.

CHAPTER THREE

Catherine
Switzerland 1992

I love thinking about my mother and yearn to relive those special times. One memory leads to another until I'm in a puddle on the floor having a teary-eyed pity party.

I rehash my decision to move to Switzerland. Truth be told, I had run away. Or better said, I was running from pain. And not from the angst brought on by the recurring nightmare or lost years.

My life had taken a sharp turn, blindsiding me, and leaving me behind. There were many challenges, too many to list, but the final straw—my ex-husband found someone else—someone whom he felt needed him.

And as bad luck would have it, that somebody turned out to

be my best friend. Oh, yes, she was great at playing the blonde damsel in distress, the needy airhead. I watched her play men for years with that age-old game. Unfortunately, I turned out to be one more fool she played.

I vacillated between loving them and hating them—my friend and husband—the adulterous gutter-slut and the deceiving liar. What kind of a friend moves in on your husband? What kind of a husband has an affair with your best friend?

When the truth was exposed, the onslaught hit me like a sledgehammer. I know I should have felt overwhelmed, betrayed, hurt, and angry. So angry, I could have spit fire. But instead, I felt nothing. Just numb.

Beaten down and not wanting to be vulnerable, I hid my wounds as best I could. The knife of betrayal cut deep. Not daring to trust either of them or give them the power to twist their *stab in the back* deeper, I avoided seeing mutual friends, because it only stirred my pain. I just wanted to get out of town. Embarrassment and shame engulfed me. But why?

Hadn't I given my all to my marriage? Weren't my efforts good enough? A more painful question—wasn't *I* good enough?

I believed I didn't measure up. I was lacking. My survival instincts set in and I took cover, hiding inside my numbness.

So, maybe I did go into hiding, all the way to Switzerland. The country needs dental hygienists, making it reasonably easy to get a job and to get out of town. Away from everything that reminded me of my divorce.

Thinking about my ex-husband drains my emotions. I'm weary and tired. My eyes grow heavy. I allow myself to rest and doze off. Soon I fall into a dream, back to a time when I was five years old.

My family is all around me…

Catie
Winter 1962

An extra scary scream comes from the back of the house. From the hallway? The bedroom? Or is it the bathroom? I can't tell. Who's screamin'?

Oh no! It's *Mommy*!

Charlotte jumps up, and darts from the dinner table, with her supper half-eaten. She points at all four of us, "Stay put! Claudia, Carolyn, you keep Catie and Charley in the kitchen."

Charlotte runs out of sight, headed toward the scary screams. I'm frozen in place. My mind talks a mile a minute. My heart pounds like it's tryin' to jump right out of my chest.

I don't like bein' bossed around. So what if Charlotte's the oldest of us five kids. Just 'cuz she's twelve doesn't make her the boss over me. I'm five now, and I don't need her tellin' me what to do.

Charlotte's always sayin' I'm actin' too big for my britches, but I know better. I'm actually too small for my britches, since all I get is hand-me-downs and have to grow into them. I might be the youngest girl, but I'm big enough to know when somethin's wrong.

I move out of my chair. Charley puts his small arm in front of me. He quietly says, "No, no sissy, Char-witt says to stay put."

Carolyn stands to block me, givin' me the stink eye, "Shhh, Catie. Listen and be still."

The screams, sobs, and loud moans keep comin'. My eyes sting as they fill with tears. Claudia and Carolyn are nine and seven. I pound them with questions. "What's wrong with Mommy? Why's she screamin'? Is there a stranger in our house? Who's hurtin' her?"

I squeeze my hands on the sides of my chair, pressin' my bottom into the seat. "Are they gonna hurt Charlotte too? Why'd she run off all by herself? What about us? I want Mommy!"

We look toward the long hallway, stretchin' our necks, hopin' to see Charlotte soon. I want to run to Mommy, but I'm not fast enough to get around my two older sisters.

Chills run down my back. *Is Mommy hurt? Mommy has to be okay.* I cover my ears to muffle her screams. I don't like feelin' scared—no, not one bit. *She must have stubbed her toe again. That's right; the one Mommy broke on the Kirby vacuum cleaner.* What had she said? *It was somethin' 'bout, the vacuum bein' built like a train, but gets the job done. Mommy said it didn't budge when she stumbled and slammed into it a few days ago, breakin' her baby toe.*

I tell Charley, "I think I know what's wrong. I bet Mommy stubbed her broken toe again."

"You think so, Catie? She didn't cry or scream last time. She just moaned real loud and hopped around." His face is blotchy, his eyes red from cryin'.

I really don't believe what I said, but I want to. I can tell Charley doesn't believe it either.

Why can't I see Mommy? Why isn't Charlotte tellin' us what is wrong? It must be bad!

All the racket is scarin' the livin' daylights out of me! I want to scream, but hold back. I don't want to scare Charley any more than he already is. I'm his big sister.

Charlotte is the oldest, she's my number one sister. Mommy says we have to look after each other. So Charlotte looks after Claudia who is my number two sister. Claudia looks after my number three sister, Carolyn. And it's Carolyn's job to play and look after me, 'cuz I'm the number four sister. Bein' the number four sister, my job is to play and look after my baby brother, Charley.

Another rule is to hold your younger sister's hand, but since I'm the youngest sister, I get to hold Charley's hand. Mommy holds his other hand, 'cuz I'm just learnin' 'bout babysittin'. And of course, Daddy always holds Mommy's hand.

Charlotte yells, "Claudia, Carolyn, go to the neighbors for help. Make sure Catie and Charley stay in the kitchen, and out of the way!"

Charlotte's a bossy meanie, not lettin' me see Mommy, but I know better than to disobey her. It'll only get me a spankin' later.

Everyone shouts and cries. I don't know what to do. *What's goin' on? What's happenin'?*

Claudia flashes out of her chair. She has me by the shoulders and looks me square into my eyes. "Catie—listen, Carolyn, and I have to go get help. You stay right here. You understand? Keep Charley back. Stay out of the way. Take his hand." She puts Charley's hand into mine. "Don't move!"

She threatens me without sayin' a word. I know if I move, I'll be in big trouble. I stand still, stiff like a tree. They run out the door before I have a chance to speak or even nod.

Before long, I hear thunder with bright, flashin' lights outside our house. It's hurtin' my ears and eyes. It's the biggest thunder and lightnin' storm I've ever heard or seen.

I don't like storms: they scare me. My body shakes. I don't like feelin' afraid. I remind myself of what Daddy said, *"Storms are nothing to fear. They're simply God bowling in heaven. The thunder is the ball going down the alley and hitting the pins. The lightning only comes when God makes a strike."*

I try to focus on Daddy's words, but they don't comfort me. It doesn't stop my shakin'. Mommy's not screamin' anymore, only loud moans. The storm outside isn't lettin' up. I can't understand why God is bowlin' and not helpin' my mommy?

I cling onto Charley, huggin' him as hard as I can, as we wait for Claudia and Carolyn to come home.

Phyllis, the neighbor lady who lives next door, bolts through our front door with two other grown-ups, lookin' for Mommy and Charlotte. Carolyn follows.

There are so many strangers comin' into our house that I can't see our furniture 'cuz of all these people. They're pushin', shovin', and all talkin' at the same time. I can't tell who I'm supposed to listen to.

21

I yell out to Carolyn. "Where's Claudia?"

"She's too afraid to come inside. She's sittin' on the next-door neighbor's porch. She says she'll stay there and pray for Mom." Carolyn walks over and stands next to me.

Charley wraps his little arms around my waist, and hangs on so tight he pinches me. I squirm a little and then look at him. He searches my face.

"What's wrong, Sissy? Why's Claudia praying?"

Tears stream down our faces even though I'm tryin' my best to be brave. I turn to Carolyn. She shrugs her shoulders.

Phyllis makes her way over to Charley and me. She pushes us out the front door and walks way too fast. She tugs at us to keep up. We run across the lawn toward her house.

I turn and see Daddy's car pull up. Someone must've called him home from his bowlin' night. He runs as fast as he can, toward the house. He doesn't even look at me or hear my cries.

I scream out, "Daddy, come get us. Help! Somethin's wrong with Mommy! Charlotte won't let us see her."

I let go of Charley's hand to run to Daddy. Phyllis tightens her grip as she pushes us up the front steps of her house. Through blurry tears, I miss a step. Phyllis lifts me into mid-air by the back of my shirt. I never fall. I crane my neck to look at her arms to see if she has Popeye muscle arms.

By now Charley has joined me with sobs and pleas for Daddy's help.

Phyllis pushes us through her doorway.

"You dear sweet babies, it will be okay. Shhhh." She puts her pointer finger up to her lips. "It's important for you both to be quiet so they can help your mom. Shhh, shhh." She gently wipes a tear from my cheek.

I'm scared, and I don't like bein' told to shhh. I wrinkle my nose and squint my eyes at Phyllis. "What 'bout all those people in my house? She's my mommy, and those grown-ups need to be quiet and get out of my house. Me and Charley should be able to stay. We live there. And…" I take a big breath. "I'm not a baby. I'm almost five-and-a-half-years old."

I cover Charley's ears and then whisper, "He's only three, but almost out of diapers. He wears big boy pants durin' the day and a diaper only for bedtime."

Cockin' my head to the side, I lower my voice even more. "He's still kinda a baby, but doesn't like to be called one, and me neither." I uncover Charley's ears once it's safe for him to hear.

"Oh, Sweetie, I didn't mean either of you were babies. It's only a term of endearment. I know you are very grown-up, especially for your age. I'm sorry. I didn't mean to hurt yours or Charley's feelings."

"I don't know what *en-deer-mant* is, but you didn't hurt our feelin's, we just don't like bein' called a baby." I turn to Charley. "Right?"

He nods his head and keeps suckin' his thumb.

I feel the warmth of Miss Phyllis's home. It's January and freezin' outside. She din't even put our coats on before she started pushin' us out of our house—away from our family. I don't like her right now. She's a big meanie too, like Charlotte. I want to make a face at her, but my ears catch the racket outside. I turn toward the noise and see the reflections of the crazy lightnin' comin' in through her livin' room window.

Her house is just like ours. I walk over to the big picture window and press my nose against the glass to look outside. I wonder why I've never seen such pretty lightenin' before. The storm of lights and thunderin' noise won't stop. The loud stormy sounds make me cover my ears. It's blurry, but I can still see the flashin' colors in the lightnin'.

I watch the strangers go in and out of our house. It's not fair. How come all these people can be there, but me and Charley can't?

I continue to yell. I beg for someone, anyone, to come get us. I'm worn out and can't holler anymore. My voice has stopped workin'.

Phyllis walks up wearin' a polka-dotted apron that matches her bright pink lipstick. She smiles and moves a plate from behind her back. "Would you like a chocolate chip cookie?"

I smell the sweet, melted chocolate. Charley looks up, but he's cryin' so hard his tears stream down his cheeks, and go right inside his mouth. He shakes his head no and cries out for our mommy. "I want my Mommy. Mommy! Mommy!"

I want a cookie, but shake my head no, then slump to the floor. I play with Charley's sandy brown hair till he falls asleep.

A while later, Phyllis moseys over, bends down and picks Charley up off the floor. He's sound asleep, suckin' on his thumb. She cradles him in her arms and nudges her head for me to follow. She leads us into an extra bedroom. It's for guests, she says. But I don't want to be her guest. I wanna go home.

With tears in her eyes, she tucks us into the bed for the night.

Phyllis kneels against the bed, hoverin' over Charley and me. She closes her eyes, and ever so quietly says a prayer. "Lord, please help this family. Help Forest to be strong for his wife and children. Assist the doctors to heal dear sweet Belle. Please make sure everything is okay. In Jesus Name, Amen.

CHAPTER FOUR

Catie
Winter 1962

I wake up with the sun shinin' bright through the window. I squint at the blindin' light, when I spot curtains with flowers. Puzzled, I glance at yellow walls and a white dresser. *This room isn't my bedroom. Where am I?*

Charley's lyin' next to me, all snuggled up, huggin' his pillow. I hear the door crack open. Miss Phyllis' face peeks into the bedroom.

Last night wasn't a dream. Oh no, it was all true. My heart hurts.

Phyllis smiles, then she whispers, "Good morning, Catie. Did you sleep well? I can see Charley's still sawing logs."

She puts her finger to her lips, tellin' me to be quiet and not to wake Charley. I crawl out of bed and follow her into the kitchen. Phyllis is dressed, her hair combed up into a French twist hairdo, and her lips are still bright pink.

After rubbin' my eyes, stretchin', and lettin' out a big yawn, I ask, "How's Mommy? Can I go home and see her now?"

"Sweetheart, your Mommy and Daddy aren't at home. They're at the hospital. Your dad telephoned Charlotte earlier to tell her the doctors are working on your mommy, making her better. I'm going to be watching you and your brother. We will probably hear something later on today."

"Will they come and tell us how she's doin'?"

"I'm sure they will, Sweetie, as soon as they know."

"Do you promise, Miss Phyllis? Cross your heart and hope to die, promise?"

"Yes, Catie. As soon as I find out, I will tell you right away. And as soon as I can, I'll take you and Charley home. I promise."

"Do you think she'll be okay? Did my daddy say she hurt her baby toe again?"

"Charlotte didn't mention anything about a hurt toe. But I'm sure hoping and praying she'll be just fine," she says smilin'.

I feel better knowin' Miss Phyllis is prayin'. Her smile looks like she believes Mommy's gonna be just fine. So, I decide I'm gonna believe it too. I feel better already.

"Catie, I went over to your house earlier and gathered your school clothes just in case you want to go to school today."

"Huh, what do you mean, if I want to go?"

"Charlotte told me your dad said if you wanted, you could stay home from kindergarten."

"What? Really?"

I think about it. We're gonna be practicin' our school show. I'm in the tumblin' group. I don't want to miss practice, bein' it's only three weeks till our big show.

"Miss Phyllis, I want to go to school to rehearse my act. I want to be the best in my group for Mommy and Daddy."

I brag a little. "You know, my mommy is soooooo talented—at everythin'. She taught all us kids how to dance and pantomime to

26

music—our favorite records. Do you want to know how I do it, Miss Phyllis?"

"Sure, Catie. Tell me all about it. I want to hear everything, just in case I might want to pantomime to a song someday. Is it easy to learn?"

"Oh, yes. Okay, the first thing is, you have to memorize the words to the song. Then you learn how to lip-sing the words, that's another word for pantomime. You just move your lips in time to the words. It's pretendin' to sing. It's easy when you know the words. If you do it just right, everyone thinks it's you singin'."

I point toward our house. "You see, we do our acts in the back yard. Grandpa made us a stage right under the bathroom window, 'cuz that's where we put the record player. We turn it up to make the music real loud. I love to pantomime with my mommy and sisters. Sometimes, I really sing, and not just pretend, but no one can hear me over the record player. The key is to keep up with the singers. I'm pretty good at it, Mommy says. You need to come over to watch one of our talent shows. I bet she'd let you be in one if you learned how to pantomime."

"Well, Miss Prissy, I've seen your talent show, from over the fence. I watched you last summer. You sang 'Itsy, Bitsy, Teeny, Weeny, Yellow Polka-dot Bikini' while wearing a smart little bikini yourself and doing a wonderful job of the twist dance."

I beam with excitement. "Mommy made me the bikini. It's my first one! She made one for each of us girls. It's blue and white seersucker, not yellow, but that was all the fabric she had. She taught me how to do the twist dance too."

I moved away from the kitchen counter to show her.

"My mommy's a good dancer, makin' it easy to learn. All you have to do is pretend you have a towel across your bottom, wipin' it dry by pullin' it side to side while puttin' out a cigarette under one foot." I demonstrate.

"Right now, I'm learnin' how to change from one foot to the other, and back again. It's pretty hard, but I should have it figured out in the next few days. Do you know how to do the twist, Miss Phyllis?"

I keep on dancin'.

"Great job, Catie. And yes, I do know how to do the twist. And you'll never guess who taught me."

Charley comes into the kitchen rubbin' his sleepy eyes. My brother isn't awake yet. He comes over and hugs me but doesn't let go. He smells a little like pee.

"Miss Phyllis, while you were gettin' my school clothes, did you get Charley some? I know he could use some clean pants. Mommy usually gets them for him in the mornin'."

"I sure did. But how about we have some breakfast first? I made pancakes. Does that sound good?"

Both Charley and me are wide-eyed 'bout havin' pancakes. It's a favorite we eat on holidays or birthdays. We finish breakfast, then wash up and get ready to put on our clean clothes.

Phyllis brings me my very favorite dress. It's white with little red hearts all over. I wonder how she knew. "Mommy sewed it for me...for my first day of kindergarten. She finished the collar, sleeves, and hem in this special red lace trim." I touch the lace and show Miss Phyllis how fancy it is. "Mommy said it took her a very long time, but she said I was worth the effort."

I tell Phyllis all about it while she helps me get dressed.

"Well, Catie, or should I say, 'Chatty Cathy,' we need to get you off to school in a few minutes."

I laugh, "That's so funny. Did you know that's the doll Santa Claus gave Carolyn and me for Christmas? We both have Chatty Cathys. But I think he gave each of us the wrong doll. I'm sure Santa knows I'm a brunette and that Carolyn's a blonde,...so why do you think he gave me the blonde doll and Carolyn the brunette?"

"I'm not sure Sweetie, but I would suggest you write Santa a letter and ask him if you really want to know. Let's get you off to school."

Dark clouds have moved in and cover the mornin' sun, leavin' the sky gray and cold. I usually walk to school, but I'm not gonna turn down a ride.

When we arrive, Phyllis walks me into my classroom. She

takes my teacher aside to talk with her while I hang up my coat and put my boots against the wall. I wave goodbye and blow Phyllis a kiss from my desk. I like her better this mornin', 'specially since after eatin' her tasty pancakes.

The school mornin' is fun. We practice our routine for the show. I'm able to do a front and back rollover the very best out of everybody. We call them 'summer salts' at home. I've been doin' them since I was a baby, so I'm really good at 'em. Besides rollovers, we're all gonna do the 'bicycle' on our backs. It's an exercise where you roll up on your back and pedal your feet in the air, like a pretend bicycle.

I tell my teacher, "I'd rather ride my real two-wheeler bike on the stage since I learned how this summer when I was only four." *It was actually a few months before I turned five.* The teacher said I couldn't. Instead, I need to practice this other kind of bicycle. I pout but obey.

School isn't quite finished when I see our other neighbor, Harry, the man from across the street, come into my classroom. He walks straight over to Miss Parker. I hear him tell her he's here to pick me up.

Harry comes up to me and says, "Miss Phyllis sent me to fetch you. They've heard back about your mom. She told me to tell you that she kept her promise to come get you. She's taking Charley home and will wait for me to bring you there."

Harry is his usual quiet self on the drive home. He has chocolate-colored hair like my Grandpa, but he never tells stories, barely ever speaks a word.

I walk through the front door, lookin' for Phyllis and Charley. They're sittin' in the kitchen with Charley on top of the table eatin' a banana. I'm hopin' for a snack too.

I send a big wave. Phyllis sends me a small smile, then stands.

Sisters two and three, Claudia and Carolyn, are sittin' on the floor, leanin' up against the livin' room wall. They both have their faces buried in their drawn-up knees, close to their chests.

I walk toward them, curious about how Mommy is doin'.

Claudia looks up and blurts out through her tears...

"Mom's dead!"

Catherine
Switzerland 1992

I'm startled awake. It was as if I'd been transported back in time, back into my five-year-old body. This revelation, or dream, or whatever it was, appeared so real, and to my surprise, it was in vivid color.

I balance myself on the edge of the mattress and grip the tussled sheets. *Am I coming or going?* My mind races to make sense of the dream. I run my fingers through my damp, tangled hair. *What the heck just happened?* I need clarity.

I shiver, though I'm sweating. My brain feels scrambled. I shake my head, hoping to shimmy my racing thoughts back into place.

I've had a breakthrough. A memory whooshed out like air released from a sealed canning jar. I felt like I was experiencing this memory for the first time, but I know it happened over thirty years ago. And of all my memories, why am I reliving this one? Mom's death.

I'm befuddled because I've always believed there was a thunder and lightning storm the night Mom passed away. That night turned our lives upside down; things were never the same.

I've spent decades trying to forget the events that followed my mother's death, erasing them from my mind as best I could. Or so I thought.

I pray, "Father God, in the name of Jesus, now what? What does this mean? What are you trying to tell me? Should I move back to the States? Is it time to go back to college? Is it time to get counseling to help me unravel this nightmare and my lost years?" My prayer continues with more questions and uncertainties.

As I pick up my journal, stacks of papers spill out onto the coffee table. I stare at a list of colleges where I've sent applications —no responses. More questions swirl through my mind. I have no answers.

My thoughts go to Charley, my sweet, innocent, vulnerable, baby brother. In the memory, he was there, right beside me, holding on to me. My hand clutches my chest to comfort the ache inside my heart. We went through so much together. I was five and he was only three—so little. I'm compelled to call him.

Opening my teal, Italian-paper address book, I run my finger down the alphabetized index page landing on the C's: Charlotte, Claudia, Carolyn, and Charley. Listed by our age, oldest to youngest. I put my pencil on the page to hold my place, thinking through the seven-hour difference in our time zones. Let's see, if it is eight a.m. here, it will be three p.m. there, which means I'll have to wait three hours before he'll be home.

I keep my eye on the clock, watching the time pass, waiting to call Charley. I distract myself by using the time to update my resume, and make a 'to-do-list' for my return to the States, which includes finding a dental hygienist to replace me at my job. The hours pass quickly.

Picking up a freshly brewed cup of tea, I walk over to the couch. I arrange the blanket over my legs. Feeling comfortable, I pick up the receiver and dial.

His phone rings, once, twice, three times. "Come on, Charley, pick up."

A fourth ring sounds. I prepare to leave a message, but then Charley picks up. "Hello." He sounds out of breath.

"Hey, Charley, it's me. Your long-lost sister, Catherine."

"Catie—I mean, Catherine. Hey. Are you calling me all the way from Switzerland?"

"I sure am. How ya doing? How's the family, the kids?"

"We're all good. Same old, same old." With tension in his

31

voice, he says, "Man, this must be important. You all right?"

"Yes, I'm fine. Nothing horrible has happened. But I do need to talk to you about something. Okay?"

"Shoot. You've piqued my curiosity. What's going on?"

"Well, without going into too much detail, I'll give you the short version because I don't want to run up my phone bill. I recently had a dream or maybe a vision, not sure which. Regardless, I've remembered everything about the night mom died." My words race. "It was so real, unbelievable."

Charley interrupts. "Sis, I'm not sure what you're saying. Where are you going with this?"

"Sorry, I'll get to the point. Do you remember the night Mom died? There was a thunderstorm, right?"

"Uh, huh. I remember. A terrible storm and the next-door lady took us to her house."

"That's what I remember too, but Charley, it was in the dead of winter. There aren't thunderstorms during that time of year." I pause, allowing my words to carry across the Atlantic.

"Charley, it was an ambulance. With me, being five, and you, only three, neither of us had ever seen an ambulance. I remembered the blaring lights and the loud sirens. I just thought it was a thunderstorm because it was the only way I could relate to the experience."

"Wow," he spouts, then whistles over the phone. "All these years, I thought it was a storm. In fact, that's the story I've told my kids. But you're right. It was January." He pauses, and the silence tells me he's soaking up all I've said.

"Do you remember Dad telling us thunderstorms were God bowling in heaven?"

"Yeah, I sure do, Catherine. The thunder was the bowling ball rolling down the alley, and lightning came when God made a strike."

"Exactly." I explain, "Ever since Mom died, somewhere deep in my heart, I thought God was selfish. I believed he cared more about bowling than he did about me, or us, having a mom. I've been so angry with him because I felt robbed. "

Tears swell, blurring my vision. I dab the corners of my eyes, blotting the droplets. I rock back and forth, consoling myself. Emotions erupt, stirred by the memories of my mother's death as well as the events that followed. Nagging thoughts scream within my mind. *I'm not valued. I'm not important.* I've carried these familiar sentiments my entire life.

Charley says, "Don't take this wrong, but I'm glad to hear you say that because I've struggled with confusion about God myself. I know I was only three, but I remember hearing something like God needed Mom to take care of the baby angels in heaven. Guess I believed Mom would rather be in heaven with the other babies than be with us. And I blamed God for taking her. Messed up huh?"

I swallow hard, feeling a huge lump, in my throat. I can't respond.

Charley continues. "And do you remember Aunt Jean promising to buy us new coloring books and crayons if we didn't go to Mom's funeral?"

"Wow...yes, I do, but haven't thought of it in years. She never followed through on her promise either."

Suddenly I visualize my aunt squatting in front of Charley and myself in our living room, telling us it would be better for us to stay home. I can see it as plain as day. There's a sting in my heart, but I'm encouraged because this memory came back with ease.

A new memory pops into my mind. "Charley, do you also recall our sisters' telling us about that old lady who asked Dad if he was going to put us in the orphanage?"

"Yeah, I remember the girls mentioning that over the years. Why would that woman ask such a thing? And at Mom's funeral of all places?" he asks.

"It was in the early 1960s. Men back then weren't equipped to take care of little kids. It was considered a woman's role to cook, clean, and raise the children. Charlotte said that after a woman's death, it was common for the children to live in an orphanage."

I twirl the phone cord through my fingers. "Keep in mind, Dad was only 33 and with five kids. Charlotte was the oldest, being 12, and you were only three and in the process of being potty-trained. Basically, still in diapers. It was a lot to take on, and Dad was instantly alone without his wife and our mother. I'm just glad he said no and that he had every intention of raising his family."

"No, kidding. That was a lot to take on. I'm not sure I could've handled that situation. Do you think he was afraid of losing us kids?"

"Yes, I would imagine he was very overwhelmed. It must have been a huge learning curve. I'm not sure Dad knew how to boil water much less about any other domestic chores."

"I'm happy that Dad valued us enough to keep us all together."

"Charley?"

"Yeah?"

"Valued." I take a deep breath. "I still wrestle with feeling unvalued by God...well, actually, I feel unvalued by a lot of people. I feel like...well...umm...that something's wrong with me." I sniffle softly, trying to hide the emotions that bubble up like the fizz in a shaken soda.

"Well, Catie, it seems to me neither one of us feel so good about ourselves. Or God. I think those early years kinda screwed us up."

"I guess you're right. We were both so young, just little kids. But I've always wondered why Dad or the other adults in our lives never explained what death meant. I eventually figured it out. I stopped waiting for Mom to return. She was never coming home."

I twist in my seat, seeking comfort from the tension. "Charley, today was a big deal for me. Remembering Mom's death showed me the lies I believed about God and myself. I suspect God gave me this memory to show me the truth. You too."

My heart breaks, knowing how stirring up the past is painful for my brother, but I need to speak the truth and get it out into the open. He's the only person who can understand because he was there. I'm fearful, yet excited.

I speak slowly. "Charley, bad things happened after mom's death. I'm specifically referring to when Dad was married to Anna." I pause and wait for him to respond. He says nothing. All I hear is the buzz on the phone line.

"You still there?" I ask.

"Uh huh."

I go on. "I've never known how to deal with what happened. I think I'm ready to go back and remember. I need to do this. I'm so tired of hiding from my lost years and being afraid to fall asleep. Memories are coming back to me—"

Charley interrupts, "I can't go there. And anytime I even think about those times with *Anna...*" He chokes up. "I can't go there. I wish you luck, Sis, but I can't do it. I hope you understand. I can't talk about the step-*monster.*"

His voice cracks. He's on the brink of tears.

"That's okay, Mc Fudd." I say using his nickname. "You don't have to talk about Anna. This issue is something I must do for myself. Are you okay with that?"

"Of course, I'm okay with it, Catie, I mean, Catherine. I can't seem to get used to calling you Catherine, but I know that's what you prefer. So, *Catherine,* I'm fine with *you* dealing...umm, with the past. You've got more courage than I do. The truth is, I don't remember much. Whenever I even think about Anna and her family, I have such horrible anxiety. Well, it's more like terror."

I hear his voice choking up again. "Let's just drop it, okay? I'm glad you remembered those things about Mom's death. I'm surprised to learn it wasn't during a thunderstorm. I'm gonna have to give this some more thought. But thanks for letting me know."

There's a long pause before he finally says, "I'm looking forward to seeing you whenever you're back for a visit. Hey, you think you'll make it to the family reunion this year?"

"Yeah, in fact I decided *today*...it's time for me to move back to the States. I have a lot to figure out, but I think I'll be home just in time for the reunion. I'll see you then. Love you, Charley."

"I love you too, Sis. I'm glad you're moving back. And I'm

feeling quite important, since you called me all the way from Europe."

"Well, I wanted you to be the first person I told that after thirty years, I finally figured out that God doesn't bowl."

Charley chuckles. "Yeah and there isn't a baby angel daycare in heaven either. Wow, I guess we weren't as smart as we thought we were. Thanks for the call. Hope to talk to you real soon, okay?"

"Sure thing, bro. I miss you. Bye-bye."

We hang up the phones.

I pray for Charley and myself, asking God to give me direction and additional confirmation on what to do next. My stomach rumbles with nervousness. I know I need to trust God with the details of moving, securing a job, finding a college, and most of all, finding the *right* counselor to help me walk through the process of remembering.

Marion
September 1992

I drive into the parking lot and glance at the sign designating my new office: *Marion Sanders, Counselor. Suite 102*. It is a brisk fall morning. My short walk to my office allows me to enjoy the change of foliage. Against the sunny blue sky, the aspen leaves reflect their beautiful golden shimmer, striking oranges, and a few pinks, which are my favorites. Autumn is my preferred time of the year. My senses delight in the crisp scents.

With great deliberation and planning, I moved my counseling practice to the local Bible college campus. I am excited to have that decision behind me. Some friends thought it risky because most counseling offices are in medical or business buildings. My logic differed. Since I practice faith-based Christian counseling, I reasoned a Bible college campus is a fertile referral base. I also remembered my college years. It was a squirrelly time in my life, when I was trying to navigate all the tough decisions. With all the pressure, I could have used some counseling during those years. I chuckle as I remember those days now long gone.

As my feet stroll along the pavement, I hear footsteps behind me.

A male voice calls out, "Hey, Marion, how do you like having the counseling practice here on campus?"

Turning, I see him. *Oh, wow, it is the cute guy.*

"So far, so good. It has only been a couple of months; however, the transition is going smoother than I had thought. Thanks for asking. Mr. Templeton, right?" I purpose myself not to stare. He is your typical tall, dark, and handsome type.

"Oh please. . . call me Mark."

"Okay, Mark. You are teaching on the book of Romans and Introduction to Basic Christian Counseling. Is that correct?"

"Yes, you have a good memory. I'm impressed." He pinches his lips together in a tight contemplative smile.

We walk. The man slows his pace to be in step with mine. He's attractive, just my type. I steal a quick peek at his ring finger. There it is. A thick gold wedding band. Darn.

He goes on, "I have to admit, I'm grateful you moved your office here. It takes the load off me. I referred two students to you. Have you heard from either a Samantha or Gregory yet?" He tucks his manila folder underneath his arm.

"No, Mark, I have not heard from either of them, but I will let you know when I do." I smile. "Thank you for the referrals. I appreciate your support. I have some business cards in my briefcase. Would you care to have some?"

Or would you happen to know any good-looking Christian single men like you, who are available? No, shut up, that sounds desperate. After all, I do not want to appear hard up…even though I am. Dang. As a counselor, it is so hard to meet anyone. Anyone who would set me up would have to admit they are receiving counseling. Lord, please bring me a good man. I long to get married.

"Sure…great, that would be helpful."

I wander off into my own thoughts, half-listening, which is now evident to Mark. He has stopped a few steps behind me with his hand extended.

How long has he been waiting and staring at me?

I hurry, unclasp the front compartment of my briefcase, and fumble around for my cards. I am mortified and feel a flush rise on my cheeks. I suspect I am beyond red-faced, probably a bright scarlet. I want to hide under the nearest bench. I finally hand my business cards to him—though it is more like a shove. I am so shaken up.

Does he notice? Or is he merely being gracious?

Relief rushes over me as we approach my office entrance. I yearn to run away. Instead, I turn to Mark and as if to make up for acting like an airhead, I say in my most professional voice, "Mark, thank you once again for the referrals."

I extend my hand. He takes it, shaking it firmly.

"Sure thing, Marion." His smile shows perfect white teeth.

I gaze back at him and attempt to cover up the nervousness behind my smile. Breaking eye contact, I look down to insert my key into the lock, and enter my office. Leaning up against the closed door, I let out a safe breath.

What an idiot, I must have made a horrible impression.

The office feels warm and toasty, a contrast to the fresh autumn air. I hang my coat and slide my purse inside the cherry credenza behind my desk, which I notice needs a good dusting. It looks like it is sprinkled with fine powder sugar. A few swipes with a fresh tissue do the trick. Now I'm ready for my first cup of hot coffee to begin my morning.

Hearing a soft knock, I furrow my brow, and then glance over at the clock. My first appointment isn't for another thirty minutes. I open the door, swinging it wide.

CHAPTER FIVE

Catie
Spring 1962

I swing open the door lettin' the screen door slam behind me and run into the house. Daddy's at the kitchen counter. The bread, peanut butter, and grape jelly are set out. I skip over and hug his waist. "I miss Mommy," I whine. "When's she comin' home, Daddy?"

"She's in heaven, Darlin'."

"How long does she have to stay there?"

Daddy's eyes start leakin' again as he walks out of the room. I follow him into the livin' room. He stands at the front picture window pretendin' to be lookin' at somethin' but I know he just doesn't want me to see him cry.

"Sweetie, I need to get busy making you kids something to eat. You hungry, Catie?"

"You know I'm always hungry, Daddy." I skip behind him back into the kitchen.

"Okay, why don't you go play? I'll call you kids when the food is ready."

I skip back into the livin' room and pick up my baby doll, Chatty Cathy and rock her in my arms.

I'm worried 'bout Charley. He's only three and seems afraid of everyone. Daddy has brought home so many new babysitters, but not a one ever stays. Probably 'cuz Charley bites 'em. He's scared of strangers…really scared. So scared that he hides under the bed. When our babysitters have gone in to pull him out—CHOMP! With some, he's even raised blood. Afterward, they all have a beautiful blue and purple bruise, but they don't think it's so pretty. Then we get *another* new babysitter.

My oldest number one sister, Charlotte, bein' twelve, acts like she's the new mommy. She says she has to keep her eyes on all of us now. Her eyes are the biggest, like Cleopatra, so I'm thinkin' she has the best eyes for the job. She looks in the newspaper to spot all the food coupons for Daddy.

My number two sister, Claudia, who's nine, prays all the time when she's not singin'. She loves to entertain us with stories, skits, and jokes. Her lower jaw is bigger and sticks out a little more than the rest of us girls. But I think that's what makes her such a good singer.

My number three sister, is Carolyn, who's seven. We play a lot together. She's a fighter, tougher than any boy. I like it 'cuz she protects me if anyone tries to bully me. She has a big heart but I think she hides it sometimes. Lately, she goes off all by herself into the closets. Sometimes she stays there for hours.

I don't like how everythin' has changed. We all miss Mommy. But I'm pretty sure I miss her the most. It makes me sad, and I cry almost every day. Grandpa says my 'eye-faucets' must be stuck. I'm figurin' so, 'cuz they just seem to leak all on their own. I see Charlotte cryin' in Mommy's room. She likes to smell Mommy's clothes. Claudia cries in her bed at night, and so does Carolyn. Charley, he's still a baby so he cries all the time. When I see them cryin', well, there I go again. I don't want to be a crybaby, but I miss my mommy…so maybe I am a sissy—a big crybaby.

I overheard Daddy tellin' Teenage Granny that he only makes sixty-five dollars a week. I can only count to twenty, so I'm not sure how much money that is, but sixty-five sure seems like a lot to me. He said he has to pay the babysitter thirty-five dollars and doesn't know how long he can keep it all goin', whatever that means. I didn't think Daddy ever got scared, but he told Teenage Granny that he's afraid the bank is gonna take away our house.

I don't understand why a bank would want our house. They already have a big place of their own. I know all about the bank's house, 'cuz Mommy used to take us there on Fridays.

God's unfair. A big fat meanie not lettin' Mommy be my mommy anymore. He can get anyone to bowl with him. I'm guessin' I must've done somethin' really wrong for him to take her away. I bet I'm on Santa's *naughty* list too. Probably won't get any presents from him. That would be fine if only I could have Mommy back. I miss her so-o-o much. My eyes sting from my tears. They won't stop, no matter how hard I try.

Catherine
September 1992

My eyes sting from the brightness of the clock as I reach over to turn off the alarm before it sounds. Rarely, if ever, do I wake before the alarm clock and often struggle waking in general.

This last month has been a busy blur, though; my life feels different—exciting. I pop out of bed at the crack of dawn, energized about my new beginning, new job, new school, and my new apartment.

I use the extra time to stop at the grocery store to pick up a few things before my Friday classes. I also hope to check out a counseling office I saw on campus. With my list in hand, I make a quick in and out, each arm toting a bag of groceries to the car. Having a store open all night, and only three blocks away still feels fantastic since most of the shops in Switzerland are locked up by six p.m.

"Born in the USA" plays on the radio. I crank it up, and sing along, bobbing my head to the music. I've changed the words to 'Back in the USA'. This is my new theme song, which has replaced, "Should I stay or Should I go? Dun, dun-dun, da, dun.."

Thumping the steering wheel, I keep the beat. It's been five years since I've driven a car and to think, I'm now cruising the streets of Denver. The views of the beautiful Colorado snowcapped mountains and colorful autumn scenery make it hard to stay focused on driving.

I manage my way home with ease turning into my assigned parking space, right in front of my apartment. Wa-lah. Easy as riding a bike.

Fumbling with my key, I insert it into the lock and open the door. My heart sings as I enter my new home.

My apartment, located close to work and school, is outrageously spacious compared to the flats in Europe. I fix my eyes upon the rich mahogany Victorian living room furniture, a glowing welcome as I enter into the foyer. All of my beautiful antiques had been in storage during my stay abroad. I thank the Lord that not a single piece was damaged.

I've spent the last two days unpacking, arranging, and rearranging to get my apartment to look like a picture from Better Homes and Garden. Thank goodness for caffeine; I couldn't relax until I got the job done.

Surrounded by all my treasures, it feels like Christmas. Such comfort. To my delight, I even have a washer and dryer *inside* my apartment, which allows me to do my laundry anytime I want, unlike my allotted twice-a-month laundry days in Switzerland. That luxury alone is enough to make me want to jump up and dance.

I carry my groceries into the kitchen and smile, pleased at the ease of my move. Everything is finally perfect, everything except the nagging voice in the back of my mind, which demands my attention. It sounds like a child's voice, crying out for help. Begging to be heard. Begging to be helped.

Marion
September 1992

I open the office door to a smartly dressed woman in her mid-thirties, smiling. "How may I help you?"

"I'm so sorry to bother you," she says. "I didn't know how to schedule an appointment. Yesterday, I saw your sign, but I didn't see a phone number. So, I decided to drop by today. You know, take a chance that someone might be here."

She shifts her books to her other arm and cradles them against her chest. "Is this a good time to schedule an appointment?" She cocks her head, eyes wide, awaiting my reply.

"Hello, I am Marion. And yes, it just so happens I do have about thirty minutes before my next client arrives. Would you like to come inside the office?"

She nods as I motion her toward the seating area. "Shall I tell you a little about the counseling ministry, or do you have any particular questions in mind?"

She does not respond. Perhaps she is distracted, or maybe she did not hear me.

I speak louder. "Would you care to schedule an appointment?" I open my appointment book. "Do you have your calendar?"

She has a dance in her step. Turning, she places her books, coffee cup, and scarf on the table. Still standing, she shuffles through her purse. The young woman pulls out her calendar and waves it in the air.

"Yes, I have my calendar. I'm one for planning. I don't go anywhere without it. I don't think I could get by if I didn't have everything written on my schedule. I guess that's an indication of my life being way too full."

Flipping her soft brown curls off her shoulders, she continues, "School is demanding, and so is work and all the other things I try to squeeze in...and of course also trying to have a social life...you know how it is."

Me, a social life? Hardly.

She looks at me through teal-colored eyes, uniquely shaped, small, but pretty.

"Excuse me, dear, but I did not catch your name."

She bobs her head, side to side, followed by a big smile. "I'm sorry. My name is Catherine. You said your name was...?"

"Marion. My name is Marion. Please, take a seat." I gesture with my hand to the seating area.

"Nice to meet you, Marion."

The leather love seat lets out a swish from under her petite frame as she makes herself comfortable.

"Catherine, the first thing I want to impress upon you is that everything said in this office is strictly confidential. It is essential for you to feel comfortable and safe. It is my desire for you to trust me with whatever it is that has brought you into the office today. Would you care to expound upon those reasons?"

Crooking a half-smile, she twists her purse strap. "I'm told you do Christian, um faith, um...spiritual counseling. Or...is it mentoring?" She crosses her legs, nervously bouncing one foot. "I'm not sure what you call it, but I'm hoping you might be able to help me. Find some answers that is."

I lean toward her, giving a soft wink. Her shoulders soften. "Catherine, I understand your confusion about the role of this ministry. There are many ways to describe what we do here. Basically, we turn to—or shall I say, depend upon God, the Bible, and prayer to seek answers for the challenges or struggles clients face. Is that acceptable to you?"

"Oh, yes, absolutely." She nods vigorously.

"Alright. Would you care to elaborate on what led you to seek counseling?"

"Okay. Well...to begin, my father wanted a son, so we ended up being a fairly large family with five children, all girls, except the youngest, my baby brother. We are all about two years apart, roughly. The oldest is Charlotte. Followed by Claudia, next Carolyn, then there's me, and the baby, Charles. But I call him Charley. My mom thought it would be fun for us to have the same initials. Dad finds our names to be a tongue twister."

"You're the youngest girl? Correct?"

She nods while glancing at the clock. Catherine's eyes widen. She gulps the air, seeming only now aware of the time.

"I probably need to get to the point of why I'd like to schedule an appointment. Um, it is...well you see, Marion, when I was five years old, my mom suddenly died. The doctors said she died from an aneurysm in her brain. My family suffered a great loss, and um...um our lives were turned upside down and continued to decline. As for mine, it was until I was almost nine years old."

I pushed the tissue box closer to her. Her eyes shine from the brimming tears, threatening to flow.

"What happened to you and your family?"

She swallows hard. "It's impossible to explain in only a few minutes."

She stiffens, crosses her arms over her chest, and straightens her back.

I smile purposely, and relax my arms on the armrests of the

45

chair, then soften my voice. "That is fine. I understand. We can address the subject another time. Feel free to share whatever you are comfortable discussing."

She nods yes, then reaches for a tissue. She rolls the edges of the tissue until it shreds. I pretend not to notice, not wanting to make her feel anymore self-conscious or uncomfortable. Catherine talks very fast, perhaps to utilize our limited time.

"Basically, I remember most of the terrible things that happened to my family. And trust me, they were horrible. But when it comes to my brother, Charley, and me, I remember some things, but as for the *secret things*...um... my mind goes black, and I feel numb. My siblings confirmed I was taken to some *special church*. It's the way they said it that makes me believe it was creepy, or something about it just wasn't right. No one in the family talks about it much. It's one of those tender spots." Upon finishing, she releases a big breath and slumps back into the love seat.

"I see." I pick up my pen to jot down a few notes. "You mentioned not remembering the *secret things*."

"Did I? I guess I was referring to the things I can't remember. I know bad things happened, but no matter how hard I try, I've no detailed recollection of what exactly occurred. To me and Charley that is." She cocks her head. "What on earth would cause me to forget, or not remember?"

"I cannot say for certain, since we have only just met and spoken for a limited period of time. However, it is possible that what you may be describing is called suppression of memory, which is a coping mechanism. It is how a person manages trauma by hiding or concealing memories that are too difficult, painful, or overwhelming to deal with at the time of the event."

She crinkles her brows, engaged in what I am saying. "Do you mean like forgetting on purpose? As if I've purposely locked up my *forgotten years* somewhere inside my brain? Perhaps like a locked box tucked away in a safe, dark corner of an attic?"

"Catherine, your example is an excellent word picture. Any reason why you picked that particular description?"

"I'm not sure. It just popped into my mind. Almost as if it

were something familiar." She cocks her head in question. "But then again…I'm uncertain. All I know is I can't remember."

"Memory suppression is not uncommon. It occurs when people are unable to understand or process a shocking ordeal, a loss, or perhaps a wound; basically, an emotionally traumatic event."

I lean forward, hands clasped against the desktop. "Catherine, you mentioned your age as being from five to nine years old. During that timeframe, your brain wasn't completely developed. When children cannot remember their past, it is often because there is a lack of emotional, intellectual, and even physical ability to comprehend what happened."

I break for a moment, allowing my words to sink in. Shifting in my chair, I reach for my coffee cup and take a quick sip, then continue.

"I personally see suppression as a gift from God. Unlike a developing child, an adult is older, more mature, and better equipped to decipher and cope with the events that took place during earlier years."

Catherine's expression withers as her upright posture deflates like a balloon. She glances at her shoes.

"I believe I've locked those memories away. On purpose. But now…" She bites on the bottom of her lip to still the quivering. "I don't have any idea how to retrieve those lost years." With her head lowered, she peers up through her wispy bangs. She edges herself to the lip of the love seat.

"I want to deal with my past. I mean…I need to. I really do."

Catherine fidgets with her ring, twisting it around her finger while she stares at the blue sapphire. She continues, "Um, um… and, there are two more things."

She lifts her head, struggling to make eye contact. "I suffer from a recurring nightmare. And I'm convinced it has something to do with that timeframe."

"It is accurate that nightmares and dreams can hold messages. They are common and can often be a good thing." I speak calmly

47

to ease her nerves, as mine are rising. I feel concerned and discern something dark hidden in her past.

"And what is the other thing that concerns you, Catherine?"

She leans in close and grasps the front of the leather cushion, her hands trembling. With eyes pleading, she studies my face as if she is awaiting my reaction.

"You see...I can see things. Things other people can't. Does that sound like I'm crazy?"

CHAPTER SIX

Catherine
October 1992

The past few weeks have been crazy, a whirlwind of new doors opening. I've jumped at all the opportunities dangling before me. I moved into my new apartment. Check. I started classes at the local college. Check. I found a new church. Check. I even met a nice guy. Well, we'll see.

Most importantly, I sought out and found a Christian counselor. Check. And I landed a job. Funny enough, my new dental hygiene position was the first job I'd ever been offered based on a question about a piece of jewelry.

Two weeks ago, during my interview, I toyed with my necklace, untangling the two charms. Dr. Fredrick, who looks to be the same age as me, thirty-something, peered over his eyeglasses, and noticed me straightening out the pieces. "Does that necklace have any specific meaning to you?"

I glanced up. "Yes, in fact, it does. Thanks for asking." I held up the cross explaining, "I bought this in Bethlehem. It's special, partly because of my trip there and also because of my Christian faith. This…" I pointed to the fish symbol, "was a gift from a friend."

I held the cross out and showed him how the fish tucked neatly into the cross as if artistically designed to intertwine.

"So, this piece of jewelry represents a lot about who I am," I said, smiling.

From there, our conversation blossomed into the beginnings of what I believed would become a good friendship.

The interview ended with Dr. Fredrick saying, "Catherine, your resume and credentials are wonderful, and this conversation is just what I needed to seal the deal. The job's yours if you're interested. The hours are Mondays through Thursdays, seven a.m. to four p.m., with an hour for lunch."

I shook his hand, happy to accept the job. What a perfect schedule, with evenings to study and Fridays off to attend school. And to top it all off, the entire staff are Christians. Sweet. I felt right at home. My first day on the job was the following Monday, two weeks ago.

Since then, Dr. Fredrick invited me to visit his church. Feeling unnerved by the rumors of the rise of the new age movement in the area, I phoned the church to ask questions. During my conversation, I inquired about the Singles Ministry, thinking it might be a great place to meet new friends.

It is a beautiful, sunny Sunday morning. While walking through the parking lot, I pause to straighten my Italian, fire-engine-red pencil skirt. I had wondered how people in Colorado dressed for church. I opted for my usual assumption—it's always better to be overdressed than underdressed.

I arrive early and walk into the sanctuary. A neatly attired man with wire-rimmed glasses steps up on the stage and thumps the microphone, to hear if it is live. A rockin' praise band practices behind him.

People crowd into the sanctuary. I funnel my way to the second row, so as not to be distracted by others around me. I close my eyes, raise my hands, worship, and dance before the Lord. I felt alive, happy, and free. Finding a church with an awesome worship band and located practically next door to my apartment sets me right into my happy place.

With the last beat of the bass drum and the final crashing of the cymbals, the band finishes playing. As I wait for the pastor to begin his message, the question lingers in my mind. "Will this be my church?"

Instead of seeing the pastor, the same man with wire-rimmed glasses traipses up on stage. He announces the available classes for the morning before he dismisses the entire congregation.

What? Am I in the wrong place? I lean over and ask the couple next to me what's happening. They are already standing and ready to leave. They take the time to explain that I'm at the Single's Ministry, which meets at the Denver Seminary. The church across the street had multiplied its attendees more quickly than anticipated, so they rented space at the seminary building to accommodate their fast-growing membership.

I stand not sure of what to do. One of the ushers, a robust man, in a brown plaid shirt with the name tag, Roger, approaches me. "Catherine, right? The couple sitting next to you mentioned a mixup with the location."

"Yes, I thought I was at the church, but that's okay. I'm here now."

"Would you like to stay and check out one of the Single's Ministry classes?"

He hands me a paper with a listing of selections.

"Thanks, Roger. I'll take a look."

I study the list. A class describing how to share your faith without an argument grabs my interest. Scanning the room, I spot a slender lady with a bobbed haircut. Greeting her, I explain my circumstance. Pointing to the class listed on the now wrinkled paper, I ask for directions.

"Oh, I'm in that class. If you wait a second, I'll walk you there."

"Sure...great, thanks. My name is Catherine. What's your name?"

"I'm Harriet."

"Thank you, Harriet, I'd appreciate you showing me to the class since I'm new."

As we walk down the hallway, I smell the familiar scent of new books and fresh school supplies. Still suspicious about the growing new age and cult movements, I interrogate Harriet with a barrage of questions—perhaps too many.

Following my onslaught, she appears a little rattled, but patiently says, "I have to admit I'm partial because my brother teaches the study. But yes, I'm enjoying the class very much. It applies to life. And it's definitely Bible-based."

Embarrassment rises to my face and I know my cheeks are scarlet red. We walked into the classroom and find seats side by side.

Her brother, the teacher, strolls up to the chalkboard and introduces himself as Hunter Stone. From where I sit, I can see his blue eyes favor his sister Harriet's. He is quite tall, at least six feet, and has excellent posture, giving off a sense of confidence.

I pull my attention back to what Hunter is saying. The first point he makes is about the importance of sharing our faith to give others hope. He provides several examples, which include a time in his life when he struggled with pornography. As a single man, his victory is a part of his story or testimony about how the Lord helped him to overcome such snares.

My mind wanders again. I wonder if his blonde hair, high cheeks, and firm jawline, are signs of German or maybe Austrian descent. But the last name—Stone...huh? I plan to ask Harriet, but as the class ends, she scurries off as if late for an appointment.

I approach the front of the classroom with curiosity about the church spilling over in my mind. I stand in line, waiting for my turn to talk with the teacher, Mr. Stone.

A short, pudgy-faced guy waddles up and starts talking to me. I can't see any details of his face, because he's standing too close. My vision blurs and my eyes cross. He talks so fast. His sentences run together like an auctioneer. On and on, he rambles, giving me a library of information about the singles group and why I should attend.

'The Gnat' is the name I've attached to this stranger. He obviously doesn't understand personal space. I wonder if he'll pass out before he takes another breath or if I'm going to fall over something as I step backward again and again. He continues moving closer, not catching on to my body language, which is screaming—back off!

Someone clears their throat. I look over in that direction. The teacher looks directly at me. He flashes a glance at The Gnat then back at me. He lowers his eyes ever so slightly, suggesting his apology for the guy's behavior. I break away and walk to his desk.

Extending his hand, he says, "Hello, I'm Hunter. How can I help you?"

"Hello, my name is Catherine. Nice to meet you, Hunter. I'm new in town and wondered if you might be able to answer a few questions about the church? I'd like to know about the denomination and theology, to start."

Looking into my eyes, he says, "I'd be happy to answer any questions you have." He smiles. "But would you mind if I contacted you later in the week when I'm less distracted and can give you some undivided attention to address your concerns?" He glances at the crowd of people, standing around, mingling, waiting for their turns.

"Sure, that would be fine." I point to the class register. "That's me, right there, Catherine Williams. All my contact information is listed here." His hand brushes over mine as he reaches for the list.

"Great, Catherine. I'll phone you next week. Is there any particular time that is better for you?"

"Yes, evenings are best." I smile and walk away.

The Gnat follows me into the parking lot. I avoid eye contact and speak in brief, yes or no answers. *Wow, how can someone be so unaware?* I wonder if maybe he's a person with special needs.

I tap my watch and tell him I need to leave, but he keeps on with his constant chatter. *Unbelievable.* Trying to be polite, I listen, waiting for any pause to excuse myself.

My eyes catch a glimpse of Hunter walking to his car with his arms around a box of books. He looks at me, chuckles a little, and shakes his head.

The Gnat notices him as well and shouts, "Hey, Hunter, how's it going?" He sends Hunter a wave. I use the distraction to dive into my car, start the engine, and drive away.

My week flies. I love living in Colorado. My workweek is behind me, it's Friday, technically my day off, except for school, running errands, and my session with my new counselor.

After classes, I have just enough time to grab a quick bite at a local fast food place before my second counseling appointment. Munching on my salad, I recall and rehash my first appointment with Marion. I was a wreck…

I clasped my jittery hands. It was as if I had too much coffee, which I hadn't. Did everyone feel like this? I watched Marion walk to her chair and sit. She organized her spiral notepad, pen, and a well-worn book on the small wooden side table. She had a pleasant, soft smile, and an oval face, framed with soft blonde waves. From where I sat, it looked like she added blonde highlights for a splash of light, like a starburst streaking from the top down along the sides. It looked darling, super cute. It was a great distraction.

Marion seemed kind enough, appearing to be within five to ten years of my age, which would make her somewhere in her forties. I'd hoped for someone older, with experience and wisdom. I admired how she carried herself, her style of clothes, conservative and professional, dress slacks and a nice blouse. She was very relaxed and comfortable. I wished I could say the same for myself.

She seemed sensitive, yet perky and light-hearted, especially after I said, "I'm a little nervous about this...I mean...um, a lot nervous. I'm hoping with you being a counselor that there isn't much you haven't heard."

I tilted my head, seeking her agreement. She didn't respond, so I chattered on. "I want to believe I can say anything and well... I hope it won't shock you."

Tension and fear crackled in my voice. "But I suppose there's always a first time." I made a weak smile.

Marion settled into her wingback chair, then addressed my question.

"Yes, Catherine, I have heard copious amounts, and I have to say I am not bothered by most things. However, I suppose there could be a first." She ended her comment with a wink and a soft laugh.

I noticed her precise speech. She didn't use contractions. It took some getting used to, but there was something about her open candor, perhaps her professionalism mixed with a playfulness, that made me feel at ease....

My mind comes back to the present. I hope today's counseling will be as comfortable. After lunch, I clear the table and toss my trash into the waste bin. I scurry to my car and head back to the campus to see Marion.

After parking, I check myself in the rearview mirror, apply fresh lipstick, and fluff my hair. I instantly feel put-together on the outside. Still feeling unnerved within myself, I focus on counseling as a new adventure. Somewhere in the Bible it says, the truth will set you free. God knows I need to be free.

Marion
October 1992

I lean forward, stretching the stiffness in my back with the hope of relief and fully awakening. Extra sleep is something I crave, besides sweets—what I would not give for a bear claw donut to sugar-me awake this morning. However, the coffee will have to do if I ever plan to take off these extra thirty pounds. I yawn widely, cradling my cup of java.

I swipe my fingers through my appointment book, then swivel my chair to unlock the filing cabinet, and remove the client files for today.

Reaching for the *Catherine Williams* manila folder, I recall meeting with her the first time. I already have my suspicions after hearing her brief description of struggles. I review my initial notes: Emotional numbness, suppression: blocking out memories (age six through nine)—a recurring nightmare.

I take another sip of coffee. Sudden loss of mother (age five). Such a young age—how heartbreaking. Has she mourned her mother's death? I jot a note to myself: Discuss grieving with Catherine.

I glance at the clock. With five minutes to spare before my first appointment, I use the time to focus and pray aloud.

"Lord, help me as I meet with my clients. Provide me insight into their needs. Give me understanding, compassion, wisdom, and discernment. Help me to teach them how to find answers that will bring them healing and closer to you and your truth."

After lunch, a soft knock sounds on the office door. I hurry to invite my client inside. Catherine stands with her arms overflowing with a journal, her purse, a bulging book bag, and a cup of coffee.

56

"Marion, is it okay to drink coffee?"

"Sure, that is fine." I place a gold glass coaster onto the cherry table in front of the love seat where she sits and makes herself comfortable.

"So, Marion, how do we start?" she asks.

"I would like to begin by gathering background information. It will help me to understand, in more detail, your struggles and how I can be of help to you. Tell me about your present status. Are you married, single, divorced?"

Catherine tells me of her failed marriage to Edward, but wishes to concentrate more on the nightmare and her lost years. I comply, but I am sure this subject will resurface.

"We will explore why and how your memories became locked and unavailable to you. Of course, we will delve into these subjects at a pace that is comfortable for you." I smile. "I will teach you how to find answers in the Bible. We will also spend time in prayer and seek the Holy Spirit's guidance and direction. Do you have any questions?"

Catherine responds. "At our first meeting, I noticed you don't use contractions. I'm just curious. How did that come about?" She crosses and uncrosses her legs.

"It is something my parents taught me as a child. It is a hard habit to break." I observe Catherine is nervous, and her question may be an attempt to divert the attention off herself and onto me.

I steeple my fingers. "If I concentrate, I can combine words, but it *doesn't* come naturally." I pause and readjust my position. "You will also discover I repeat myself. It is another bad habit, but it works well in counseling because it has proven to be an important learning tool. I find repetition brings the point home. Shall we begin?"

Catherine smiles. "Yes, please. I'm ready to get started. Just a little anxious."

"Have you ever had counseling before?" I ask.

"No, not really."

"I see. I think you should start. Shall we say...at the beginning?"

Catherine takes a deep breath. "As I look back, I see my life as a jigsaw puzzle. With too many pieces—some missing. It's hard to make sense of it all. I have numerous pictures in my head, some full memories, others incomplete, and many are black voids locked away—and have been for years." She looks down and flicks a loose thread off her slacks. "And I've lost the key. I have no idea how to retrieve them."

I make eye contact with Catherine to let her know I am fully engaged, listening to her every word. "You are doing fine, Catherine. When do you believe your struggles began?"

"I believe it was, well…when my mom died. I was so young, only five, but I have many memories of her. They're my treasures. My siblings and I used to put on plays, talent shows, and perform pantomime singing acts. Mom encouraged us to use our imaginations and to dream big. I miss those magical days and grieve their passing all the more, because of what was to come."

I lean toward her and inch to the edge of my chair.

Catherine's jaw tightens. "Then Anna crashed into our lives."

My eyes dart to her cheeks. "Catherine, what is causing you to cry?"

"Oh…uh…am I crying?"

She touches her face, looking surprised at her wet fingers.

"I wasn't aware." Catherine continues. "It seems I have a pattern. Whenever emotions arise, such as grief, anger, fear, or anything intense or overwhelming, I push them down. I've practiced this my entire life."

She shakes her head. "Even now, Marion, I'm pushing down the lump in my throat. I stuff my feelings to compose myself. I believe if I allow myself to feel or express my pent-up emotions, I'll never stop crying. I'm afraid if I unlock the door to my past, I believe I'll go crazy."

I am quick to jot down notes, and return my focus to her. "Tears are a part of the cleansing process. I believe God gave us the ability to cry to help wash away the pain and suffering associated with crippling beliefs that hold us in bondage."

I allow Catherine time to soak in the message. I nod, encouraging her to keep sharing.

"I want to believe you about the benefits of emotions and tears." She sniffles. "But it's hard to believe when I'm on the edge of losing it."

"Thank you for your honesty. Fear is a strong emotion, but I hope in time, I will be able to help you overcome that struggle. Please go on."

"When I first met Anna, she came over to babysit. My sisters were carrying on...."

Catie
Summer 1962

I hear giggles from Mommy's old bedroom. My curiosity sparks. I skip down the hall to see what my sisters are busy doin'. Charlotte's strappin' on some white contraption with silver loops danglin' from her waist. She models whatever it is. Claudia and Carolyn study her every move.

I nose my way into their room. "What's that, Char?"

"It's a garter belt."

"A garter belt? Like a garter snake?"

"No, Catie, It's a ladies' undergarment made to hold up silk stockings, like these." She holds out a pair of suntan-colored, see-through stockin's—leg-shaped.

My eyes widen with the same interest as my sisters. Char rolls and gathers the soft silk down to the ankle then slips her petite foot inside. Slow and steady, she glides the stockin' up her slender leg and then fastens the silver loop onto the top. Her ivory leg turns tan, as if she's been to the beach all summer. I stand back and watch each of my sisters take turns tryin' on these beautiful stockin's.

Charlotte poses, placin' hands on her hips, with one leg bent at the knee, restin' her foot on a pointed toe. She's so sophisticated and grown-up. I'm all google-eyed 'cuz I want to be just like her. I wait, hopin' for a turn. It's so excitin' and cool.

I want to be as old as Charlotte so that I can wear silk stockin's. She's almost a teenager (next month) and in Junior High school. For me, playin' grown-up dress-up is way up there with fairytale princess stories.

I ease my way and slowly nudge into the middle of them.

I point to Claudia's and Carolyn's calves. Then I tell them, "I'm ready to stop wearin' these anklets, skip the knee socks, the kind you guys wear, and be just like Charlotte so that I can wear silk stockin's."

I make big puppy dog eyes. "When's my turn?"

I'm in my own dream world, when I'm shaken out of it by my sister's words. "Catie, you're too young, too small, too, too, too ..."

"Just let me try. What harm would it be? Let me try. Come on, for grins and giggles?"

I make faces to make them laugh. I keep on askin' and beggin'.

"Catie, No! Quit bugging us! You're in the way."

"Come on, you guys. I'm your little sister. You should feel bad pushin' me out of the fun. What if I tell Daddy? Please, pretty please? Cherry on top? Come on."

No response.

"You're treatin' me the way the wicked stepsisters treated Cinderella. I want to go to the ball too!" I spout, and then walk away, 'cuz I don't want them to see my tears. I just know I'll die if I can't feel those magical silk stockin's. And so what if my legs are skinny little girl legs?

I crawl up onto the livin' room couch. Ouch, ouch, ouch. My tummy rumbles. I rock myself to stop the aches and knots that grip my belly. I don't go to my sisters. They've already made it very plain—I'm unwanted. They treat me like I have cooties. The cramps get worse. Sharp—stabbin' pains take my breath away and I double over.

Anna, my daddy's new friend, is babysittin' tonight. Charlotte says she looks just like Marilyn Monroe. I'm not sure I like her 'cuz she's not my mommy. Besides, she wears too much perfume, and too much lipstick. Her lips are as red as an apple and the whole house smells like her, even the back bedrooms.

I try harder to make the pain go away, but rockin' doesn't help.

Anna watches Charley in the corner, who's playin' with his blocks, as my sisters continue to prance and primp for their pretend grand gala.

Another sharp pain rips at my insides. I gasp and cry out in pain. I don't want to cry, but I can't help myself.

Anna whirls her head my way and rushes in my direction. "Are you okay, Catie? What's wrong?"

I can't get the words out. The pain steals my voice. I mouth the words, "My tummy."

My sisters; Charlotte, Claudia, and Carolyn appear. Claudia runs over with the garter belt and stockin's swingin' from her hand. The other girls tuck behind.

Claudia offers, "Catie; you can put on the stockings. Maybe we can find a safety pin or two to make the garter belt small enough to fit you. We're sorry. Come on; please stop crying. It's your turn. Now get up."

Claudia's tear-filled eyes watch me, strugglin' on the couch. I can't breathe, much less talk. I push the stockin's aside. I gasp for air with the next stabbin' pain. Anna puts her hand on my stomach, then presses on different parts of my belly.

"Does this hurt?"

I scream and pull up my legs, wrappin' my arms around my shins to protect my belly from her smushin'.

My sisters gather around. Anna jumps up and rushes toward the wall phone. I hear her askin' the cab company for a ride to the local hospital. Her next phone call is to the bowlin' alley, where she leaves a message for my daddy.

The cab ride speeds by. My stomach aches, but Anna's hugs make it feel a little bit better. She pets my head. "It's okay, Angel Baby. I'll get you to the doctor, and it will be okay. You'll see. It will be okay." Anna holds me in her arms, caressin' my back and brushin' the sweaty bangs off my forehead.

A plump, dark-haired doctor pulls the curtain closed. He enters with a nurse, her curly hair peekin' out from her nurse's cap. She follows him, carryin' somethin' in her arms. They introduce themselves as Dr. Wilson and Miss Nancy. He presses around my tummy, layin' both his hands firmly across the area. "Um-hum...Um-hum."

Through an openin' in the curtain, I squint, and see my daddy hurryin' across the hospital room toward me. I lift my arms to him.

"Daddy, Daddy, somethin's wrong with my tummy. It hurts awful bad."

He hugs me tight. Turnin', yet still holdin' on to me, he looks at the doctor. "What's wrong with my little girl?"

"Hello. You must be Catie's father? I'm Dr. Wilson."

Daddy lets go to shake the doctor's hand.

"Based upon my examination, I have found Catie's intestines to be in spasm. This condition is often brought on by stress. Is there any anxiety, tension, or conflict going on in her life presently?"

Daddy sends me a soft, warm smile and a wink. He makes his way over to the doctor and nurse, then motions for them to follow him. They leave the room.

Anna stays with me. "Catie, Angel Baby, your daddy's just talking to the doctor about how to make you feel better."

"Miss Anna, do you think he's tellin' the doctor 'bout Mommy goin' to heaven?"

Her eyes narrow. She tries to look away, but I see her. A shiver runs up my spine. The room feels colder. I wrinkle my nose. Anna doesn't smell like perfume anymore, she smells funny—stinks, but

I don't say anythin', 'cuz I know Mommy would say I was bein' rude.

"Anna, did you know my mommy? Did you not like her?" I stare.

Her smile looks fake. Seems to me that she's pretendin' to be nice.

"No, Catie, I didn't know your mother. But let's not talk about that now. How are you feeling?"

I don't believe her. The hairs on my arms stand up, the same way it did this summer when cousin Jeffy was tellin' ghost stories. I pull my hospital blanket up around my shoulders. The room feels icy cold now, but Anna doesn't seem to notice. *Somethin's wrong with her.*

The nurse walks back into the room, carryin' a tiny tray with a clear cup filled with a red liquid. Daddy and the chubby doctor return. Dr. Wilson takes the cup from Miss Nancy into his huge hands and brings it to me.

"Here you go, Catie. This medication is for you. It's sweet cherry-syrup, and I think you'll like it. Most of all, it will make your tummy feel better. Does that sound good to you?" He tussles the top of my head, and then watches me drink the red liquid.

CHAPTER SEVEN

Catherine
October 1992

My dang nose is as red as Rudolph and runs like a faucet—allergies. I don't know what I'd do without this medication. I pop the small red pill and swallow. It usually only takes bout 20 minutes to work, but I keep the tissues nearby just in case.

In the meanwhile, I sort my school papers into three stacks, one for each class, and then insert each bundle into their proper folder inside my notebook before tucking everything into the book bag. I'm finished for the night, and it's only eight o'clock. Thank goodness my nose has finally stopped running.

I catch the phone on the third ring. "Hello."

"Hello. Is Catherine Williams there, please? This is Hunter Stone, calling from—"

"Hey, Hunter, this is Catherine. How ya doing?" I twist the cord with my fingers.

Hmmm, the teacher followed through with calling me. Wow, this may turn out to be my church, after all.

"Oh...um, I'm great. Ah, I'm calling to see if I can address your concerns about the church."

"Sure thing. That would be helpful. Now let me see..."

Hunter is kind enough to answer my questions about the church: their denomination, mission, vision, purpose, and statement of faith, as well as a few other details of interest.

Time sails away with ease as we gab about a multitude of subjects. He offers to show me around town, as well as introduce me to some of his friends. Like me, he loves the outdoors: skiing, snowshoeing, hiking, biking, and even rock climbing. Hunter talks about Colorado like it's a giant playground. I'm excited to hear about the opportunities at my fingertips.

My throat feels parched. I walk into the kitchen. With the phone held to my ear, I pour myself some orange juice. My eyes catch a glimpse of the clock.

"Oh my goodness, Hunter, do you realize what time it is?"

"No idea."

"Ten-thirty. We've been talking for two and a half hours." I race toward my bedroom. "I have to get up at five-thirty. Sorry, I need to get off the phone."

"Well,...okay...ah...how about we go to dinner and finish our conversation?"

"Okay. When?" I ask without thinking, then hesitate, because I've only seen this man once. Numerous questions race through my mind.

He seems nice and also sounds like he'd be a ton of fun. Is this wise? He could be a weirdo, like The Gnat.

"How about Friday night?" Hunter asks.

How else am I going to meet people?

I say yes before I have a change of heart. "Sure. Any suggestions as to where to go?"

"Where do you live? I'll pick a restaurant somewhere in your area," Hunter politely offers.

Don't tell him. After all, for all I know he could be an ax murderer.

"I live very close to the church, I mean, the seminary where the singles ministry meets. I'm not sure where the church is located."

He laughs. "I live nearby as well. How about this cute Italian restaurant up off Jefferson? Do you know the place near the Swedish Hospital?"

"As a matter of fact, I do. I was just there. It was great, but do you mind if we go to someplace else since I'm trying to get to know the area?"

"Sure, that's fine. How about the 'Fresh Fish Company' up on Hampden and Tamarac?"

I giggle, "Can you believe it? Been there too." I look at the clock, anxious to get off the phone.

"Wow, Catherine, for being brand new to town, you sure get around. It sounds like you have a lot of guys pounding at your door. I take it you've been on quite a few dates?"

Although his assumption isn't correct, I ignore his question. It isn't any of his business. Besides, men love mystery. I remain silent, knowing he will feel awkward and move on in our conversation.

Hunter rattles off two more suggestions of restaurants in the area, both of which I have eaten.

"Well, let me give this some thought. Can I call you later this week?" His voice remains upbeat and patient.

"That would be fine." I laugh. "Sorry, Hunter, I'm not trying to be difficult. I just want to try someplace new."

"Hey, no problem. I'm drawing a blank and know you need to get off the phone. You've got an early morning, and I'm glad it's you and not me," Hunter teases.

"Thanks a lot." I tease back. "It was nice talking with you.

And thank you for taking the time to phone me. Really, Hunter, I appreciate it. I'll talk with you later this week."

I hang up and hurry to make my lunch and get ready for bed. By the time I've washed my face, the clock glares 11:15 pm. I groan at the idea of dragging myself out of my comfy bed to a blaring alarm. My last thought is about my next meeting with Marion. How do I tell her about Anna, my wicked stepmother?

Catie
late Autumn 1962

D addy married our babysitter, Anna. She's his wife now—makin' her my stepmother. Anna has two daughters who now live at our house. Daddy said they got married by a judge at the courthouse in town. None of us went to the weddin'. There was no room for seven kids. That was a whole week ago.

I head outside and let the screen door slam. We're goin' to collect pretty autumn leaves. Even though the peak has long passed, I'm still hopin' to find a giant-size pinkish red maple leaf to iron between wax paper.

Charlotte stops in her tracks once we're out of hearin' distance of Anna. Her face looks all red and shiny. Yikes, she looks mad. Her hands wave, goin' in all directions, and now she's pointin' her finger at Claudia and Carolyn. She's waggin' her finger in their faces.

"Well, I don't care what anyone says, they've both disrespected Mom by not waiting a full year to get married." She squints her eyes and wrinkles her face like she's 'bout to spit.

"But Charlotte, it's been eleven months, that's pretty close," I say, steppin' back a little.

"Exactly! So, what's the big deal? Why couldn't they have waited? I bet Mom is rolling over in her grave at the idea of Dad getting married so quickly. Even Granny Grunt and Grandpa say they should've waited longer."

She pushes her bangs off to the side, showin' her pretty blue eyes. "It's downright disrespectful. Anna's acting like a female dog in heat."

"Huh?" I say. "Char, what's that mean? Anna doesn't have a dog. Plus, it's November, so it's not hot."

"Never mind, Catie, you're too young to understand. Let's just say; it means they're thinking more about themselves than anyone else. It's not right, nor proper." She scoffs. "And after all Mom did for Dad and us kids. It's dishonoring. And it's all Anna's fault."

She stomps her foot, hard enough that her gym shoe comes untied. Claudia listens while she pulls on a pair of pink socks over her hands for gloves. Carolyn starts unfoldin' the brown paper sack we're gonna use to hold our leaves.

I don't understand the grown-up things my big sister is goin' on 'bout. All I know is I don't want Charlotte mad at me, givin' me the stink eye and silent treatment the way she does Daddy and Anna. If Charlotte, Grandpa, and Granny Grunt are all mad at Daddy, I'm thinkin' Mommy's probably mad too. But I don't want to be angry at Daddy, 'cuz he has too many people already upset with him.

Melinda is Anna's oldest daughter. She's almost eight and has dark brown hair and big green eyes that bulge like a bullfrog. I'm not 'pose to notice, 'cuz starin' is bad manners.

Shawnee is the same age as Charley, turned four last month. She's the pretty one, with bright brown eyes and silky yellow-blonde hair. I don't know them very well, but I hope they like to play games so we can have lots of fun together.

Right now, all I want to do is go on a treasure hunt for beautiful leaves. But Charlotte keeps on jabberin'.

"Anna's been married too many times, that's what Granny

69

Grunt says. She wouldn't tell me exactly how many husbands she's had, but she says Anna's been married as many times as Henry the eight, whoever he is."

We call my Mommy's mother, Granny Grunt, 'cuz she grunts so loud when she's in the bathroom. And it always takes a long time. Grandpa and Granny only have one bathroom. I had to go out in the bushes one time,' cuz I couldn't wait any longer for Granny Grunt to finish.

"Charlotte, we are wastin' the mornin' away. Let's get goin'. You can walk and talk at the same time." I whine, then tug at her sweater.

"Well, you'd better enjoy our time together because it won't be long before Anna's brats are going to have to be with us *all the time*. We're just lucky they're at their dad's house today."

Melinda and Shawnee always brag 'bout their Daddy Douglas. He buys them beautiful dresses, lots of candy, and always shows them a good time. I hope after he meets me, he'll send me candy too.

Shawnee and me are the same size, even though I'm two years older. Everyone says I'm small for my age. Anna promises she'll let me wear some of Shawnee's pretty dresses on special occasions. Her dresses are beautiful—like what a real princess would wear. I'm not sure when those special occasions will be, but I can't wait.

Carolyn and I skip far ahead, so we don't have to hear Charlotte complain. We spot the park. It's right across the street from the house with the wishin' well pond. It's one of my favorite summer swimmin' spots. But it's too cold today for any splashin' in the water.

We cross the street, lookin' at all the beautiful trees. I see one of my favorites, a maple, and it's still sheddin' its leaves. We squat, and scurry along the ground, lookin' for special leaves. I'm gonna take an extra leaf for Charley, who's back home takin' a nap. We hit the Jackpot as Charlotte walks up, still yappin' 'bout Daddy and Anna.

Marion
October 1992

C atherine enters the room carrying a beautiful reddish-pink maple leaf. She says she found it on the ground while walking to the office.

"I like the colorful leaves from the hardwood trees. Rich colors like these are hard to find in Colorado." She follows the veins of the leaf with her fingers. "The tree must have been planted by the college. This leaf brings back memories of how I loved to play in the leaves when I was a child."

Catherine takes a seat and crosses her legs. With each appointment, she appears more comfortable. I offer a welcoming smile while I gather my thoughts.

"At our last session, I was moved by your vulnerability and desire to be open and honest. I can see you are motivated by what you have remembered. The recalled details of your mother's death and when your dark dreams first began are very promising and a wonderful start."

I swallow a quick sip from my water bottle.

"However, moving forward will entail a discussion about the process of remembering."

"Okay." Catherine looks at me like a lost puppy yearning to be found.

"What has impressed me so far is your ability to identify the untruths of your child-like perception of God. You stated that you perceived the sound and lights of the ambulance to be a thunderstorm; therefore, you concluded God had taken your mother to heaven to bowl with him. Those impressions led you to believe the Lord was selfish. You also mentioned that you believed

God cared more about having a bowling partner than you having a mother. Is that accurate?"

"Absolutely. It sounds silly to think such things, but as a kid—it seemed and felt extremely real. All of a sudden my life unraveled and I felt robbed."

"Yes, I would imagine it would have been a genuine belief for a five-year-old. So much so, even today, with you being well into your thirties, I question if, at some level, you may still believe God is selfish?

She shrugs. "Possibly."

"It is essential to understand that additional suppressed memories, once recovered, may also be from a child's perspective. This point of view, based on your age and your ability or *lack of ability* to reason can be limited and skewed. Logic and reasoning are significant concepts because of the possibility of additional false beliefs being embedded in your unrecovered memories. We will address those child perceptions on an ongoing, as-needed basis. How do you feel about this?"

"It's all new to me. I'm not sure what you're describing. Much less what it will look like."

"To put it simply: Catherine, whatever you *believe*—whether true or not—creates emotions. And from there, your actions will follow. One example is your belief about God regarding your mother's death. You believed God was selfish, which awakened the emotion of distrust, and then your actions followed. You moved away from God. Does that ring true to you?"

"Oh...that makes it clearer. I think I get it now. And yes, most definitely, I want to know the truth about what happened in my past. And Marion, doesn't the Bible say somewhere—the truth will set you free?"

"Yes, in the book of John, 8:32." I open the Bible and read the verse aloud.

"Be encouraged, the fact that you were able to recognize the lies associated with the trauma of your mother's death is quite an accomplishment. And Catherine, I am truly sorry for your loss. It must have been hard to lose your mom at such a very young age."

"Thanks, Marion. To be honest, it's been so long that the sting has left. But I appreciate your compassion."

"Catherine, to clarify, you mentioned the details of your mother passing came to you in a dream? Is that correct?"

She nods. "It was the dream that gave me hope. The very reason I sought help." She raises her shoulders. "So here I am."

Her eyes shine, her smile is genuine.

"Dreams can be very revealing, as you have experienced. You have also commented more than once that you are plagued with an ongoing dream ever since childhood."

I check my watch to make sure we have ample time before posing my next question. "If you are ready and agreeable, would you mind describing the recurring nightmare?"

"Ah, um, ...sure. I can do that. I know this dream by heart, but I want to make sure I don't leave anything out. And I'm hoping you might be able to help decipher its meaning."

Catherine closes her eyes to concentrate as she reclines into the cushions.

"It begins with fragments of pictures flashing quickly, like watching a program in fast-forward. Nothing is detectable because it moves so fast—until it stops—and the images rest on a likeness of my hands. Yet, they aren't entirely mine; rather, there's a large pair of hands on top of mine. Similar to a transparency in an old anatomy book, placing one image over the other. Both are visible." She pushes her bangs to the side, out of her eyes.

"Then, it changes to our combined hands holding a soft fabric, a pure yellow satin. The man compresses my hand. Hard —he takes control. Then a crushing and kneading of the satin begins. Over and over. Bundling the cloth tighter and tighter."

Catherine moves her hands in the same motions she describes.

"With each gnashing of the fabric, deep dread and anxiety envelop me. I hear the rustling of the fabric, followed by the sharp pitch of it being torn. Ripped. It hurts."

Her face grimaces. Her hands cradle her stomach as she describes the details.

"I'm tempted to look toward the sound, but I can't. I set my focus on the satin. It has somehow, in some way, become my safety net—my anchor. I'm too afraid to look elsewhere. To take my eyes away, I sense—I know—would be much worse."

I watch as Catherine's face shines with perspiration. She winces as if in pain. Even telling the dream is causing her to react physically. She pauses briefly.

"I feel loss. Remorse." A tear balances on the corner of her eye. "My heart aches for the yellow fabric. Robbed. Ripped. Plundered of its original beauty. Now, ugly, defiled, and disheveled. I rivet my head to the side. I can't stand to look at the image any longer."

She pinches her eyes tight, then her mouth. She forces several determined blinks to fight off the tears running down her face.

"Catherine, please go on. You are doing great. Take a breath, and please continue."

"The scene changes without warning. A box of wooden matches comes into focus. I stare at the matches, relieved the satin has left my sight. Urgency. Panic. There's no time. I can't catch my breath. If I can only get ahold of the box of matches—even one match, to hide it, I might be able to stop what's about to happen. I reach. My fingertips are so close. But I can't."

She stops to blow her nose, keeping her eyes closed and her head low.

"I can't reach them. I feel pressure, knowing I must! An encroaching horror is drawing close. Too close. I tell myself to run. Hide. Fight. Wickedness surrounds me. Pitch-black darkness swallows me."

Catherine places her hand on her chest. She swallows a deep breath as if it might be her last. She continues.

"Panic sets in—my heart races. I can't breathe. I'm sure my chest will explode. Shifting my body, I struggle to wrench myself free from the paralyzing hold…"

Lifting her head, she opens her eyes. She stares. At me—no through me? She glares. Her words come slowly.

"Then, I wake up…I'm choking, and gasping for air. My

energy is gone. Stolen by the nightmare...again and again. Without fail, the same dream, the same order, with the same terror."

She drops her head, resting it in her hands. "Marion, it's exhausting." She takes a drink from what must be tepid coffee. "I live in fear of never knowing when this nightmare will rear its ugly head."

I listen intently. I am on pins and needles after hearing Catherine describe the dream. I write her description in the file. I remain silent, allowing her to elaborate on any further details.

She explains, "I know it's connected to my past, but I can't remember why or what happened."

She clenches her hand and bangs her fist against the air. "I'm so frustrated. I have no idea what it means. Only that it's hauntingly familiar."

I glance down, scripting the last word of her description into my notes—*hauntingly familiar.* Shivers slither down my spine. Her nightmare and its undisclosed meaning unnerve me. I compose myself before responding to her comments.

"Thank you, Catherine. After hearing your dream..." I pause. "I, too, question if it is linked to your suppressed memories. The unknown is something we will pursue, but I cannot say an exact time frame. I am trusting the Lord to lead us. All in time. I believe God is faithful. The meaning will be revealed when the time is right."

CHAPTER EIGHT

Catherine
November 1992

Whew...what a day! My life has taken on the theme: *Remembering the unknown*. My thoughts swirl as I look at the many handouts I'm trying to memorize. My classes demand me to cram new information into my brain, while counseling sessions require me to dig-up and unearth the past from my mind. Everything's wearing on my nerves. *Am I doing too much?*

A small squirrel outside my window battles an acorn among the autumn leaves. While my eyes follow the frisky fellow scampering away, I catch a glimpse of the clock. What? 6:04! I jump up disregarding my notes spread across the dining room table and fly into the bedroom.

I'm supposed to meet Hunter at seven. Jetting into action, I dive into black jeans and boots and complement them with my fitted dressy teal sweater. There's no time for accessories. A spritz of perfume will have to do before grabbing my black leather Jacket. Dashing to my car, I run a brush through my hair for a quick fluff.

Driving to the address Hunter gave me goes without a glitch. The restaurant sign confirms I've arrived at the right place. Three minutes to spare. Great.

I pull up to a parking space directly out in front of the main entrance, but it requires me to parallel park. To my surprise, the motions of parking come back naturally, like riding a bike. After locking the car, I smile at the sign above the marquee, which reads, 'If you don't like garlic…Go Home!'

Hunter must have paid attention to our conversation about how much I love garlic and Italian food.

I feel almost fanciful. Here I am living in Colorado and about to have dinner with my new friend. A new friend that is spiritual and knows the Bible well—a bonus. And an extra bonus, I'm enjoying his class at church. My world is coming together with unexpected fun and excitement.

An older woman with kind eyes and a friendly smile greets me at the hostess table. She takes my name and informs me of a five to ten-minute wait before I can be seated. I take note of her giving instructions to the wait staff and cooks in her native language, Italian, while she speaks English to the customers. I suspect she's the grandmother of this family-run restaurant. It's warm and quaint, which melts my heart, making me feel at home like I'm back in Europe.

It's my turn to be seated. Gesturing the hostess, I refer to the couple standing behind me.

"Please let them go. I'm waiting for a friend to arrive."

I check my watch at ten minutes after seven. I peek at the many souls now standing behind me in line. I motion yet again, this time, to a couple with their teenaged daughter. My smile, strained, as I look around for Hunter. He isn't here.

Is he standing me up? He has five more minutes before I'm out of here. I

78

understand being a few minutes late. But fifteen minutes is downright rude. What's up with these American men?

I shuffle my feet, switching my purse from one shoulder to the other while battling the feelings of anger paired with downright embarrassment. I've never been stood up. The thought of rejection stirs with a painful stab. Gritting my teeth, I search for the door, ready to run out of the restaurant.

Marion
November 1992

Catherine runs into the office, apologizing for being a few minutes late. She sits watching as I carry out our beverages. I know her well enough now to remember what she prefers to drink. After we have settled, I pose a request.

"Catherine, I have heard you refer to your lost years. What exactly, if anything, do you remember about that time frame?"

"The memories I do remember are becoming more explicit, but I rarely talk about my lost years. Not even with my family—it's just one of the many concealed skeletons in the closet. The subject makes me—us uncomfortable. Only on rare occasions have I shared any details with my closest friends. But they either ask too many questions or none at all and then change the subject, making the conversation awkward and uncomfortable.

"I remember most of what happened to my sisters. However, when it comes to Charley and me, my mind goes black—empty, numb. And this whole idea of memory suppression makes me nervous. Based on what you said, Marion, *if* I were too young to handle what happened, well then…I'm afraid I won't be able to handle it now. I may look like an adult, but I feel like a little kid inside when it comes to the years with my stepmother, Anna. I'm not sure if I dare to face whatever it is I've purposely forgotten."

Tension and stress rake over her face.

"Catherine, how about we begin with your history with Anna? Tell me what you do remember, and we will see where it takes us."

Catherine chews the inside of her cheek while gathering her thoughts.

"My first impressions of Anna were that she knew my mom and disliked her. I asked her, and she denied both questions. Being so young, vulnerable, and desperate for a mom, I hungered for a close relationship with Anna. My wishful thinking was only a child's dream." She looks down, rubbing her palms together. "Actually, it was a nightmare." The sides of her eyes crease with sadness.

"Anna and Dad were married in November of 1962. Our first holiday together was Christmas…"

Catie
Winter 1962

It's our first Christmas since Mommy's gone to heaven. I still miss her so-o-o-o much. Daddy will be home soon. He took time off work so that we can decorate our Christmas tree. And it's with Anna, Melinda, and Shawnee too, 'cuz it's our first Christmas together as a new family. We have nine in our family now. One, two, three…I love to count.

I bet we'll have our tree up rocket fast with all of us decoratin'.

I hope for cookies and milk afterward. Hot cocoa—even better. Candy would make a perfect night. I twirl around, dancin' with my sisters, singin' our favorite Christmas carols—the ones Mommy taught us. We love to dance, sing, and laugh.

I hear a car rumble. Pullin' back the curtains, we peek out to the driveway watchin' for Daddy. Charley slips beside me, on his tippy toes. We're giddy about Christmas, Jesus' birthday, and Santa, who brings gifts to all the good kids.

Melinda and Shawnee are wearin' their pouty faces. They want to be at their Daddy Douglas's house, 'cuz he gives them candy and gum. Melinda says they can have sweets whenever they want.

I ask, "Really? Even if you wanted one hundred pieces?"

Melinda says, "Yep. Even two hundred."

Shawnee nods her head in agreement.

"Wow, you're lucky. I can't imagine havin' a daddy like that. My daddy doesn't let us kids eat much candy. Plus, we're supposed to brush our teeth afterward."

Claudia dances over and offers a hand to the girls, to dance with us. Shawnee scoots to the front of the couch. Melinda pushes her back. "We don't want to sing any of your stupid songs. And you all look like dumb monkeys dancing around."

I ignore Meany Melinda. "Come on, Shawnee. It's fun. I can teach you the twist."

I extend my arms and bop around, motionin' her to join us.

I bet she wants to dance, 'cuz who would wanna sit with old frog-eyes grouchy Melinda anyway?

Melinda yells, "Leave her alone, Catie. Can't you see, we don't want to be here? Especially with any of *you*! It's not fair. We want to be with Daddy Douglas." She crosses her arms. Shawnee lowers her head and looks sad.

Claudia tries to reason with her. "But Melinda, you and Shawnee will still get the presents. You only have to wait a day or two after Christmas."

I add, "You're the biggest lucky ducks, 'cuz you'll have an extra Christmas."

Melinda hollers, "Mommy, Catie and Claudia are bothering Shawnee and me. They won't leave us alone."

She starts fake cryin'—loud, tryin' to get us in trouble. Good thing Anna doesn't hear. My sisters pull Claudia and me back into the circle of dancin'. We sing louder to cover up Melinda's phony tearless cries. We're thrilled 'bout decoratin' the tree.

Daddy slips in the front door, surprisin' us. We run over, screechin', "Daddy's home, Daddy's home!"

After collectin' our hugs, he writes our names on pieces of paper and puts them into a red cereal bowl. Coverin' his hand over the top, he picks out the four names of who will get to go with him and Anna to pick out the Christmas tree. It's a super-duper big deal. With seven kids, Daddy says, it's just too difficult to fit all of us into one car. He opens each of the four pieces of paper revealin' who's won. My name comes out first.

"I get to go!…I get to go!"

I'm over the top singin' and twirlin' around. Charley's name is next. He jumps up and down, over and over, his version of dancin'. I grab his hand, and spin him in a circle, while we chime together, "We get to go-o! We get to go-o!"

The next two names are Melinda's and Shawnee's.

What?

Charlotte winks at me. That's when I know; it's fixed. They must've decided for us younger kids to go.

Melinda will ruin everythin'.

We park the car at the tree lot, and Melinda, Shawnee, Charley, and me pile out and race toward the trees. I run back. "Daddy…Daddy, I want to look at *every tree* so that we can pick out the *very best one.*"

After we browse through trees, Daddy sets out three good ones for us to pick from. Me and Charley sniff the pine scent deep into our noses.

"Smell, Daddy. The trees you picked all smell just like Christmas."

"You've got that right, Catie." Daddy chuckles. His eyes sparkle like the stars.

It isn't an easy pick, 'cuz they're all so beautiful. Daddy, along with the scruffy, bearded, wrinkly man at the tree lot, tie our best tree onto the top of the car. They pull hard on the ropes makin' sure they're tight.

Charley and me walk to the car, pretendin' we're smokin' cigarettes. The cold Christmas air looks like smoke when we blow air from our mouths.

Melinda says, "You both look stupid."

"No, we don't," I say. "You're just jealous 'cuz we're havin' fun."

She crinkles up her nose and sticks out her tongue.

"Daddy, Melinda just stuck her tongue out at me." I tug on his coat. "Tell her to stop. That's not nice."

Anna butts in. "You kids—shut up and get in the car." Her face looks cross.

I don't know why she's yellin' at me. I din't do anythin'. I obey. We crawl up onto the back seat. Again, Melinda sticks out her tongue. This time it's at her mommy behind her back.

"Anna, Anna. Melinda just stuck out her tongue at you."

Anna turns, pointin' her finger at me. "Enough!" Her eyes bulge.

I jump back. "Daddy," I whimper.

"Come on, everyone," he says. "It's almost Christmas. Let's have some peace and quiet around here." His face tightens as he looks at Anna.

It's a quiet drive home. I pull Charley close, right up next to me and as far away from Melinda as possible. We don't want to catch her cooties. She's a brat and looks like a frog-face and not very nice at all. For an eight-year-old, she must drink a lot of pickle juice, 'cuz she sure is sour.

Arrivin' home, we cheer and clap as Daddy pulls the tree off the car roof. We stand on each side of the tree and hold tight onto one of the branches. We lift the limbs as best we can, to help carry it inside.

Melinda opens her big mouth *again*. "Catie, you and Charley are just in the way."

I frown at her, still walkin' in step with Charley and Daddy. *I wish she'd just shut her big fat frog-face mouth.*

Charlotte, Claudia, and Carolyn run out into the yard to help. They grab the trunk, makin' it easier to carry. The branches scrape along the sides of the front door as Daddy pulls the tree, top first, into the house. A trail of pine needles falls onto the floor.

It feels toasty warm inside our livin' room. We pull off our coats, mittens, and scarfs, and hand them to Charlotte, who hangs them in the hall closet.

Our tree looks even bigger inside our home. We gather around as Daddy and Anna steady the stand. Charlotte and Claudia scurry on their bellies under the tree. They twist the screws tight into the trunk. Carolyn walks in from the kitchen carryin' a pitcher with aspirin and sugar added to the water. Daddy says that's what Christmas trees like to eat. I can understand the sugar, but the aspirin, ICK! Well, unless it's yummy baby aspirins. They taste like sweet tangerines.

Us girls grab the stacked boxes from the corner. Each kid is assigned somethin' to do. My two older sisters, Charlotte and Claudia sort out the decorations. Carolyn, who is the middle child, fluffs the branches. Charley and me unwind the garland. Everyone is helpin' except Melinda and Shawnee, who are still wearin' their pouty faces.

Daddy's job is to fasten on the lights; red, blue, green, yellow, and purple. We take turns puttin' on Christmas ornaments. They're a rainbow of colors. I'm little and short, so I can only place bulbs so high, but my sisters are tall enough to reach almost to the top. Daddy finishes attachin' decorations on the very top and then lifts Charley to place the angel on the tippy top. Beautiful!

I scratch my arms. "This sure is an itchy Christmas tree."

Daddy overhears. "Catie, come over here. Let me take a look at you."

I skip over to him. He checks my arms, my legs, neck, tummy, and everywhere. I have red welts and little blotchy spots all over me. He takes one of the fallen needles from the floor and pokes it on my arm. Within a few seconds, another blotch wells up. It itches.

"Daddy, I think this might be a mosquito Christmas tree."

Through his smile, he says, "No, Catie, that's not the problem. You're allergic to this tree."

Carolyn walks up to Daddy. "I think I'm allergic too." She shows him her arms. Yep, Carolyn has red bumps and welts all over her too.

Anna acts all concerned, lovin', and supportive. Everyone else laughs and thinks it's funny. Only at first, though, 'cuz none of us has any idea that bein' allergic to the tree means we'll have to take it down and start all over.

But I'm happy, 'cuz Carolyn and me get to go in the car with Daddy and Anna, all by ourselves. Everyone else has to stay at home. Charlotte babysits.

As it turns out, we're not allergic to all Christmas trees, just the pretty kind. At the tree lot Daddy pricks our arms with every type of tree. We end up with a long needle type with thin branches, wide apart. Orphan lookin' if you ask me.

When we arrive home with our new tree, Carolyn, who's never afraid to say what she thinks, says, "It's the best ugly tree."

We all laugh and start the decoratin' all over again. It's already dark outside. Everyone isn't quite as excited as before.

Soon after, we all have sleepy eyes. My eyes feel heavy too. I din't quite remember finishin' trimmin' the tree. And most important, I din't remember any cookies or hot cocoa.

The next mornin', after breakfast, I'm colorin' at the kitchen table. Daddy and Anna are talkin'.

Daddy asks, "Anna, why don't you like Charley?"

"I like him, okay. I'm just not used to boys." Anna stirs her coffee and sets the spoon to the side on her saucer.

Still colorin' and not lookin' up, I *think* out loud. "No, you don't, you always yell at him and pick on him. You know, he's only four. You don't treat Shawnee like that, and she's the same age—"

SLAP! My head jars. My face stings. *I can't believe it. Anna slapped me across my face.*

I turn to Daddy. Tears flow down my cheeks. "Daddy," is all I muster out. I reach out to him—sobbin'.

"Catie, give Daddy a minute to talk with Anna." He wipes the tears from my face. His jaw's tight, his teeth gritted. "You go play with your sisters. Okay?"

CHAPTER NINE

Catherine
November 1992

S till vacillating between embarrassment and anger, my jaw
tightens, and I grit my teeth. I feel foolish for having waited
so long. I turn to bolt out of the restaurant just as Hunter opens
the entrance door. Our eyes meet, and he smiles. I frown at him,
fuming.

He glides over to my side. "Hey, Catherine. I was just—"

"Where have you been?" I interrupt, tapping my watch.
"You're lucky I didn't leave. I was giving you five more minutes.
You arrived just when I was turning to go," I spout with my hands
on my hips, my eyes bearing down on his.

"Wow." He steps back, smiling. A nervous laugh bubbles up.

"I've been in the parking lot for the last fifteen minutes, waiting for you so that I could walk you into the restaurant."

"What parking lot?" I cock my head. "I pulled up right in front and parked on the street."

I point to my car, visible through the glass panes on the front door.

He throws his head back and his laughter heightens. "The parking lot is on the side. You lucked out, getting a spot out front. I've been outside, sweating it, thinking you'd stood me up."

My anger drains away and I join in his laughter. The misunderstanding is resolved, immediately breaking the ice.

"Here I was thinking the same thing," I admit.

Arching an eyebrow, he says, "Guess that explains why you scolded me when I came through the door."

"You bet!" I smile, pretending I'm fine. But on the inside, my emotions holler at me like a bullhorn. To distract myself, I focus on what he is wearing. I can't help but smile. Hunter is also wearing a sweater with dressy black jeans. We look like twins, but instead of teal, his sweater is ultramarine blue, which compliments his bright blue eyes.

"Excuse me, please." The hostess politely grabs our attention. "Are you ready to be seated?"

Hunter nods. "Yes, please,…and if possible, could we have the table upfront in the bay window?"

"I'd say luck is in your favor today." She glances at me and winks. "That particular table just opened up. Follow me, please."

Hunter flashes a wide grin of triumph, taking credit for our happy fortune. He orders the house specialty, lasagna. I request spaghetti, Bolognese, and a house side salad. We dive into our meals, both being hungry. Immersed in conversation, we talk nonstop throughout the meal until the waitress returns, inquiring if we would care for any dessert.

"No, thank you, just the check, please." Hunter turns toward me, "Catherine, I thought it would be nice to have coffee and dessert across the street at this cute little French place called *Pour*

La France. I want to give you a taste of being back in Europe—here in the good old US of A."

I smile, feeling impressed he'd put some time into planning tonight's date. Or rather, *our meeting* to further discuss my questions about the church.

"Sounds fun," I say.

While signing his credit card receipt, Hunter looks up at me and says, "I enjoyed dinner. I'd have to say I've never been out with such a petite woman who can eat so much."

His observation is sincere and not offensive. I can see he is genuinely surprised—curious.

"Well, I did tell you I ate like a bird. But I guess I forgot to mention it was a vulture."

Hunter rears his head back, laughing.

"I'm not the type of girl who orders a piece of lettuce with two croutons."

"That's what I like about you, Catherine, you're comfortable with being you."

He walks over, rests his hand on my chair-back, and assists me from the table, then helps me drape my coat over my shoulders.

Ahh…the perfect gentleman.

I stiffen, my back straightens, and I remind myself. *If only men were as honest as their mothers taught them to be. Be cautious, don't trust just any handsome stranger.*

The French bakery cafe' is a pleasant reminder of living in Europe. The French pastries, desserts, and coffee are all wonderfully familiar, and their aromas fill the room. My stomach, although full, finds room to enjoy the sweetness of a Crème' Schneider, washing it down with bold, French pressed, hot coffee.

We take our time, and when done, we stroll back across the street, chattering as if we've known each other for ages. After we reach my car, I rustle around in my purse and pull out my keys.

"Great sporty car." Hunter nods and grins in approval.

"Yes, and it's red." I blurt out enthusiastically, without thinking.

"Yes, it is." His face looks puzzled by my comment.

"Umm…uhh, it's my first red, umm, anything. I haven't always liked the color. Actually, I've found the color irritating, unnerving, and just downright disturbing." I smile, feeling my ears burn with the flush of embarrassment for having said so much— too much.

"Oh, yeah? Why's that?"

"Hmm…I'm not sure," I lie, then shrug my shoulders, not disclosing how the sight of red triggers anxiety. "But I decided it was high time to move beyond that challenge, so I purposely bought a red car."

"That's cool. Kinda like facing your fears, like in one of those Outward-Bound classes?"

"Yeah, something like that." I turn toward Hunter and smile, then without thinking, I casually rest a hand on his shoulder. "I had a wonderful time. We need to do this again."

Hunter's eyes widen, "Oh…okay…sure." His pause makes me blush. My face burns. I pull my hand back, realizing I just asked him out. *On a date!*

He opens my car door. "Drive carefully, Catherine. I'll give you a call about getting together." There's a sparkle in his eyes, a shy grin on his lips.

I climb in, crank up the engine, and watch him walk with confident strides towards the side parking lot before I drive away.

Will he call? Did I totally blow it? He probably thinks I'm forward or loose like the women who sunbathe topless in Europe. And why did I bring up the thing about the color red? I'm such an idiot.

90

Marion
November 1992

C atherine sits down, draping her book bag to the side of the love seat.

"Marion, you have a way of making me feel understood and accepted." She leans forward, her hands folded around one knee. "I wasn't sure if I'd like having two-hour appointments, but I'm finding I need that much time to relax. I've programmed myself to forget for so long; there's a learning curve to cooperate and focus on remembering. I guess I'm just afraid."

Catherine pauses. Her brow furrows, then relaxes along with her shoulders. "Being honest with myself is refreshing. I have a sense of empowerment when I admit I'm afraid and uncertain."

She takes out her journal, ready to start. "This tormenting nightmare is exhausting. It seems like fear's always lurking. I never know when it will rear its ugly head. The nightmare somehow connects to my lost years, but not knowing the meaning unnerves me. I don't expect others to understand. After all, even I don't understand." She tilts her head, squeezing out a faint grin. "I'm thankful I have you and that we can talk."

I return a warm smile. "I am here for you. Based upon the experiences you have shared, this discussion is not your average, cup-of-coffee conversation." I say, trying to lighten the moment. "With the Lord's guidance and counseling, I hope you will find clarity."

"Me too."

I lean forward. "I would like to help you understand how you developed a belief system using the example of your mother's death."

Catherine nods.

"Your perceptions were from a child's point of view, which led you to believe you were unvalued, not good enough, and questioning if something was wrong with you. Therefore, you have filtered your life and circumstances through these untruths. Does that make sense to you?"

She shrugs her shoulders. "Maybe. I'm not sure."

"Let me explain. It is like a coffee pot; the drip system with the filter above." I place my hands into the shape of a filter to illustrate my example.

"The clear water represents life, which is poured over coffee grounds, which are merely circumstances. The filter represents your beliefs about yourself, others, and God."

I continue to make hand gestures throughout my explanation.

"The collected brewed coffee represents your conclusions or how you have interpreted your life situations. It appears your filter is one that believes you are not valued and do not measure up. You have filtered those beliefs into all your experiences. This belief is conscious, as well as subconscious. This process, in your past, as well as the present, skews, darkens, and taints your understanding, resulting in misconceptions. These misconceptions are not only about yourself, but also about God, and others, including their motives. Does this comparison make the concept a little clearer to you?"

Catherine nods, a cue for me to continue.

"What you believe governs your emotions and actions. False beliefs can lead to inappropriate reactions. You may even overreact."

I purposely wait as Catherine finishes her notetaking. After a few minutes, I continue.

"Some of your beliefs will most likely be proven to be lies or a carried-over flawed perception of a child." I tilt my head. "Can you recall a time when you may have overreacted or when inappropriate reactions have happened?"

She shakes her head as if disappointed. "All too well. You remember Hunter, the guy I told you about? The one who teaches the Bible class, where I had the Gnat-Experience?"

I nod.

"Well, he asked me out to dinner, and there was a mix-up with the parking lots. He was waiting for me outside, and I was waiting for him inside. We both thought we were stood-up. On the inside, I was fuming. I wouldn't have been surprised if there was smoke coming out of my ears."

I interrupt. "Exactly what were you feeling?" Believing? What is the first thing that came into your mind?"

She pauses to take a deep breath. She stiffens.

"Come on, Catherine, do not overthink the question. Just say your response."

"Okay." Her expression hardens, her brows come together, and her voice tightens with anger. "I'm not good enough. Something must be wrong with me. I don't measure up. I will never have what it takes. No matter what, people leave me."

I send her a gentle smile. "Catherine, although you are feeling an array of emotions, this is progress. I am proud of you for being so transparent. It takes courage to be this vulnerable and real."

She sighs, her eyes scanning the ceiling. "It stirred up the rejection I felt from my ex. I tried so hard to be the best wife. And where did that get me? He saw me as too independent. He felt unneeded, so the man ran off with my *needy* ex-best friend. I'm damned if I do and damned if I don't." She sinks further down into the love seat, closing her eyes.

She opens her eyes, turns her head, and says, "Marion, counseling is tough."

"Catherine, seeking help, as you have, requires strength and is not for sissies."

Her smile is a positive response.

"What happened with Hunter?" I continue writing notes.

"Talk about emotions. I was feeling so rejected I jumped all over the poor guy when he finally arrived."

"Did he ask you for a second date?" I ask, with a smirk on my face.

"Yes, no…umm, I think I asked him out. That's something I've never done." She crosses her legs. "It was a bit confusing, but overall we were able to sort out our misunderstanding. He was charming about the mix-up. Although initially, I had to pretend. You know, cover up how mad I really was."

She squirms. "Perhaps I was feeling hurt. Regardless, my reaction was over-the-top and didn't make sense for the circumstances. Thankfully, we enjoyed a nice dinner and dessert. Hunter had put a lot of effort into the planning, which I appreciated. Talking about filters, the whole time I kept questioning if Hunter—or any man for that matter—was trustworthy. Whenever I had a nice thought about him, I'd question it, bringing back my world of suspicion and distrust of men."

Before I can interject, Catherine adds, "Heck, not just men, women...well, I'd have to say, people in general."

I raise my brow. "Trust issues? Judgments? Accusations? Without proof?"

She presses her lips together. "I suppose you're right when you put it that way." She jots down some notes.

"Catherine, it is prudent for people to assess their situations. While collecting information and opinions about others, it is wise to be aware of your unique filter and how it works. It is important to consider your triggers or the things that set you off." I reach for my Bible and start flipping through the pages.

Pausing, I say, "Here is a great quote from James 1:19, 'Everyone should be quick to listen, slow to speak, and slow to become angry.'"

I close my Bible and set it back on the desk. "Being a good listener affords you and others the ability to build friendships and relationships."

"How do you do that? I mean, not react?" Catherine asks.

"Just like it says in the quote. Be quick to listen. Pay attention to what is said, and what you are saying. Ponder your thoughts before you respond. As an assignment, I would like you to write down your thoughts and try to identify the lies you are saying, hearing, and believing. Train your ears to listen."

"Okay, I can work on that. Marion, I hate to admit it, but you're right. I need to get a grip on this reacting stuff."

She sets her open journal to the side, revealing how her doodles have turned into hard straight lines scratched deep into the paper. She tosses her pen down onto the cushion and her jaw tightens.

"I don't have any confidence in my judgment of people. Not only my ex-husband, Edward, but I suppose everybody. It isn't something I like about myself. I'm skeptical. As far back as I can remember, I've believed people are pretenders. Not only about who they are but also about their circumstances—maximizing and minimizing—to downright denial about what's true. As a child, I thought it was me who was confused. Now I see it as people lying about themselves."

I tap my pen against my lips. "When was the first time you remembered feeling uncertain, leery, or distrustful of people?"

"When I was a kid, with Anna and her family…"

Catie
Winter 1963

My sisters, Charley, and me, all dart out the front door, racin' one another. Gravel spits out from under our feet as we sprint to be the first to get to the car.

Melinda and Shawnee lollygag behind, draggin' their feet. They never want to have fun. Well, Shawnee wants to, but Melinda never lets her.

Daddy and Anna aren't even down the front steps when Melinda starts in with her usual whinin'. "Mom, it's mine and

Shawnee's turn to sit in the front seat." She fake pouts and pushes out her lower lip. "Besides, there's no room in the back."

Before waitin' for Anna's permission, Melinda shoves her way into the front seat with her little sister. While Anna is distracted, closin' the car door, Melinda wrinkles up her nose, sticks out her tongue, and mouths, 'na-na, na-na, na.'

Who cares? I dint' want to sit with her anyway.

I turn away to take a look out the window. It's Saturday mornin'. Bein' February, the air is chilly with scattered spots of snow on the ground. I love seein' the sun. I miss it 'cuz the winter skies are almost always gray or gloomy, from November till May. But, today is a bright sunny day, meltin' the snow and makin' lots of mud. I love mud and am excited 'bout stompin' around in it with my yellow rubber boots.

We're all squished into the back seat—oldest to youngest: Charlotte, Claudia, Carolyn, and me. Charley snuggles up on Charlotte's lap. Wearin' winter coats sure makes it hot. That's the problem with early spring. You're cold in the mornin's and burnin' up by the afternoon. We wiggle out of our jackets the best we can with the five of us all bunched up in the back seat.

Anna tells us 'bout her mom, who we'll meet today for the first time.

"My mother's name is Ivy, but you may call her Granny Ivy."

Melinda jerks on Anna's sleeve. "No, Mom," she whines. "That's what we call her."

"Oh, my darling, it's okay for them to call her Granny Ivy. Don't you worry one bit; you and Shawnee will always be her favorites."

Anna twists her head to look at us in the back seat. Her eyes are bright likes she's excited to tell us a story or maybe a secret. Bein' curious like George the monkey, Anna has my full attention.

"My mother lives in the country, on a farm, with her husband, my stepfather, Buck." She loosens her scarf. "Dean is Granny Ivy's dad, my grandfather. He also lives there."

She runs her fingers through Shawnee's blonde hair, seemin'

pleased with the smile and excitement in her four-year-old daughter.

"They have beautiful fields and—"

Shawnee interrupts, tips her head, and looks up at Anna. "Don't forget to tell them about the barn cats and kittens. And..." she pauses, catchin' her breath, "butterflies, lots of butterflies, bumblebees, June-bugs, and lightning bugs at night."

Charley leans into the front seat. "Can you catch 'em?"

Anna pipes in, "Shawnee, those are summer bugs, so you'll have to wait a few months before you'll be able to do any bug catching."

Shawnee giggles. "I like all the creepy crawlers. When the weather gets warmer I can ask Granny Ivy to give us some jars to put the bugs inside."

Charley bounces on Charlotte's lap and she lets out a moan. "Charley, you're about to bust my legs, little buddy."

Anna eyes us. "No bug-catching today, but exploring is fine, but only *after* you've met my family. Keep in mind, this time of year, the farm is very muddy, so take your boots off at the back door. Don't be tracking mud onto my mother's kitchen floor. You hear?"

My sisters all nod, and I start dancin' in my seat.

"Yay, Charley." I lean forward to see him. "Did you hear that? It's gonna be muddy." I scoot to the edge of the seat and reach over the front seat to tap Shawnee on the shoulder. "Do they have any sand so that we can make sugar cookies?"

Shawnee turns and smiles. "They sure do."

Melinda pipes in. "Only buttholes like *you* would want to make sugar cookies out of the dirt."

"Dad...Melinda just called me a butt hole."

Anna grumbles. "Now, Catie, you're going to have to work at getting along better with Melinda." Anna gently pats Melinda's hand. "Now, Darling, be nice."

I scoff. "Ahk...she started it."

Charlotte puts her finger to her lips, signalin' me to shush. "Hey Catie, I think you, Charley, and Shawnee are going to have a great time playing in the mud and exploring. I'm sure Shawnee will show you a good time."

Charlotte winks at Shawnee, who's now completely turned around. She looks happy and chirpy. Her hands are perched on the top of the front seat, and with that yellow hair of hers, she reminds me of a cute canary.

Melinda glares at Charlotte, givin' her the stink-eye. Carolyn asks Anna a phony question to distract her, while Charlotte moves her face closer to Melinda, givin' her the same look—right back. She also shows her teeth, remindin' me of my grandpa's dog, Poncho. Everybody knows a dog shows its teeth before it bites. That's the exact message Charlotte's givin' frog-eyes-Meanie Melinda.

I'm dancin' in the backseat again. Anna probably thinks it's 'cuz I'm excited about meetin' her family, which I am. But I'm more excited 'bout Charlotte lettin' frog-eyes know she has it out for her if she keeps messin' with me.

My excitement grows as Anna describes her parents' home. She talks about a barn, horses, and a cow, with lots of cats and dogs. Most of the cats live inside the barn, but some live outside if the weather's warm. Anna says it's the cats' job to keep the mice under control. This means the cats kill the mice and eat 'em. I know 'cuz of cartoons.

Sometimes grown-ups say things to make the real stuff sound better. Or don't say anythin' at all if it makes them uncomfortable, even if it's somethin' horrible. They just pretend it's not there.

Teenage Granny told me about the make-believe game grown-ups play. She said it's like ignorin' the elephant in the room. How can anyone pretend there's not an elephant in the room? It's so big; it would squash you.

We arrive at the farm. I squirm to sit up taller, givin' me a better look out the window. Daddy drives slowly, followin' the long dirt driveway curvin' back behind the farmhouse. A big red barn and a barbed-wire fence sit beyond the house. Squintin', I can make out some animals roamin' around but can't tell what they are.

We pile out of the car. Daddy gives orders to Charlotte and Claudia to keep an eye on Carolyn, Charley, and me, so we don't touch or get into anythin'.

Melinda and Shawnee run ahead, yellin', "Granny Ivy, Granny Ivy!"

Anna follows behind.

We gather into a small back entryway and balance off one another, to take off our boots. We line them up carefully along the wall, followin' Anna's instructions. Then we remove our jackets and hand them to Charlotte and Claudia, who hang them on the high coat hooks.

Charlotte still isn't happy 'bout Daddy remarryin'. He knows it, too. Charlotte stands with Carolyn, their faces lookin' all snarly. Carolyn doesn't like Anna. She doesn't even try to hide how she feels. Neither are thrilled about meetin' our new grandparents.

Claudia, Charley, and me are hopin' they'll be as sweet as Mommy's parents, Granny Grunt and Grandpa, and my favorite, Daddy's mama, Teenage Granny.

We walk into the kitchen in our stockin' feet. Wow, this kitchen seems a mile long. My eyes widen with curiosity. *What could be in all those cupboards?* I point and look at Claudia, to see if she's wonderin' the same thing.

Claudia's starin' at somethin' altogether different. I move from behind to see where she's gawkin'. All I can see is Melinda and Shawnee huggin' their grandma. I can't see her face on account of it bein' buried between the girl's hair and necks. She's a tiny woman, just like Anna.

Her dark red hair is pulled up in pin-curls with two bobby pins in each of the many circles coverin' her head as if she were 'bout to go to bed. Din't she know we were comin' to visit?

I hear her ask, "Do you have room in your bellies for some cookies? I baked your favorite."

My ears perk, and without thinkin', I hear myself shout, "I like cookies!"

Anna and Ivy look at me. Anna smiles. "Catie, come over here and meet my mom, Granny Ivy."

I stand frozen in my tracks, unable to move closer to Anna's mother. A long gash runs from the bottom of her eye, down her cheek, all the way to her jaw. Her face is full of icky stitches. She looks like Frankenstein. There's no way I'm goin' over to that scary woman.

Daddy puts his hand on the back of my waist and gently pushes me toward her. I stiffen. I stare straight into her face while reachin' back frantically to catch hold of Claudia. I fumble in the air till I feel a button on her sweater. I yank her close, then whirl around searchin' for Claudia's help. She's wide-eyed and starin' straight ahead. My eyes dart toward Charlotte and Carolyn, who are standin' still, too. They're real quiet, also gawkin' at the gigantic red gash cuttin' its way down this strange woman's face. Charley hides his face in Carolyn's light blue slacks.

Granny Ivy speaks, and her voice sounds hoarse like she has a sore throat. "Now, kids, don't be shy. I have enough cookies for all of you."

Did whatever cut her face also cut inside her throat?

Thankfully, Claudia bravely steps forward. "Hi, Miss Ivy. I'm Claudia. It's nice to meet you." She offers out her hand, and then makes the slightest dip, like a small curtsy.

"Nice to meet you too, Claudia." Ivy shakes her hand and raises her eyebrows, noddin' at Anna. Seems like she's impressed with Claudia's manners.

Suddenly, we all become a shy bunch of kids. Dad spreads his arms, herdin' us closer toward the creepy old woman.

"Ivy, I'd like you to meet my children." Lockin' eyes with Charlotte, he gestures for her to move forward. "This is my oldest daughter, Charlotte, who has recently become a teenager—thirteen." Charlotte glances up with a strained smile. And you've already met Claudia, who has never met a stranger. She's ten, eleven in a few months."

Daddy and Claudia both smile at Ivy.

"This is my middle child, Carolyn, who's eight."

Carolyn stares up at Ivy. Her unfriendly stubbornness speaks as loud as a bullhorn, even though she doesn't say a word. She crosses her arms over her chest and then looks down at the linoleum-tiled floor.

Daddy places his hands on my shoulder. "And this is my baby girl, Catie. She's six and isn't normally this shy, but I'm sure it will be short-lived once she has one of those delicious cookies on the counter."

Daddy urges me forward. I don't budge.

Charley pushes up against Daddy's leg, looks at him and then nods toward the cookies. Daddy let out a chuckle. "And this is my boy, Charles, but we call him Charley."

Ivy takes the plate of freshly baked cookies from the cupboard and lowers them in front of me and Charley, who has inched himself next to me. The smell of chocolate reaches our noses. We both inhale deeply. Charley stretches out his little hand, palm up, while his other hand is hangin' on tight to my shirtsleeve.

Melinda barges in. "Me first, Granny Ivy. Me first. Come on, Shawnee, get some cookies before they're all gone."

Melinda elbows herself between the plate and Charley and me while we wait.

Daddy says, "Come on, girls, I'm sure there's plenty for all. Don't crowd your grandmother."

We scoot back. Each takes a turn acceptin' a cookie, followed by, "Thank you."

When it's my turn, I reach for a cookie. The old woman leans closer. UGH! I cringe and pull my neck back. Her ugly, scabby scar is inches from me. It looks like the bloody gash just happened, except for the sewin' thread that's holdin' it together. I dilly-dally tryin' to focus on her eyes and think 'bout what I'm 'pose to say. "Thank you, Miss Ivy."

"You can call me Granny Ivy."

But I don't want to. I look back at Daddy, pleadin' for him to say somethin'.

"It's okay, Catie, You can call her Granny Ivy. She's your *new* grandma. We're all family now."

Somethin' 'bout this doesn't feel right. I take a bite of the cookie.

Charley is handed a second cookie. "Thank you."

I grab Charley's hand and dash toward my sisters, who are at the far end of the kitchen. Carolyn stands next to me and turns her back to Anna and her daughters. "Look, Catie, the big fat pig, Melinda, has three cookies." She narrows her eyes. "That's not fair."

Carolyn deliberately twists around, firin' a dirty look directly at Melinda. She doesn't even care if Anna sees her, which she din't, but it still makes me nervous when Carolyn acts this way.

Charlotte chimes in. "You're right, it isn't fair."

Carolyn takes a bite of cookie and frowns. "*Poison Ivy's* cookies aren't any good anyway. They're dry. They'll never be as good as our mom's no-bake chocolate or oatmeal raisin cookies."

Anna sprints across the kitchen, comin' right at us and shoutin' orders.

"Gather up, kids. Put on your boots and coats, so we can all go outside for a tour around the farm."

After grabbin' my boots and jacket, I run out the back door with Carolyn. I snuggle up close and whisper into her ear. "Did you see her cut up face? She looks like Frankenstein. Why'd you call her Poison Ivy?"

Carolyn snarls, "First of all, she *isn't* our grandmother; she's Anna's mother. She's not our family! She's not our blood. She's only our *step-grand-monster*. And I don't like her. She gives me the heebie-jeebies and makes my skin feel creepy, so she's poison to me. That's why I'm calling her *Poison Ivy*."

Carolyn's quick-witted and clever with makin' jokes. I laugh, at first, 'cuz I think it's funny. But now I'm not so sure, 'cuz Ivy really does look like a monster. Real creepy like.

"So…I don't get it, Carolyn. Why's everyone pretendin' she looks normal?"

"Well, I sure didn't. We were all standing there, gawking at her, Catie."

"Yeah, I know, but Daddy, Anna, Melinda, and Shawnee din't say a thing. It looks like someone has taken a butcher knife to her face. They're all pretendin' the scary woman din't...." I stop mid-sentence, puttin' the pieces together.

"Carolyn, this is what Teenage Granny calls 'the elephant in the room'. Somethin's happened to that old lady, and no one wants to talk 'bout it."

I got it! I got it! I'm tickled at myself for figurin' out the riddle of the let's pretend game. But it also scares me. "Why are they pretendin'? What do you think happened to Ivy?" I ask my sister.

CHAPTER TEN

Catie
Winter 1963

Melinda and Shawnee are bein' their usual snotty, bratty selves, always spyin' on us. I don't like the way they creep up from behind.

"We heard what you said. You better stop talking about Granny Ivy, or we're gonna tell, and you'll both be in big trouble."

Melinda points her finger at us. "You should know it's bad to talk about people behind their backs."

Carolyn din't miss a beat. "You do it all the time, Frog-Eyes."

I change the subject to avoid a fight. "Melinda, what happened to your granny?"

Shawnee or Melinda couldn't resist tellin' us the story, even though a few seconds ago Melinda was preachin' 'bout it bein' wrong to gossip.

In her four-year-old-baby voice, Shawnee blurts out, "Grandpa Buck's son knifed her."

"What?" I say, wide-eyed. "Who's Buck's son? Why'd he do it? What kind of knife?"

"Grandpa Buck's son doesn't like Granny Ivy, on account of he says she took something that didn't belong to her—she stole his dad away from his mom."

Melinda barks at her sister. "Shawnee shut up. Let me tell them what happened. I'm the oldest."

Carolyn and me move into a huddle with Melinda and Shawnee. We stand, our arms on top of one another's shoulders, squeezin' in, eager to hear all the gooey details. Charley runs over and pushes his head between our legs.

"What's you's doin'?" he says.

Melinda waves him into the huddle.

"I'm getting ready to tell them about what happened to my Granny Ivy's face."

Charley looks up, squeezzin' tighter onto our legs. His eyes are big and watery with a puzzled look on his face. I think he wants to pretend that what he saw wasn't real, just like the grown-ups.

"Mom says Grandpa Buck's son, Darryl—that's his name— got into a big fight with Grandma Ivy. They don't like each other much, just like Shawnee said. To hear Darryl talk, he said some stealing and cheating was going on, but Mama says it ain't true."

"Charley stands on his tippy-toes and whispers in my ear loud enough for Melinda and Shawnee to hear. "What did Granny Ivy steal?"

Shawnee answers. "Darryl said Granny Ivy stole his dad's cart."

Melinda snarls. "No, stupid baby, that's wrong. It was his heart."

Charley cocks his head, not followin' the conversation. Me, neither. I shrug my shoulders. Carolyn shakes her head and rolls her eyes.

Melinda jabbers on. "I told you, Mama said it ain't true. Mama says Darryl is just like his dad, having a red-hot temper. He's big and strong, the same as Grandpa Buck."

Shawnee butts in. "I don't like him very much. He's too bossy and mean. Every chance he gets, Darryl pinches me. Real hard like. He always does it when his dad, Grandpa Buck, isn't looking. Then he lies about it. Mama says he's a grown man and should know better."

"Shhhh…I'm talking," Melinda scolds. "She's right. Granny Ivy doesn't like Darryl to come around. Says she's had her fair share of trouble with Grandpa Buck's temper and doesn't need Darryl to add to her misery. Every time he's here, he drinks too much, and gets all mouthy, saying things Granny Ivy doesn't want to hear. And that's when the fighting breaks out. Mom says she thinks Granny Ivy has had enough of his bull, and that's why she stood up to him."

Buck and Ivy's voices come out from the back door, so we freeze like squirrels—really quiet and still. Melinda motions for us to move toward the barn. We follow her like we're hypnotized.

"Darryl didn't like Grandma Ivy telling him to shut his big fat trap."

Shawnee picks up the story. "Momma said Granny hollered a bunch of the f-words to him."

Charley asks, "Do you mean fart?"

Me and Carolyn snicker, 'cuz the only word we'd taught Charley to spell was 'fart.' Before Melinda or Shawnee can reply, Carolyn gives them the stink eye and cuts them off.

"Charley, it's a bad word that only adults use, and they shouldn't," Carolyn explains.

Charley picks at a scab on his elbow. "Did our mommy ever use the f-words?"

Carolyn lies. "No. Never." She ruffles his hair, then tells Melinda, "Go on with your story."

Melinda continues. "Like I said, Darryl's a fighter. He started pushing Grandma Ivy around. She got as mad as a hornet. Momma said she started fighting back, and that's when Darryl got real mad. Then all hell broke loose. When Buck heard all the commotion, cussing, and banging, he came running into the room. Granny Ivy looked over at him. But…it was too late. Darryl already had the butcher knife out. He was coming at her."

My heart pounds. "Was he gonna kill Ivy?"

Melinda replies, "I don't know, but he —"

Shawnee pipes up and makes the motion with a swipe of her tiny hand.

"He knifed her in the face!"

We jump 'bout a mile straight into the air.

Buck and Ivy come out of the house and walk in our direction. Charley instantly buries his face into my belly. We turn, look at them, with wide-eyed stares.

I bend down, whisperin' into Charley's ear, "It's fine, buddy. We're okay, but stay close." Carolyn leans over and rubs his back. He cuddles close between us.

Buck barks. "What are you brats doing? Why'd you jump?"

We stand still. Don't say a word. Melinda laughs.

"Oh, I was telling them a ghost story when you came out. It scared these chickens."

She's so convincin'. She seems too good at lyin', probably 'cuz she does it a lot. Her storytellin' makes me even more nervous 'bout this new icky family.

Buck yells toward the house, "Hey, Anna, you and Forest, hurry up and get out here. Ya hear?"

"Coming." We hear Anna's voice from the house.

Buck invites everybody into the barnyard to show us how he can crack his bullwhip. We follow, unsure of what's to come.

A bad stink comes out of the big barn door. I pinch my nose and breathe through my mouth. So does Charley. We all circle inside the barn. It's dark, except for a beam of light comin' through the top window. My eyes need time to adjust. Buck makes his way to the center, raisin' his arm. He whirls the whip in a circle over his head.

CRACK, echoes throughout the barn. We all jump, includin'

Granny Ivy, Anna, and Daddy. Buck laughs hard. I can tell he likes to scare people.

To my side, a cute little brown dog with floppy black ears walks out into the clearin'. I bend offerin' the little fella a sniff of my hand. "Come here, little buddy." I let out a little squeak to get its attention.

Buck says, "That would be my dog, Sadie. She's a good mouser. Spends most of her time out here in the barn."

The sweet little dog tiptoes over to me and licks my hand.

"Oh, would ya look at that; Sadie just gave me some baby kisses." I beam in excitement. I hunker down on the ground to play with the little dog, pettin' her back and ears. I hear the shufflin' of dirt behind me and I turn to look.

Hidin' in the shadows, a pair of eyes peer in my direction. I stand, then stiffen. I reach out to grab Daddy but accidentally catch Ivy. She looks in the direction of where I'm starin', wide-eyed.

She pauses. "Oh, Catie, that's my father, Dean."

I make the connection in my head. He is Frankenstein Ivy's father and Melinda and Shawnee's great-grandpa.

"Dad, why don't you come out and meet Anna's new husband, Forest, and his children?" Ivy asks.

A small man creeps out from the dark corner. His eyes look black. He doesn't say a word, only nods. His stare is yucky. Makes me feel ice-cold. He looks at me, up and down, then stops and stares at places that aren't my face.

While Buck shows Daddy how to crack his whip, I catch the old great-grandpa starin' at me. Then starin' at all of us. But it's not like a great-grandpa or any grandpa should. He doesn't even try to hide it. Somethin's wrong with Anna's family.

Can't Daddy see how spooky this creepy man acts? How come he's pretendin' Anna and her family are normal?

Marion
November 1992

"Hi Catherine," I smile, setting my pen down to greet her. "Come in." She makes her way into the office, looking refreshed even after spending a full day in classes. She sits, removes her tall boots, fluffs up a pillow, and then places it behind her back.

"Do you mind if I stretch out? My back and neck are exhausted from sitting in those hard chairs all day. I like your navy suit by the way. It looks great on you. Blue is definitely your color."

I rub my hands down my navy slacks. "Oh, thank you."

Letting out a deep breath, she sinks into a full recline.

"How do you do it, Catherine? Your hair seems brushed, your makeup is crisp, and your clothes are always stylish like you just came off the runway. After a long day? I am amazed."

"Want to know my secret?" Catherine asks playfully. "I cheat. I stopped in the bathroom and freshened up before coming here." She twists a curl between her fingers. "Sounds silly, but if I feel like I look good on the outside, it makes me feel better on the inside."

"Why do you think you feel that way?"

"Because...well, honestly, I feel such ugliness on the inside, like something slimy is trying to seep out. Makes me feel bad. Not sure why. It's just always been there."

Catherine's words stick in my head. I make a note and follow it with a question mark. "This evening, we will start by reviewing our last session. Any questions or comments?" I ask.

Catherine hurries to open her floral spiral journal. "I'd like to read the nugget I took away from our last meeting." She reads from her notes. "Whatever you believe—that's what creates your emotions. And from those emotions, your actions follow. Even if what you're believing is a lie. And after a while, those false beliefs may become your truth. Like me, thinking God was selfish."

She thumps her pen on her leg. "I've discovered more." She stretches each leg, one at a time. "I did as you said. I've spent time examining my thoughts. I'm really trying to become aware of what's going on in my head. I wrote them down."

She points to her journal. "I've been surprised at the things I tell myself, accepting them as truth."

"Please expound. Tell me what negative self-talk you were able to recognize."

"Negative self-talk, huh? Great description—you call it what it is. I like that about you, Marion."

She turns to a paper-clipped page.

"The haunting thought that keeps coming up is—I don't expect to have a lasting relationship. I've told myself not to love because those I do love—always leave."

I know she is referring to her mother and ex-husband. "Are those thoughts true?"

"Weird—I hear them as lies. Yet somehow, they also feel true. My mind and emotions feel disconnected."

She squeezes her temples as if trying to join the two together.

"I can't count how many times I've felt unvalued, unloved, not considered, rejected, abandoned...the list goes on. Perhaps my entire lifetime. Wow, working through my thoughts is like trying to straighten a skein of yarn unraveled by a bunch of kittens."

She sits, stretches her back, and falls back into a slump.

"Yes. Analyzing your thoughts is a part of the journey to healing. You are already doing so by listening to yourself and paying attention to what you are saying. The battle is for your mind. And you are absolutely right in your discovery. Whatever you believe, that is what creates your emotions, and your actions follow. Catherine, be encouraged—being aware is the first step."

"I try not to entertain lies, but sometimes I react to them. I hate it. I can act like a total idiot. Like when I jumped all over

Hunter at the restaurant." She makes a flat smile. "I think there's a double meaning to when you counselors ask, 'Did that trigger you?' You bet I was triggered. The poor guy, I was ready to shoot him." She giggles. "He was a good sport, making light of the whole ordeal. Or at least I hope he was."

Her smile fades. "Maybe Hunter was pretending too? I can't pretend that I'm not disappointed. The entire week has gone by without a word from Hunter. No phone call. No voice mail. Nothing. My worse suspicions are confirmed. Hunter found me unacceptable. Even as a friend. After all, he didn't call."

CHAPTER ELEVEN

Catherine
November 1992

Still, no phone call. I've had a week-long rollercoaster ride of self-bashing. Such insecurity. I rehearse everything I hate about myself. This battle for the mind that Marion mentioned has become so apparent, as a constant invasion of my thoughts. Lies. I fight back, insisting I have value. I toss proclamations around in my head, and they ping-pong doubtfully between belief and disbelief. I sound like a broken record telling myself repeatedly: I am valuable, I am lovable, I am—

The phone rings. I jerk, grabbing it on the third ring, then cradle it to my ear while balancing the laundry basket on my opposite hip.

"Hello."

"Hey, Catherine. It's Hunter. Sorry, I took so long to call you. I was slammed with work this week. I can't tell you how many times I thought about phoning. It always seemed too early or too late. Boy, I'm glad it's Friday. I could use some fun this weekend. How was your week?"

My words stick in my throat. My emotions run in opposing directions. I muster out a lie.

"Uhh...fine. Busy week, too. Of course, my weeks are always busy with work, school, and the adjustments of living in a new place. I'm looking for a doctor now. I've found a hairstylist and a girl to do my manicures."

"Oh, yeah, the critical stuff, huh?" I hear the smile in his voice.

Our chat takes off, and my self-imposed mental harassment of the past week fades away. We gab about one thing, then another. I twirl a curl between my fingers, laughing in amazement at Hunter's entertaining stories.

The buzzer on the dryer goes off. I ignore it, remaining reclined on the sofa with my legs elevated and bouncing my feet to the beat on the radio. Somewhere in between swapping stories, I happily agree to go sledding with him early tomorrow morning.

———

While on our way to Evergreen, Hunter lets out a satisfying breath of air. "I call this morning a bluebird day."

"This is beautiful, Hunter. More like periwinkle...one of my favorites."

"Periwinkle?"

"Yeah, it's a color. One that looks blue yet purple. Great hue that's surrounding these snowcapped mountains."

I point at the drifts of snow on the side of the road. "The snow is so deep. But already? It's only November. How deep does it get here?"

"Every year is different. It's unusual to have a foot or more on the ground already, but it's a great base to build upon for the upcoming ski season. I'm stoked." He pumps his arm into the air like he's scored the winning point.

Turning to me, he asks, "So, do you ski?"

"Yes, I love to ski. I learned in Switzerland. I've only been skiing for the last five years. How 'bout you?"

"Twenty years or more."

I peer out the window at the beautiful mountain views in the distance. Fear grips me as the snowy narrow roads drop off without any guardrails.

"I guess the trees growing up the sides of these roads will break our fall if we skid off? Right?" I glance at Hunter, then back to the road. "It's not a very comforting thought."

"I've been driving these hills for decades without an accident. Besides, these roads are nothing compared to the mountains." Hunter assures me. "There's nothing to worry about."

I focus straight ahead, gripping the seat cushion. "This is going to take some getting used to."

We arrive at the sledding area, surrounded by beautiful wooded hills. Hunter tucks two black plastic rollout sleds under one arm while dragging a size-able yellow inner tube. We climb to the top of the hill. With his face grinning ear to ear, he seems excited to make the first tracks in the snow.

He sets his sled on the ground and settles down with his legs crossed and arms out to the sides in preparation for a fast push off.

"Are ya ready, Catherine?"

"Hey, hang on." I position myself onto my sled. "This isn't a race, you know."

"What? It isn't?" Hunter gestures a challenge. "On your mark…get ready…get set…go!"

We fly down the hill, whooping and hollering. The snowy ground speeds by faster than I remember as a kid. We both catch air, soaring up and off the ground. A loud THUD echoes as I collide with the now-packed snow. My sled skids out from underneath me. I continue sliding, my arms flailing. I flash by

Hunter in a spin until coming to a stop, covered in powdery snow.

"Olympic landing, Catherine." He stands, clapping. "Sorry, I forgot to mention to hang on to the sled at all times or..." He covers his mouth to muffle a playful laugh.

"What?" I pack a snowball and throw at him.

He smiles, arching one brow. "Ready for round two?"

"You betcha." I rise to his challenge.

After a couple of hours of sledding and circling down the hill on the inner-tube, we head back to the nearby town of Evergreen for some hot chocolate and muffins.

All-day long, I catch myself feeling cautious, fearful he might try to put his arm around me or hold my hand, which would ruin the day for me. We're only friends, merely trying to get to know one another. I don't care for pushy, assuming men. Hunter keeps his distance and is very polite; plus, he's a ton of fun.

Maybe he is a nice guy... No—don't go there! It's not like you to have the best judgment in men.

I immediately check myself on the negative self-talk.

Marion
November 1992

"Catherine, the last few sessions we have focused on listening, identifying the lies you have accepted as truth and how those beliefs have affected you.

She leans forward on the love seat, nodding. "Uh, huh. I'm getting a handle on sharpening my ears. I would've never guessed that I play such a big part in my own deception through my thought life. Or *negative-self-talk* as you call it."

"The next step is to replace those lies with truth." I move over to the credenza to retrieve a file. I offer Catherine a handout entitled: *My New Identity*. "These verses address how God sees you. You are his child, accepted, significant, and secure. Most of all— you are loved. I find security in these truths. If you do not mind, would you read aloud Romans 12:2?"

"Sure." Catherine opens her Bible, turning to the scripture. "And do not be conformed to this world, but be transformed by the renewing of your mind." She looks up, puzzled. "And?"

"The goal is to insert what God says about you into your new belief system." I take my seat, sinking into the chair cushion while laying her file on the side table.

"Exposing lies and replacing them with truth is a subject we will visit regularly. God has many ways to teach us his truth. One way is through his word, the Bible."

"I hear you, Marion, but I find it hard to believe God loves me, much less *values* me." She shrugs her shoulders.

"His word says he does." I point to a verse on the handout. "Would you read Romans 8:38–39?"

She complies. "For I am persuaded that neither death nor life, nor angels nor principalities nor powers, nor things present nor things to come, nor height nor depth, nor any other created thing, shall be able to separate us from the love of God which is in Christ Jesus our Lord." Tearing a small piece of Kleenex from her pocket, she places it on that page of her Bible. "It sounds great, but it doesn't feel true."

"I understand. It may not feel that way, for now, Catherine. You have been telling yourself that you are unlovable and unvalued for a very long time. That lie has become your truth."

She looks up, her teal eyes intent. "I know. You're right." She looks down at her hands, resting in her lap.

"Would you be willing to tell yourself what God says about you?"

"It sounds so simple. How do I start believing something I've never believed?"

"Catherine, have you ever heard the saying: garbage in, garbage out?'"

"Yes. Tsk...do you even have to ask? I've been spoon-feeding myself lies for decades. I'm a regular garbage can."

I smile, letting out a soft laugh. "Based on the same principle, God's truth in, God's truth out. It is something you will eventually come to believe. Your emotions will follow, as will your actions. What I am describing is referred to as mind renewal. This is where we need to start. Are you willing?"

Catherine's brows furrow. "Yes, alright. But, when can we address the nightmare?"

"The nightmare is something we will pursue, but I cannot say an exact time frame. I am trusting the Lord to lead us as to when. Be encouraged, Catherine, one thing I can guarantee is the more you tell yourself the truth by reading, saying, writing, and hearing it, the faster the truth will be incorporated into your mind and heart. After all, the Lord is the one who created you, so his opinion is what matters."

"You know I've considered myself a Christian for a long time, but...it has never crossed my mind to ask God his opinion of me. I didn't know you could." She tilts her head to the side. "Can you?"

"Of course you can. You can ask the Lord anything. However, the key is to listen to his answers." I wink.

"Well, I guess I better get started. I have a lot of lost time to make up. Marion, I know you already told me, but I lost the paper. Where does it say, 'the truth will set you free'? I want to add that to my list to memorize." She picks up her pen.

"That would be John 8:32. A great verse to learn." I love her enthusiasm but feel a check in my heart, saying it will be short-lived. I discern there are deeper issues to uncover.

"Catherine, if you don't have any more questions, I'd like to move along with your family history."

She nods in agreement.

"How would you describe the emotional effect your stepmother, Anna, and her parents had on you?"

Without hesitation, Catherine blurts out, "Major confusion and fear. They were unlike any adults I'd ever met. I was too young to realize my family had dysfunctions, but even as a kid, I knew right away Anna and her family were way off. I sensed I wasn't safe."

Catie
Spring 1963

Another visit to the farm and I've collected nearly a dozen cool bugs from Granny Ivy's and Buck's fields. I've placed each one real careful in the Mason jar my new granny gave me. Granny Ivy said we're lucky because the grasshoppers are hatchin' early this spring. Charley, Shawnee, and Carolyn are nearby lookin' for flyin' grasshoppers. Sadie, Buck's dog, scampers along with us catchin' a few bugs herself. Her black ears flop up and down as she runs and jumps. The sun beats down on my back makin' me all sweaty—thirsty too. I scurry closer to the ground, tryin' to spy out just one more bug. I try to work up some saliva. Nope, my mouth's too dry.

"Hey, I'm gonna go back to the house, get me a drink, and show Daddy my bugs."

Charley looks up. "You ain't gonna try to catch one of those flyin' hoppers?"

"Maybe later. I'm too thirsty. But you can catch one for me if you want."

"Okay, but after I get me one, first." His head turns back and forth as he crawls through the grasses to sneak up on a prize bug.

"I'll snatch you a grasshopper, Catie." Carolyn says, "I've already captured two. Told Charley I'd give him my second one if he doesn't catch one for himself."

"Thanks, Carolyn. That's good 'cuz those bugs are hard to catch." I skip away, headin' toward the barn. Sadie runs alongside me.

"Come on, girl. You sure are a good dog."

Buck, Ivy, Anna, Daddy, and Dean are standin' in the barnyard, leanin' over the wooden fence lookin' at the beautiful sunny fields. Buck points to the woods behind the pasture. He's tellin' everyone about the different kinds of trees that grow out there. I see so many different colors of greens underneath a big— huge, beautiful, blue sky.

"Daddy, I sure like this country place." I push my sweaty bangs out of my eyes and flash a smile at Grandpa Buck and Grandma Ivy and ask everyone, "Why's the sky so much bigger here? And the blue looks kinda like purple. It goes on and on, farther than I can see."

"It's because of the view." Daddy spreads his arms like an eagle. "At home, there are houses, stores, and buildings blocking us from seeing the sky in one big piece, like what you see here."

"Hmm. I like it here. Why don't we live in the country with a big sky?"

"Umm...maybe someday, Darlin'." Daddy looks at Buck, noddin'. "A place like this would cost a lot of money. I'd have to work hard and long to afford this much land."

Buck nods. "Your father's right, Catie, acreage costs money. And with seven kids to feed, it might be a while before buying land happens."

He looks at Daddy. "Hey, Forest, you and your family are welcome to come out to our farm anytime."

"Grandpa Buck, the country sure is pretty, even though it smells like poop." Then rememberin' my thirst, I gently tap

Grandma Ivy's arm. "Excuse me please, may I have a drink of water?"

"For you or them there bugs?"

"For me, please," I say, smilin' at her teasin'. "Thank you for the jar. It works real good." Turnin', I lift my jar displayin' my bugs.

"Look at all the bugs I caught, Daddy."

"Wow, now that sure is a bunch of fine bugs."

Ivy motions me to follow her to the side of the barn. Sadie tags along. "Catie, over here. I've got something to show you."

Takin' Daddy's hand, I pull him along. The old woman's Frankenstein face still scares me.

Ivy squats in the grass and picks up one end of a tangled, green garden hose. She holds it toward me.

"No need to ask for a drink when you're thirsty, Catie." She grabs hold of the water spigot. "Just turn it on and get yourself a drink right here out of the hose. It's clean, and it's cold. That way, you don't have to be tracking in and out of the house. But make sure you remember to turn it off. We have a well here and don't need to be wasting water."

Water squirts from the hose, makin' an arc as it falls to the ground. I glance over at Daddy. He gives me the go-ahead to take a drink. Leanin' forward, I take several gulps, then wipe my mouth with my arm. I cup my hand under the hose to give the dog a drink. She laps up the water as fast as I did. She must be thirsty too.

"Thank you. That sure is some good water. Can Charley and Carolyn get drinks this way too?"

"Sure, all you kids can. You don't need to be asking every time either. Just make sure to turn the water off, so I don't have to tan your hides, yah hear?"

"Okay. Can I show my brother and sister how to do it?"

"I think you can manage that."

Buck saunters up next to Ivy. He stares hard at her. She winks at him, then looks at somethin' real quick, so fast I can't tell what. Buck smiles at her. It's like they're talkin' without words.

121

Buck ruffles the top of my head, messin' up my hair. "Catie, have you ever been on a horse?"

His eyes flash my way. They're a soft light brown with specks of darker browns and gold in them. The colors aren't like my family's blue eyes, but somethin' 'bout his eyes are different. He won't look at me like most adults, and his eyes dart around; they're too jerky. It feels creepy, but I let it go, 'cuz I'm curious 'bout the horses.

"Nope. I've never ridden a horse, but they sure are beautiful." I peer into the pasture.

"How 'bout I saddle one up—right now?" He makes a loud whistle.

Daddy clears his throat. "Is it safe, Buck? I mean to ride a horse in the spring? Is the ground dry enough?"

"I ride my horse year round. It's safe. Don't you worry."

"Can I, Daddy? Can I?"

Before he has a chance to answer, Anna interrupts. "Now, Catie, this is extremely kind of Grandpa Buck to offer you a ride on one of his horses." She points to a horse gallopin' toward the barn. "Don't you think that black horse is a beauty?"

"Is she Black Beauty? Is she the horse in the book? The famous Black Beauty?" I start dancin'.

Ivy answers, "No, it's not that silly horse. He's a male. His name is Black Night."

"Oh, like a knight in shinin' armor? Or a prince, Ivy?"

"Catie, you call me Granny Ivy," she barks. "His name is Black Night as in the darkness of the night—black."

I look at my dad, 'cuz I don't want to call her granny. She's not only icky lookin'. She's bossy. So I ask him, "Can I go on a horse ride?"

"Sure, Sweetie. Have a great time. But hang on tight." He smiles, clenchin' his fists in front of him, showin' me how to hold my hands.

I run to Buck, squealin'. Jumpin' up and down in excitement, I try to listen to his instructions.

Buck climbs up onto his horse, and waves for Ivy to lift me to him. Anna steps up to assist her mom. I straddle my legs in the saddle and nuzzle in front of my new grandpa.

Buck's boomin' voice shouts out orders. "Catie, you hold on real tight to this wooden knob on the front of this saddle. It's called a horn. You hang onto it with both hands and try to hug the horse with your legs. That way, you'll stay on. Yah hear?"

"Okay, like this?" I grasp the wooden knob with both hands, one over the other, and squeeze my legs as tight as I can while grittin' my teeth at the same time.

Anna laughs, "You're doing great."

Buck lifts the strap, or rein, as he calls it, and walks the horse in a bunch of full circles in the barnyard. I see Great Grandpa Dean in the shadows, watchin' us.

I yell out, "Hey, G.G. Dean, look at me." I surprise him 'cuz he jumps.

Ivy waves her dad over. No smile, just his grumpy face as he shuffles over. I don't care 'cuz I'm on my first horse.

"Today's my lucky day!" I shout. "I wish Charley and Carolyn could see me. Do you think we could ride out to see my brother and sister?"

"We can take a ride, but not in the fields where they're catching bugs. It's too dangerous riding that close to a bunch of kids scrambling who knows where. Charlotte and Claudia are in the house playing cards, but you can tell them all about it later."

Anna cuts her eyes toward Ivy and Buck. They're talkin' without words again. Bucks catches on. I'm watchin' them. He tips the corner of his black cowboy hat at Daddy, then tells me to turn around and face forward. I wave goodbye wildly with one hand, the other graspin' hard on to the saddle horn.

Daddy waves as we leave the barnyard. The horse walks in a gentle soft gait, as Buck calls it. It's a little bit scary at first, but I'm gettin' used to the motion and bein' so far up off the ground. Black Night is strong. His muscles shine in the sun. Ridin' a horse is so much fun.

Yay! I'm on my very first horse ride.

A soft breeze blows across my face, and the countryside is all around me. Feelin' safe with my new grandpa, I lean back and snuggle into his chest.

We approach the end of the barn, then turn the corner. The back of the barn blocks the view of the house and Daddy. Everyone is out of sight.

Buck rides toward the back pasture, leadin' out toward the forest. The horse picks up speed, causin' me to bounce up and down. My bottom slams hard down onto the saddle no matter how hard I squeeze my legs.

The coziness I felt disappears and turns into fear. The scenery blurs. I can't focus. The horse is flyin' through the air—my tears start to spill. I can't breathe. I gasp and scream as loud as I can. "My hands are too small to hold on."

They pull off the horn as I fly into the air. I panic. Fumblin' in midair, I reach out and grab the horse's black mane. My body sails up and down into the saddle.

I beg. "Please, Grandpa Buck, stop. Please stop. Please. Please—"

"Black Night, faster, faster!" He commands.

I scream louder. Pl-eee-a-seee st-o-p. Plee-ease. My words stutter from under my sobs. I squeeze my eyes shut. *Am I gonna die?* I hang on, fearin' for my life.

"Faster, Black Night!" His voice echoes. "Faster!"

CHAPTER TWELVE

Catherine
November 1992

The alarm didn't go off! My adrenaline-filled body jumps out of bed, moving fast, like the crazed person I am at the moment. Faster, faster, I tell myself. I wash my face. Check. Thankfully I took my bath the night before. Put on my makeup, fly into my ski clothes. Check—check. I run a brush through my hair and fluff the ends. Check. A quick spritz of perfume before looking at the clock. Wow, the time leaves me amazed at the speed I got ready. *Why does it usually take so long?* As I make my way into the kitchen to make coffee, the question lingers.

The doorbell chimes. "Hey, Hunter. Come in. I'm ready," I say as if I've been up and at it for hours. *Hah!*

Hunter enters dressed in warm snow gear. His parka unzipped.

"I made us a mixture of coffee and cocoa for the road."

His eyes follow my hand as I casually point to my red plaid thermos.

"Thanks, Catherine. That's nice of you to bring that along. I packed us a lunch. Nothing special. Peanut butter and jelly sandwiches, a couple of apples and some GORP."

"GORP? What's that? Doesn't sound very appetizing."

"You've never heard of GORP before?" He cocks his head to the side, spreading his hands out, palms up, as if amazed.

"Nope. Some Coloradan food staple, I gather?"

"Some say it stands for good ole raisins and peanuts, but my concoction is made of nuts, dried fruit, and candy-covered chocolate. It's especially good after building up a sweat snowshoeing." He pulls a large slip-sack from under his arm, "I brought the snowshoes in; I want to make sure they'll fit. With this early snow, we should have a great day."

"Is November early to have snow?" I sit on a dining room chair and lift my leg.

"It's different every year, but I'm glad we've had some good dumps." He adjusts the snowshoes, sizes me up, and slips them back into the bag for the drive.

I grab my scarf, purse, and thermos, and we're out the door on our way to meet up with his friend, Doug. We rendezvous at the Morrison exit, on I-70, then ride together to Guanella Pass, near Georgetown.

Doug, a tall, fit, and friendly guy, hit it off, making the drive go quickly as the three of us chat the entire way. Hunter parks the car, and we gear up. He helps me put on the snowshoes and tighten up the straps.

Doug teases Hunter. "All the times we've snowshoed together, never once have you offered to tighten my straps."

"That's right, Doug. Ever check out that mug of yours? Not quite my type, man."

Snowballs start flying. I join in.

Walking in snowshoes proves challenging. "Hey guys, am I doing this right? I suddenly feel like a wide-legged duck."

They both chime in. "You look great; it just takes some getting used to the shoes."

Our trek begins on a well-beaten snowmobile trail. It doesn't take long to get the hang of snowshoeing. The beautiful rock outcroppings, various animal tracks, and winter wonderland views of sparkling snowcapped mountains set against sunny periwinkle skies, scents of pine, the crunch of our tracks, and the sweet taste of mocha are all so captivating.

Time whirls so quickly, although several hours have passed. Halfway into our hike, Hunter suggests we stop for a snow picnic. I follow him and Doug to a boulder overhang, where Hunter spreads a blue snow blanket.

"Catherine, we'll take off our snowshoes and have our picnic here, out of the breeze."

"Wow, Hunter. Thank you. I'm impressed. I've never had a picnic in the winter. And a snow blanket?"

He nods his head. "You're welcome." Taking credit for having thought of all the details.

Doug pipes in using a high-pitched girly voice. "Oh, yes, Hunter. What a beautiful snow blanket you have provided for today's adventure." He pretends to fluff the side of his light brown hair and bats his big hazel eyes. He then glances my way, sending a wink.

"Okay. It's a tarp, but it will keep us dry and give us a place to sit and eat our lunch."

Both Hunter's and Doug's cheeks are pink from the cold. I'm suddenly aware my face is cold, but I find it more refreshing than uncomfortable.

"Wow, this is so special. I don't think I'll ever grow tired of the mountains. I came to Colorado in the summer once, when I was eighteen. I remember telling my girlfriend I could live here. This place is wonderful. Too bad it took me so long to come back."

Holding a handful of GORP Hunter is the first to reply. "Yeah, it's great here. Being from the flatlands of Nebraska, I had my nose over the fence, longing to move west to the great Rocky Mountains but didn't make it until I came for a job after college. Then I got drafted during the Vietnam War, but as you see, I came back." He points to Doug. "He's from the East coast. Not too many natives live here. It seems like everyone is a transplant."

Before long, we finish our PB &Js, then hit the trail to return to the car. Hunter suggests we try some off-trail shoeing. He's the first in line, busting the trail. He turns slightly, talking over his shoulder. "Catherine, you'll find the snow's softer but harder to move through. The nice thing about being off-trail is you'll see places, nestled underneath the trees, untouched by any visitors."

"This is cool."

"For now," Doug jokes. "Once it's your turn to go in front and bust trail, you'll see it gets hot and sweaty fast."

I marvel at how the snow sparkles from the sun's reflection. We take turns leading so I can experience the feeling of making first tracks. At times, my snowshoes sink deeply up to my thighs. I use my ski poles to pull myself up and out. Hunter offers to give me a hand several times, but I decline, wanting to figure it out on my own, so I'm prepared for future treks.

Doug was right; it is challenging. I unzip my jacket to cool off, then hike back up onto the firm snowmobile path. Hunter's still on the soft snow with Doug following. Suddenly Hunter post-holes. His right leg sinks fast, all the way to his upper thigh, throwing him headfirst into the snow. He jerks up, revealing his entire snow-covered face. I break into laughter, and Doug chuckles. Together we make fun of Hunter's face-plant. He's a good sport and enters the fun.

I hear myself saying, "Awww."

Hunter and I exchange smiles. My heart stirs. I'm not ready for the familiar emotions rising to the surface. I immediately react. Gripping my poles, I say, "Hey guys, I think I'll hike ahead a bit. I want to see how much speed I can maneuver in these contraptions."

I turn on a dime and bolt off—away from Hunter, but mostly away from these unexpected emotions.

The self-talk lecture begins inside my mind. *What? Get ahold of yourself. You did not come here to fall in love. You came here to go to Bible College. Stay focused. All you need is some guy distracting you. Focus on accomplishing your goals. You have horrible taste in men. Don't get derailed now.*

I arrive at the car a few minutes before the guys come sloshing up. Hunter questions, "Everything okay, Catherine? Watching your arms swing away made me wonder. You looked like you were a part of an army regiment."

I lie. "Everything's fine, Hunter. I was only trying to see how fast I could move. A new sport for me and all." I change the subject. "So, are you guys ready for Christmas?"

Hunter huffs. "Are you kidding? No. Not at all. I mentioned we'd be stopping in Georgetown on the way back home. They have a wonderful Christmas Mart right now. I thought we could do a little shopping for our families."

Doug adds, "Sounds good to me; my folks love all those wooden ornaments from Austria."

I beam with excitement. "Oh, I love the Austrian Christmas Marts. I use to go to Austria every year when I lived in Switzerland. There's something so special about those homemade ornaments."

We walk through the snowy streets of Georgetown, arriving at a section of town lined with decorated booths, all accented with fresh evergreen, pinecones, and bright gold metallic ribbons. The vendors display beautiful ornaments and numerous gift options. The aroma of tempting sweet desserts fills the air. A band in the background plays a variety of cheerful music.

My emotions feel like a rollercoaster, rising and plunging with fear and delight. Taken up in the moment, I grab Hunter by the hand and ask, "Sir, may I have this dance?" I bow my head and make a slight curtsy.

He looks puzzled, surveying the crowd. "But Catherine, no one is dancing."

"Does it matter?" I tug his hand, leading to a shoveled off grassy area where we glide and twirl to the music. Before we know it, others join in, filling up the makeshift dance floor, which puts a smile on my face.

Hunter looks over to Doug. His head turns so quickly; I'm unable to read his face. *Is he embarrassed?*

He glides us over toward the walkway—away from where everyone's dancing. "How about looking at the ornaments?"

Great. If my face wasn't red earlier, I'm sure it's the color of beets now. It looks like I screwed up again, forcing Hunter to dance and all. *Great job, Catherine.*

Marion
November 1992

"Hi, Catherine, it is great to see you. Come in and make yourself at home."

She enters, her hands full and both shoulders loaded, one with a book bag and the other with a leather purse.

I inquire, "How was your week?"

"I'm not sure. The nightmare continues, so I'm losing sleep. Last week was bad, three nights. Last night was one of those evenings: same dream, same emotions, same frustration. I struggle to wake myself, but when I finally do, the dream always finishes in the same place—feeling terrorized."

The sun shines through the window highlighting Catherine's face. The unexplained dream is having its toll. Puffiness and dark shadows circle her bright teal eyes. She looks up from her folded hands, cradling a tissue.

"On a slightly better note, I saw Hunter again. I also met one of his friends. We all went snowshoeing. Have you ever done that?" She seems bubbly again, able to distance herself from the effects of the stressful nightmare and lack of sleep. I make an entry in her file.

"Snowshoeing? Hmm, I cannot say I have, but I would like to try it sometime." *That is as soon as I take off some of this weight.*

"Well, um...I had some unexpected feelings rise. Emotions I don't know quite how to handle." She cocks her head and raises her shoulders while scrunching her face. "Basically, it was the feeling of affection towards Hunter. You know, like—romantic feelings."

I raise my brow, "Oh, and...?"

"It scared me. Set me off-kilter. It's not why I came here. I have a firm intent to go to Bible College, study biblical counseling, and accomplish my goal. I need a boyfriend like I need a hole in my head." She rolls her eyes.

"I understand your desire to achieve your goal. However, I was under the impression you wanted to marry someday and have children. Is that correct?"

"Yes, but..." There is a long silence.

"But what...?"

"I lack confidence in choosing the *right man*. I don't trust myself to pick a healthy and dependable guy. I don't trust my ability to recognize poor character even when I'm staring at it square in the face. My track record with Edward is proof." She breaks eye contact, glances down, and rakes her fingers like a comb through the ends of her hair.

"I see. Catherine, I would like for you to sit or lie back, whichever you prefer, then close your eyes and connect with the emotions. Are you okay to do so?"

"Sure." She leans back into the corner of the love seat, crossing her legs.

"Focus and connect with the emotions you are feeling presently, as well as the emotions that were triggered when you were with Hunter."

She closes her eyes, concentrating, "I feel...afraid, uncertain, umm…inadequate to make a good choice, embarrassed, and I have a strong desire to run away."

"Run away from what?" I probe.

"Getting hurt again!" Anger rises in her tone. She spits out a list. "Being lied to, deceived, cheated on, betrayed. Doing a repeat of Edward."

"Hang on to those emotions. From one to ten, ten being the highest, how true does that feel?"

Her answer is instant, "Eleven!"

Her white knuckles hang fiercely onto the accent pillow, as if her life depended on its grip.

Catie
Spring 1963

My hands snatch hold of the saddle horn. I grip as hard as I can—my body trembles. Buck brings his horse to a sudden stop. My body flies forward. I expect to fly off. He grabs my shirttail and slams me into his lap. I stiffen. Me and the horse breathe hard. Both gaspin'.

Buck jumps to the ground, leavin' me in the saddle. He stands, legs apart, hands-on-hips, glarin' at me. I'm afraid—frozen with fear, like a squirrel. His glare pierces me like a sharp stick.

My eyes dart around, searchin' for the barn, the house, and Daddy. Nobody is in sight. We're so far away. My body trembles. I can't control my shakin'. I grip the horn harder. The ground is too far down to jump. I wheeze—my nose bubbles. I try to suck air. My face is covered in snot from cryin'. I don't dare let go to wipe it, in case I fall.

Buck glares. Doesn't blink. There's somethin' wrong with his eyes. They're no longer soft brown eyes. They are black with pupils like diamonds—like a snake. There's a darkness in his eyes that stares back at me. Weird. Scary. Somethin's livin' inside of Buck's eyes, glarin', like it's lookin' through windows. It's bad. Not to be trusted. Shivers slither up and down my back.

Buck laughs. An uncontrollable, wicked, bone-chillin' laugh. He throws his head back. His laughter echoes around me. Louder and louder. After each outburst, he gives me a devilish smile. He likes scarin' me.

What's wrong with this man? What kind of a monster lives inside Buck? What's happened to him? Why's his heart so rotten?

Fear crawls over me like a slimy snake. Waitin' for the right moment to bite. I can't move. I won't take my eyes off Buck.

He grabs me. His fingernails rake over my shirtsleeve.

"Let go of the horse!" The crazed man demands.

He yanks at my arm. I won't let go. Instead, I hold on harder, with all my strength. He rips me off. I fall, hittin' the ground—hard. Pain spikes through my hip.

I scramble to a stand—ready to run. But w*here? What direction?* I stand tall and force myself to make my hands into fist, stackin' them on my hips. I glare back. Pretendin' I'm not afraid, I wait. *What will he do next?* He won't stop starin'.

I have to pee so bad; I worry I'll go in my pants. I move my hand from my hips to between my legs, squeezin' hard to hold it in. I muster all my courage to speak.

"I need to go to the bathroom."

Buck laughs and calls me names. He motions for me to do my business elsewhere. He's not like any grownup I've ever known. *Creepy.*

As I'm walkin' away, I hear him mumble, "Weak, brat, pussy, sissy, pain in the…" His words drift away.

My legs wobble as I walk. The ground is uneven with all sorts of weeds and grasses scratchin' my bare legs, makin' me itch. My stomach tightens. I feel the creepy man's dark stare at the back of my head. Somethin' tells me he's lookin' for any reason to hurt me. I bet he enjoys bullyin' kids. I wish my daddy were here. I bite my lip to force back the tears.

I squat coverin' myself in tall grass, not too far away. I'll get in trouble if Buck can't see me. Not too close, either. I watch him, makin' sure he doesn't sneak up on me. I wouldn't put anythin' past him. I don't like bein' alone with him.

Is this how crazy people act?

I trot back, thinkin' of a way to put him in a good mood. As I walk closer to him, I see this plant that looks like a fuzzy cucumber with white stuff drippin' out the end.

"Grandpa Buck, what's this plant?" I point to it.

His eyes follow my finger. "Oh, Sweetie, I don't know the name of that plant, but us folks in these parts call it a Milkweed."

He called me Sweetie. Huh? Has his mood changed?

"What's a Milkweed?" I ask.

"It's a plant that makes milk. If the cow quits producing milk, we can always use these milk plants. These fields are full of them. Didn't your parents ever tell you about a milk plant?"

"No, we don't have those kinds of plants in the city. I've never seen any before. It's my first time to see one!"

"Why don't you take a big bite? I think you'll love it."

"Okay, I'm thirsty anyway and really like milk."

My mouth waters. There are so many oozin' plants to pick. I pull back the leaves lookin' for an extra big one. "Is this a good one?"

"That's a doozy. Now, take a big bite and suck the milk right out of it."

I bite into the furry plant. White milky stuff squirts into my mouth. It's slimy. Disgustin'. Bitter. So bitter, I gag. I heave. My stomach jerks in waves. Watery stuff comes out of my mouth and nose. I spit. Again, and again. I wipe my tongue off with the bottom of my shirt.

Buck stands so close; his shadow darkens over me. The air suddenly grows cold. I shiver. He laughs, then bends over and holds his big belly while he points at me. His laughter turns to a wild roar. He's actin' crazy.

I stand watchin' till he gets normal again.

Buck boosts me up on Black Night, then mounts the horse himself. I can't wait to get back to Daddy. I keep my eyes shut the whole way with one hand clutchin' the horn and the other on the horse's mane. Buck slows the horse. The stink of poop drifts up to my nose. I know we're close to the barn.

I pop open my eyes. Daddy stands wavin' and smilin'. I burst into tears.

I'm gonna live.

Buck brings the horse to a stop next to the wooden fence where Ivy, Anna, and Daddy are waitin'. Buck digs his clawed hand into my shoulder, holdin' me tight in the saddle. I don't like this man. He's a mean, icky grandpa. I turn around and glare at him.

"Well, I'm thinkin' Catie here might be a bit too young for horse rides."

Everyone sees my tears.

Daddy looks right at me. "Are you okay, Catie?"

"I am now." I sniffle. "I want down!"

Buck lets out a slight chuckle. "Black Night had a hankering here to sow some wild oats. He sprang into a full gait. Sometimes horses will do that, and it's good to let them run a bit. I stopped as soon as I realized Catie was afraid. By next year, you mark my word; she'll be begging me to take her fast on this horse. Kids have a way of overcoming little frights like this one. She'll be fine." He lowers me down to my dad, then says, "You'll see, Catie, you'll be just fine."

Melinda walks up as Buck lowers me off the horse. Daddy takes hold of me. I grab onto him—tight. My tears flow and my body trembles.

"Catie, you're such a crybaby! I could've told *my* Grandpa Buck you're too much of a chicken-scaredy-cat to go on a horse."

Daddy corrects Melinda. "That is not necessary, young lady. Enough. Can't you see she's upset?" He grits his teeth.

Anna remains silent. Melinda tucks behind her mother and

grandmother. Both look at her while she mouths, crybaby, crybaby, then sticks out her tongue. They watch but do nothin'. I squeeze harder onto Daddy's neck. He calms me, then lowers me to the ground.

Anna's grandfather and Granny Ivy's daddy shuffles over toward us. I call him GG Dean 'cuz he is my great grandfather. He walks closer, speakin' to me for the very first time. "Not so much fun, huh? How about you come into the barn with me? I'll get you some jacks and a ball to play with till the other kids come back."

"I don't want to play with Melinda. She's too mean," I say with my head down, waitin' to be scolded for speakin' the truth.

"Aww, she can be a brat sometimes. You and I can play together, that is, if that's okay with you?"

I look up. GG Dean's sourpuss face has a smile on it. He extends his hand. I look at my dad. He nods his approval.

The two of us walk hand-in-hand into the barn to play. "You know, GG Dean, you're awful nice to play a game with me."

"I reckon so." He squats down and fumbles through a wooded box underneath the workbench. A small cloudy window in the wall separates the barn from the bunkhouse. For a quick moment, I see a boy with dark hair peerin' through the window, watchin' GG Dean and me. He smiles and waves, followed by puttin' his finger to his mouth, motionin' me not to say anythin'. The old man stands up, and the boy instantly scrams. Poof, he's gone.

My new great-grandpa hands me a small pull-string bag. I can feel the jacks and ball. I take a peek inside.

"Thank you, GG Dean."

"How 'bout you give yer old great-grandpa a big kiss for those jacks?"

He spread his arms wide waitin' for a hug and kiss. I walk up. He places his hands on the sides of my face. I smile. He comes in and kisses my lips.

His hands tighten. He forces his tongue into my mouth. I pull away. He pushes his tongue deeper. I gag. I push him. Hard. Droppin' the jacks, I hightail it out of the barn.

I see Daddy in the backyard still talkin' with Anna and her parents. I screech, "Daddy, Daddy, that old man put his tongue in my mouth!" Tears gush.

Ivy speaks up. "Your great grandpa's just a sloppy kisser. Don't be acting like that, Catie," she scolds. "You probably scared the old man half to death. And after he offered to play a game with you." She shakes her finger at me. "Shame on you!"

Anna pipes in. "There's just no pleasing this one. Buck takes her on a horse ride, she cries. GG Dean tries to play with her; she cries. Forest, your youngest daughter is quite spoiled and doesn't appreciate anything. I won't have it." She turns to her daughter and mother. "I think Melinda is right." Melinda wrinkles her nose and mouths, *crybaby*.

I bite my lip to fight back my tears. "Please, Daddy, let's go home. Please."

"As soon as the other kids get back, we'll head out. It's been a long enough visit." He pulls me closer to his side. "You're fine now. I'm here."

Charlotte and Claudia come skippin' out of the house. They see me, whimperin'.

"What's wrong, Catie?"

"I'll tell you later. I want to go home."

I cling to Daddy. We all turn as we hear Charley runnin' towards us, laughin', and holdin' up his jar of prize bugs. Carolyn and Shawnee scamper right behind.

CHAPTER THIRTEEN

Marion
December 1992

C atherine scampers into my office, clinging onto her wool coat. She brushes sprinkles of snow off her shoulders. "Wow. Your office feels so warm and cozy compared to the blistering cold outside." She slips off her gloves, scarf, and coat. "This is my first snowstorm since moving here, and the news says we're supposed to get a ton of snow over the next day or so. Is this normal for December?"

"It can be, but the snow usually melts pretty fast. You are welcome to cover up with the blanket to warm yourself." I point to a soft cream coverlet on the love seat. "I can see you have a thermos of something, so I will not offer you a drink."

"I'll take you up on the blanket. I brought a couple of muffins. Would you care for one?"

"Oh, no. I am not eating sugar. I have several pounds to lose."

Catherine snuggles up, and we begin.

"We have been working on your family history. You left off with getting to know Anna and her family."

"Yeah, I remember." She pulls the throw up over her shoulders. "They were weird. Buck, Ivy, and GG Dean were confusing to me as a child. The whole horse ride and the poisonous plant didn't make sense. I couldn't understand why Buck would do such mean things."

"What did your father say about what happened?"

"I watched Anna's family spin their cover-up stories like a black venomous spider. They were able to tangle my dad into their web of lies. Or maybe he was in denial and wanted to believe Anna and her family. My father was so overwhelmed with having a new wife, two extra kids, and now a family of nine. He worked awful hours, the graveyard shift for the extra money, trying to make ends meet. I suspect he was still in shock from losing my mom."

I shift in my chair. "I am sure it was extremely stressful to lose his wife and the mother of his children. Her unexpected death must have been unfathomable for your father as well as for you and your siblings."

"Yes, it was sad and hard for everyone. Dad was desperate and probably remarried too quickly. Anna was disheartening for me; because I wanted…no, I needed Anna and her family to be sweet and loving. I missed my mother so much. Her death left such an empty void. I was so young, only five when she died, and very dependent upon her. Another sad thing was my mom wasn't there to explain to me what was happening. I only knew it wasn't good."

"Catherine, you were a child when you met Anna and her family. Six or thereabout, right?"

She nods. "Yes."

"At that age, your mental and emotional development would not allow you to use logic or reasoning to decipher the dynamics unfolding before your eyes. Self-doubt, second-guessing, and confusion would have been a normal reaction. In a loving family, children instinctually trust and depend upon their parents, family, and other adult friends to care for and protect them. The deliberate intent to cause hurt is too complex for a child to understand."

I check my notes as to where Catherine had left off on our last visit. "What happened when you returned home after you told your Dad about Dean thrusting his tongue into your mouth?"

"Anna tried to make it sound like it was a big misunderstanding. When Dad questioned her, she got angry and accused me of being nothing more than an ungrateful brat. My sisters believed me, which made me feel better. Dad didn't know what to think. It wasn't like I had a voice in the matter. I just thought Anna's family was weird, possibly crazy."

She takes a bite of her muffin, washing it down with a big gulp of warm coffee—my mouth waters. I fight the temptation, resisting the craving to ask for a bite.

Catherine continues talking about her life with Anna, her kids, and the rest of Anna's family. Her experiences were not the average adjustments most blended families encounter. I allow her the time she needs to share, knowing the process of healing involves the opportunity and affirmation of being heard.

"And one more thing I've mentioned to you before, Marion, is that I see things. Things others don't seem to see. It started on the horse ride with Buck. I saw something in his eyes, something wicked looking back at me. I wasn't able to express myself as a kid, but as a woman, I know what I was seeing." She sweeps crumbs off her lap onto her napkin.

"Catherine, Satan, and evil are authentic. Your ability to discern what you saw is supernatural. However, before we dive into that subject, I need to build up to that topic by gathering more information about your past history. We can discuss spiritual abilities and gifts at another session. Is that agreeable?"

"Will my history help you and me to understand why I see and sense things?'

"Yes, that is my hope."

"Okay, then." She scoots to the edge of her seat, with pen and paper ready.

"Let us begin with Lucifer. I will try to keep this very simple." I take a deep breath, searching for the right words to simplify a very complex subject.

"Lucifer was an archangel. He started a power struggle with God. To pick a fight with your Creator, one who is all-powerful, all-knowing, and ever-present, was not the brightest decision. Lucifer was kicked out of heaven, taking with him one-third of the angels. His name was then changed to Satan, the dragon, the serpent, the devil, and our enemy, only to mention a few."

"Oh yeah, I've been studying this in school. I know Satan hated Adam and Eve. Do you think he was jealous of the love and relationship they had with God?" She takes another sip of coffee.

"Probably. I know the devil hated God and declared war, wanting to overpower him. I would say Satan targeted what God cherishes—us. He wants nothing more than to cause God pain and to kill, steal, and destroy us. He will try anything to come between God and us."

"So, this battle is for my mind that we've talked about, meaning the lies. Is the devil behind them?"

"Catherine, the Bible refers to him as the 'father of lies.' In my opinion, Satan's most powerful lie was and is convincing people he does not exist."

"How does that work?"

"After Satan was cast to the earth, he lurked in the garden. He was spinning his lies, flaunting temptations, and scheming against Adam and Eve to eat from the only tree that was forbidden and off-limits."

"Satan's such a slime."

"Well said." I smile. "Adam and Eve were instructed by God not to eat of the tree. However, but because of their disobedience —they died—which means spiritually and eventually physically. They were separated from God and removed from the garden from where they once walked freely with the Lord." I read her face to make sure she is engaged and tracking with the information.

"Unfortunately, we, as Adam's and Eve's offspring, inherited their condition. But the Lord, out of his love, could not and would not leave us in such a darkened condition. He had a remedy —Jesus."

"How did Adam's and Eve's death affect us and our relationship with God? What do you mean when you say a darkened condition? And what about Jesus?"

I confer with my watch. "I want to answer you, Catherine, but our time is almost up for today. We will have to address your questions at your next session.

Catie
Spring 1963

My question got answered. It turns out Daddy was right after all, he doesn't have enough money. I wasn't at home when the bank came to take our house away.

Daddy tells me all 'bout it, as he hands me three small cardboard boxes to pack up my clothes and toys. I feel sad, 'cuz somehow it makes Mommy feel farther away.

I ask Daddy if this means we're gonna have to live in the orphanage, since we're broke, and have almost no money. He says not to worry that Anna is our new mother and will help him take care of us kids.

We have another home now, but it looks dumb, like a white barn. Anna says it's a new style. Maybe? I think it's the style for poor people.

I'll be honest. I like one thing. It's the front steps. The wood is gray with bits of white paint, pretty worn out all right, but the middle step has a big hole, right smack dab in the center. It's our pretend fishin' pond. Daddy can't find our fishin' pole. He says it was probably lost in the move. That's okay, 'cuz we found a nice stick and tied some kite string on it with an open safety pin as our hook.

Fishin' reminds me of my mommy's parents—Grandpa and Granny Grunt. I don't get to see them much as I want now that Daddy is married to Anna. They taught us to love fishin'.

There are all sorts of treasures under these porch stairs. We spend a lot of time fishin'. We take turns. I love to catch anythin', even leaves. It's a good thing that we like to be outside 'cuz Anna doesn't want us in the house, botherin' her.

After we finish supper and our chores, we all gather around the front steps, seein' what we'll catch. Charley pulls the fishin' stick up carefully, and to our surprise, a shiny red candy wrapper dangles off the safety pin hook.

"I caught me something!" he shouts, "I caught one, I caught one!" Charley shines with happiness.

We all join in. "He caught one...Charley caught one. Yay!" We prance around pretendin' it's a real fish!

Now it's my turn. I lower the string in the hole. Carolyn holds my hair back so I can see better as I stoop down, peerin' into the darkness. I lay the safety pin down just right to snag me a good catch.

Claudia asks, "Catie. You think Dad is gonna make us go back to Anna's folks' farm after what they did?

"I sure hope not. I'd rather visit Teenage Granny and Grandpa and Granny Grunts anyway. They're normal and not weird, like Anna and her family. I don't care if I ever go back to Grandma Ivy's house. Ivy *is* poison. And GG Dean and Buck are plum crazy. I don't care what Anna says. She wasn't there. I din't misunderstand. I know what happened. They're bad grown-ups."

I drop the fishin' pole to my side. I'm not in the mood to fish anymore. My stomach churns. It's the same squirmy feelin' I had after seein' Frankenstein Poison Ivy's face, Buck's devil eyes, and hearin' Buck's spooky laugh. Same as when GG Dean put his icky tongue in my mouth.

Carolyn picks up the pole for her turn. "Anna's nuts. Teenage Granny says the apple doesn't fall far from the tree, meaning, if Anna's nuts, her folks are too. I bet they're the ones who taught Anna to be mean. And Poison Ivy's father, Dean, is a creep." Carolyn points the fishin' pole at me. "We know, Catie, because it was that same day that jerk tried to put his tongue in all our mouths. I told Dad too. What I don't understand is why he can't see it. I guess he believes Anna and her folk who said the old man was just a sloppy kisser. YUCK! I know better."

Claudia explains, "Dad's a fool for love. He's gone blind with love and thinks the best of Anna and her family. Mom would want us to pray for them."

Charlotte puts her two cents in, "What? Pray for them? No way, Claudia." She clenches her fist and grits her teeth, then hollers, "Carolyn is right, Claudia. Did you know Anna asked for a date with Dad only three weeks after mom died?" Charlotte doesn't wait for Claudia to answer and goes on complainin'. "I tell ya, I hate her. Aunt Jean said it was Dad who called off the first date, *not her*."

Charlotte's temper is gettin' hotter by the minute.

I chime in. "But he din't go on any dates with her till right before we met her, Charlotte. Mommy was long gone by then."

"Catie, it only felt like a long time. It was a short six months. What kind of a woman would ask to go out with a man only three weeks after him losing his wife and *our mother*? I'll tell you what kind—a floozy, that's who."

The front door squeaks open. Daddy steps out. He waits for us to stop playin' so he can get down the stairs. He has his lunch bucket in his hand, his midnight snack. He's workin' an extra job, the graveyard shift, to make sure he has enough money to keep the bank from takin' away this house too. I'm not worried. I know the bank wouldn't want this stupid barn house.

"You kids gather round." He raises his arms, invitin' us in for a hug. We snuggle him like a litter of puppies, squeezin' him with the bestest hug ever.

"Now listen to Anna and do what she says." He smiles. "She has planned something special for you, calling it Friday game-night. Have fun, and don't be up too late."

Charlotte, Claudia, Carolyn, Charley, and me, all pipe in, "Okay, Daddy, we'll miss you. See you in the mornin'."

He waves while backin' out of the driveway.

The sunlight goes away 'bout the same time the street lights come on — meanin' it's time to go into the house.

The smell of popcorn stops me in my tracks. Anna calls from the kitchen. "You kids get upstairs, wash up, and put on your PJs. I'm making popcorn for game-night."

I race up the stairs, squealin', takin' two steps at a time. I scurry into my PJs then run downstairs to see what Anna has planned. I'm excited 'bout playin' games. I love to play and make fun out of ordinary things. Why walk when you can skip, hop, or bounce?

Bein' curious, I look on the end tables and coffee table expectin' to find my favorite games. But the tables are dusted clean. I check the dinin' room buffet table, carefully pullin' out each of the three drawers—no games in sight.

We played games with Mommy. She loved games too. Our favorites were Candy Land, Old Maid, Fish, Pick-up-sticks, Tinker Toys, and Lincoln Logs, besides playin' with my favorite baby doll.

Dancin' around the room, I swoosh into the kitchen with my imaginary dance partner. Anna breezes by headin' for the livin' room. The sound of the coffee table scootin' across the floor tells me she's movin' things around for our night of fun.

This new barn home is small, but Anna calls it cozy. I like bein' cuddly close with my sisters and Charley. And tonight we're gonna be extra snuggly close with Anna and her girls, makin' eight of us all in the same room.

Melinda and Shawnee start nibblin' on the warm popcorn from the bowls settin' on the kitchen countertop. Another giant bowl brimmin' with popcorn is on the stove. I count small colorful dishes of popcorn with my pointer finger. 1, 2, 3, 4, 5, 6, 7... there's one bowl for each of us kids. I find it fun to count, as I recount the dishes once again, but from the opposite direction.

Meanwhile, Melinda and Shawnee grab at the popcorn, shovin' handfuls into their mouths, chewin', and swallowin' as fast as they can.

As Anna rounds the kitchen corner, I reach out for a few kernels.

SMACK.

She hits my hand and knocks it into one of the bowls, spillin' the popcorn over onto the counter.

"Catie Kay, did I tell you it was okay for you to eat this popcorn?"

She jerks me around facin' her and slaps me across the face — my cheek stings. I look wide-eyed at Melinda and Shawnee, who quickly wipe their faces clean of any crumbs. My attention flings back to Anna as she shakes my shoulders.

"You are lucky I don't send you straight to bed right now!"

"Anna, I...I...thought it was okay 'cuz Melinda and Shawnee—"

Melinda cuts me off. "I already told her, Mom, but she kept eatin'. She took popcorn from almost every bowl except these last two bowls."

Anna hands her daughters the only two full bowls of popcorn. Just then, Charley and my sisters file into the kitchen, all hungry and eager to get some popcorn.

I'm the last to be handed a bowl, half-full. Anna gathers the spilled popcorn from the counter, cups it into her hand, then tosses it into her large bowl.

Silent tears spill from my eyes. I start to open my mouth in an attempt to explain. Anna puts her face close to mine, almost nose-to-nose. She's so close, my eyes cross.

She shouts, "I don't want to hear it. You have to learn the rules. You should feel lucky I gave you any popcorn. Now get in the living room with the other kids before I change my mind. You hear me?"

I purse my lips, not sayin' more as I walk into the livin' room, balancin' my bowl of popcorn, afraid of what she'll do if I spill a single kernel.

All of us kids sit on the livin' room floor, and everyone is munchin' on the buttery sweet treat. Melinda and Shawnee sit leanin' up against the couch next to their mom, whose long, slender legs stretched out over the full length of the sofa. Anna's arms wrap around her huge bowl of popcorn. All three look down at their heapin' dishes and then back at mine—half-empty. Melinda's smile is too big. She makes yummy faces at me.

On purpose?

I have questions I want to ask my sisters. But Charlotte, Claudia, and Carolyn are busy gigglin' about some story, not noticin' the red welt on my face. Charley hovers over his bowl with butter smeared on his cheeks and tiny fingers.

I cross my legs and sturdy my bowl in the small openin' in front of my legs. My tummy starts to churn. I'm too afraid to ask. *Why's my new family so mean? Did I do somethin' wrong? Why did Anna hit me? I miss bein' happy, the way it used to be. I miss Mommy and our special fun times like Christmas when we would all sing and dance together.*

Catherine
December 1992

The Christmas season surrounds me, even at the grocery store. Everywhere I look, bright signs advertise turkeys, hams, and all the fixings. Even stocking stuffers, hats, gloves, and lots of candy are in unlimited supply. As I come out of the store, toting my bags, I notice a man setting up a Christmas tree stand.

"Excuse me, Sir. Will you be selling Christmas trees here?"

"Well, young lady, I will be just as soon as the trucks arrive. I'm expecting a batch of fresh trees any minute now."

"Sounds great." I check my watch. Only 5 p.m. "I'll be back. Say in an hour or so?" He gives me the thumbs-up and nods.

I arrive home wondering how I'm going to get a tree back to my apartment. How can I rope a tree on top of my car? While searching inside the closet for my ornaments and Christmas tree stand, the phone rings.

"Hello." I recognize his voice on the line. "Hey, Hunter."

"Hi, Catherine, how are you doing? I'm calling to confirm our ski plans for tomorrow. It looks like the weather's going to be perfect. A wonderful day to hit the slopes."

"Yes, I'm excited about going."

CLICK. CLICK. CLICK.

"What is that clicking sound?" Hunter asks.

"It's call waiting. I must have another call coming through."

"Do you want to answer it?"

"Do you mind? I'll only be a minute," I promise.

"Umm…sure. No problem."

I click over to the other call. "Hello."

"Hi, Catherine, it's Patrick. I met you at Diane's dinner party."

"Well, hello, Patrick. Yes, I do remember you. You're the FBI guy. I remember teasing you with the nickname of secret agent man." I let out a quick giggle.

"That's right." He laughs. "I was calling to ask if you'd be interested in going shooting with me sometime?"

"You mean shooting the machine gun you mentioned? The one you possibly have access to through the FBI?" My heart races. I know I need to get back to Hunter, but this is a once-in-a-lifetime opportunity.

"I'm still working on that deal. I was referring to an afternoon at the gun range."

"Patrick, it sounds like fun. I'm on the other line right now. Can I give you a call back when I have more time?"

"Sure, that would be great."

I hang up and click back to the line where Hunter is waiting.

"So sorry, Hunter. It took a little longer than I planned."

"Who were you talking to?"

"Oh…no one, you know." I leave the answer short and sweet.

I rummage through the boxes, trying to spy out the tree stand.

"What's that racket in the background?"

"Sorry. I'm looking for my Christmas tree stand. Safeway, the grocery store has fresh trees arriving tonight, so I'm getting my stuff out in preparation. I'm excited about my first Christmas back in the States."

"Cool. Sounds fun."

"Speaking of fun, Hunter…any pointers on how to rope a tree onto my car?"

"Isn't your car new?"

"Yeah."

"When do you want to do this?"

"Tonight. Now. I like to let the tree stand upright for a few days allowing the branches to relax before I trim off the excess." I cross my fingers, hoping he will offer to help.

"Well, I don't have anything going on right at the moment. I could throw it into the back of my Wagoneer. That car's a real beater. So, no worries about your car getting scratched up."

"Really?"

"Sure."

"I'll take you up on that offer!" I spot the silver stand squished up into the corner. "Found it." I lean over, pulling it out.

"What?"

"My tree stand. I found it. How about going to pick out a tree at seven?"

Hunter and I pick out the prettiest tree on the entire lot. We have it loaded up in the back of the Wagoneer and inside my living room in less than an hour. Hunter steadies the tree, engineering it perfectly straight. He holds it straight while I fasten the screws into the trunk.

I breathe deeply, enjoying the scent. "Doesn't my apartment smell like Christmas?"

He nods in agreement, taking a long whiff. "Sure does."

"How about some hot cocoa to thank you for your help?" I wink as I walk toward the kitchen.

I carry a tray into the living room with two mugs brimming with cocoa, topped with small marshmallows. A small plate of cookies sits to the side of the drinks. I'm careful as I place our goodies on the coffee table in front of the sofa. We sit, admiring the beautiful tree.

Hunter takes a big bite of a cookie. "These are tasty. Did you make them?"

"Yes, I did." I boast. "Glad you like them."

"When do you have time to do this? Fridays after school?" He examines the cookie, spying out a group of chocolate chips and takes another bite.

"Actually, I go to see my counselor on Fridays after class. I'm usually pretty tired by the time I get home. So any baking done in this house is on the weekends."

"A counselor?"

"Yes." I hesitate. "I hope that's not a problem. You know I am studying to be a Christian counselor?"

"No problem. I've just never seen one. What's it like?"

His answer calms my concerns. "Well, at first, I went because I was having problems adjusting to living back in the States."

"That makes sense, but why do you need a counselor for acclimation?"

"When I moved here, I didn't know anyone. Guess I needed to talk with someone." I shrug my shoulders. "But… I have to admit that one of the reasons I came back to the U.S. was to seek out counseling as well as to go back to college."

"Oh." His brow furrows.

"Hunter, you see…" I bite the right side of my lower lip. "I have a recurring nightmare. The same one—ever since I was around nine years old. And I believe it has to do with a particular time in my childhood…" Second thoughts crowd my mind, but I take a breath, then push through my fear. "It was after my mom died. I remember most of the bad things that happened to my sisters, but as for my baby brother and myself, I've blocked it out, and I suspect it isn't good."

Hunter leans forward, his elbows resting on his knees, listening intently. He appears to hang onto my every word. He nods a couple of times, smiles, and even squeezes my hand. "Catherine, I can respect that you're seeking help."

My back stiffens. "It's all about the healing, Hunter."

I feel awkward. After all, I just met this guy. I don't want to scare him off or make him think I'm crazy. I change the subject. "Thank you so much for all of your help with the tree. It's wonderful."

Hunter points to the Douglas fir. "So when do you plan to decorate this beauty?"

"Day after tomorrow. Sunday. Want to help? I'll treat you to dinner and wine…and perhaps cookies and milk afterward." I playfully punch his arm.

"Who'd turn down such an invitation?" He glances at his watch. "I need to head out if I plan to get some sleep before tomorrow's skiing." Standing, he looks toward the coat closet.

After handing him his coat, I walk him to the door. "Thanks, Hunter."

He draws me close and hugs me. His comfortable and tender touch still makes me edgy. I pull away.

"Catherine, I won't take that personally." He chuckles. "See you bright and early tomorrow morning, seven a.m., for some fun in the sun." He closes the door behind him.

CHAPTER FOURTEEN

Catherine
December 1992

D aylight has barely dawned, and the sky is still hazy as I open the door at 7 am to greet Hunter. He loads my gear into his car, and we drive off, heading for the ski resort.

It isn't long before the sun is bright, and we're flying down the slopes. We carve our way down the mountain, passing each other in between S-turns, making a two-strand braid in motion, leaving our tracks in the snow. The breeze is perfect; the snow is soft but firm. It couldn't be a better day.

Hunter is very easy to be around. Perhaps too easy? My mind battles against conflicting thoughts as I search for things to dislike. I know the protective wall I've erected is wrong, but it feels safe, familiar, and comfortable. I fight the temptation to hide behind my emotional distancing. In all honesty, Hunter deserves a chance, a clean slate, not one littered with my baggage—the distrust from Edward's betrayal.

When we arrive back home, Hunter is quick to help me carry my skis, boots, and poles into my apartment.

"Whew, what a day!" He draws near. I avoid him as I dance away.

"Can I offer you anything to drink?

"Just a big glass of water. I'm parched. Skiing dehydrates me. Probably because I forget to drink."

"Sure thing." I come out from the kitchen carrying a glass of water for each of us. "Cheers, Hunter, to a successful day of skiing!" We clink our glasses.

"To tomorrow," he volleys back. "To decorating your first Christmas tree in Colorado."

"Yes. And afterward, how about playing a game? I love games. Do you?"

"Games? Play? Me?" He grins. "Does that include popcorn?"

I shake my head, tossing him a grin as I walk him to the door.

Catie
Spring 1963

It turns out I have enough popcorn, 'cuz I'm not hungry anymore. I look around. "Anna, where are the games? We have a bunch of fun ones. I like Candy Land the best." I prop myself up onto my knees, leanin' toward her. "It only has five markers, but we can use different colored Tiddly-Winks, so we can all play."

Anna springs up on the sofa, sendin' me jerkin' backward. "CATIE, I'm the parent here. I will determine what games we will play. If I wanted your opinion, I would've asked—which I did not! You need to keep your little mouth shut unless I ask you a question. Understand?"

I din't understand. I turn my eyes to Charlotte for an explanation. My big sister is 'bout to blow. Her eyes are bulgin' and her hands are fisted. Claudia takes Charlotte's hand to calm her, pettin' it like a puppy.

Claudia, the second oldest, has the biggest and bestest kind heart ever. She always laughs and tickles Charley and me whenever we're sad or cryin'.

Anna stands. Her shadow looms over us. "I have a special game for tonight. I'll pick one of you to lie on the carpet." Her eyes move slowly over each one of us, finally restin' on Melinda.

Figures. She's one of the big kids. I wrinkle my nose. I want to be picked. I'm often the last one chosen in games 'cuz everyone says I'm too little.

Anna moves to the center of the room, motionin' us to gather around. A pukey odor seeps into the room. It smells like farts, but worse. I pinch my nose. "Hey, you guys, who farted?"

Everyone swears it wasn't them. Melinda, Shawnee, my sisters, and Charley all say they can't smell anythin'.

Anna interrupts. "Enough. I don't smell a thing. And Catie, use poot or fluff when referring to gas."

"You can't smell that poot?" I cock my head in disbelief. "What? Your nose must be dead 'cuz if you lit a match, the whole room would blow."

Everyone bursts into giggles, except Anna and her daughters, who are dead quiet.

"Enough, Catie!" Anna shoves her finger in my face. Her teeth are clenched. I stiffen and pull away.

Her voice suddenly changes. It softens. She speaks calm—too calm.

"Now, children, Melinda will lay on the floor. I will tell each one of you where you'll sit on the floor next to her."

Anna instructs, "Charlotte, I want you to sit at her head. Claudia, you sit at her feet. Carolyn and Shawnee, sit on Melinda's right side. Catie and Charley, sit on her left side."

She tells us exactly what we are to do.

"Now, children, place your pointer and middle finger on each hand underneath Melinda as she lays on the floor."

I look at my sisters with questions, but still obey.

Anna yells, "Melinda, be still!"

"Sorry, Momma, but it tickles."

"Hush!"

Anna never yells at Melinda. We slide our two fingers underneath her.

Anna says, "Okay, try to lift her."

We all try. It's impossible 'cuz Melinda's too fat. My fingers are gonna break off. I knew she should've used me, Charley, or Shawnee. We're the littlest.

Anna interrupts. "Alright, alright. Stop trying. Now I'm going to have you repeat a chant after me."

Carolyn asks, "What's a chant?"

"Shh, Shush." Anna put her finger to her lips. "Just do it!"

Our new stepmother gets mad so easily and is mean so fast. Her moods change as quick as lightnin'. A lot like Buck. Scary.

"Now, each one of you repeat this after me. Charlotte, you go first." Her voice is calm again.

"She looks dead."

We all say the words, as told. It is repeated six times.

"She feels dead."

Again, the six of us speak the words, six different times.

"She is dead."

Another six times.

"Now, move your fingers out until only your fingertips are touching her." She waits, watchin' to make sure we follow her instructions. We do as we're told. "Now lift her."

We obey.

What? Huh?

Melinda floats up in the air as if she's light as a feather. Wow!

156

Floatin' must be that magic stuff. Now I understand why she picked her, 'cuz she's the heaviest. A big fat pig, to be honest, but Anna would never say that about her precious girl.

"I want a turn. Me next." We all shout, raisin', and wavin' our hands.

Anna teaches us, one by one, how to lead the chant, as well as lettin' us take turns floatin' for the next couple of hours. It's fun, but at the same time, I wonder why and how it works. I ask Anna, but she never really answers, only says, "It's a secret for me to know, but I'll tell you the name of the game. It's called levitation."

———

The next mornin' while we're all gathered around the television, watchin' *The Huckleberry Hound Show*, I hear Anna and Daddy talkin' in the dinin' room.

"Forest, the kids and I had a gas last night. They were going ape. We ate popcorn and played games till ten o'clock."

"Even Charley and Shawnee? Up that late?"

"They were both sleepy-eyed but didn't want to miss a thing. I think Charley fell asleep while I carried him to bed."

"Did everyone get along?"

"Yes, of course. I told you game-night would be a great way to bring the children together."

I walk into the dinin' room on my way to the bathroom. Daddy and Anna are still eatin' their breakfast and sippin' coffee.

"Hey Catie, I heard you all had a fun time last night. What'd you think?

"It was fun, Daddy! I like Anna's floaty game. You should play it with us sometime."

"I wish I could, Darlin', but Friday nights are Daddy's double shift night, remember?"

"Uh-huh. Maybe we could play on another day?" I turn to Anna. "Does it work on grown-ups as big as Daddy?"

I have to pee real bad, so I cross my legs and hold myself.

Anna notices. "You need to use the bathroom. Go on before you have an accident."

I hurry off, but not before I hear Daddy ask, "What's the floaty game?"

I keep the bathroom door open to eavesdrop.

"It's just a little game we played. Although, that's a good name for it, the floaty game."

I hear her chair scoot back and the clankin' of plates and silverware. I watch her from the bathroom as she passes, carryin' dishes into the kitchen. She sees me on the potty.

"Catie, you need to close the door when you're using the bathroom."

"Sorry. Had to go too bad."

Marion
December 1992

Catherine takes a bathroom break after telling me about the long-ago game night Anna planned. Such favoritism is hurtful and hard for a child. Yet Anna's choices stir my suspicion. I fear where this is going. If my intuitions are correct, they would confirm the reasons for Catherine's suppression.

"Marion, when we were together last time, you explained how Lucifer was kicked out of heaven and ended up deceiving Adam and Eve, so they died spiritually. What exactly did you mean by spiritual death and something about a darkened condition?"

Catherine pulls out a notebook from her college classes. "We're studying about our identity in Christ in school, and I think this plays into that subject." She crosses her legs and leans into the cushions.

I explain. "Adam's and Eve's spiritual death affected our identity and our relationship with God. Like most questions dealing with God and the Bible, the answers can be quite lengthy, but I will do my best to keep my answers simple." I hand her a diagram. "I hope these illustrations will help. As for our identity in Christ, we are made in God's image. His essence is a three-part being; Father, Son, and Holy Spirit."

"Oh, yeah. I remember learning about this as a kid in Sunday school. The Trinity—three parts, the same, but different. Somewhat like water. All H2O, in different forms. Fluid, ice, or steam, representing the Father, the Son, and the Holy Spirit."

"Yes, I recall learning that explanation as well; although simple, it will suffice. We also have three parts—body, soul, and spirit. Our body is the visible physical part and how we interact with our environment. Our soul consists of our mind, will, and emotions, and it enables us to interact with others. Our spirits make us different from anything else God created. It is through our spirits that we interact with God." I point to the diagram.

"To recap, due to their sin, Adam and Eve spiritually died, meaning their spirits were darkened and separated from God. We, as direct descendants of Adam and Eve, are born in this very condition with darkened spirits or separated from the Lord. The Bible refers to it as living in our *flesh*, meaning we try to meet our own needs without God."

Catherine adds. "That's very hard to do, and it brings along terrible consequences." She pats her heart. "Speaking from my experience."

"I think 2 Corinthians 5:17 will bring clarity and good news." I will read it aloud. "Therefore, if anyone is in Christ, he is a new creation; the old *darkened spirit* has passed away, *died*, but the new has come, *the Holy Spirit*!

"So Catherine, when we believe in Jesus Christ, and invite him into our hearts and lives, we receive the Holy Spirit, which is referred to as salvation or being saved. Prior to that, we were spiritually dead with a darkened spirit separated from God. This condition is described as having an Adamic spirit. I like to refer to it as an Adam-ick spirit, as in icky, because we are separated from God."

"That's cool, Marion, I love word association."

"Me too." I smile. "Now, for the significant part. 'The new has come.' The Lord sends his Holy Spirit to live inside us, giving us a new spirit, which replaces the old dead, darkened spirit. We are now able to converse with God 24/7. Do you understand?"

Catherine nods. "You bet I do. However, I need to check in more often. I have a friend who shares everything with the Lord. That's my goal. I only need to get it into my head, and then remind myself that I have unlimited access."

"Exactly. That is a wonderful goal for me, as well. Perhaps applying a sticky note here and there would be an excellent reminder. Some people do not realize as Christians; we can pray-talk to God, ask him for guidance, direction, and depend upon him for anything and everything." I glance at the following verse 18. "We are reconciled or brought back into relationship with God, meaning—"

"I get it!" Catherine jumps in, "We are reconciled back to God through Christ. It—the reconciliation undoes what Satan did in the garden with Adam and Eve." She lifts her hand into the air. "We need to high-five on this fact."

We slap our palms together. Moments like these make my job worthwhile.

I swivel my chair in the direction of my ottoman. "Catherine, do you mind if I put my leg up? I twisted my ankle last weekend." I lift my pant leg, showing her. "It is swollen, again, and beginning to ache." I grit my teeth.

"Eww. That doesn't look so good." She shakes her head. The concern is drawn on her face. "Do you have any ice in the lounge?"

"I have a polar pack in the freezer. Would you mind getting it for me?"

Catherine is up and back within a couple of minutes. I ease

my leg onto the ottoman. She gently applies the cold compress to my ankle before she takes her seat.

"Aww. Much better. Thank you. I stepped off the curb and lost my balance."

"Marion, please make yourself comfortable. As you see, I'm all into comfort."

Catherine is very relaxed and sprawled out on the love seat. I heed her advice and settle into my chair. We continue our discussion.

Catherine shares a crooked smile. "I can't imagine trying to get through life without the Lord, especially with what I'm facing."

The ice is soothing. My ankle feels better already. "I love how God uses so many special and unique ways to communicate with his children. However, obtaining relational intimacy is more than what many think. I am not saying that going to church, listening to a sermon, or engaging in a Bible study, are not important because they are, very much so. However, relational intimacy with God is more like pursuing any love relationship."

"I agree. My favorite part is my conversations with God. I know I tend to talk too much." Catherine throws her head back, laughing at herself. "But when I do listen or when I'm fighting my fears and doubts, he meets me right where I am. I love hearing his still, small voice. It booms with arm-in-arm-ness—if that's a word."

She hugs her legs, snuggling up in the blanket. "It's hard to describe, but lately, my time with God has been warm and cozy, filled with his lovely fragrance. That sounds weird, I know. Right?"

I shake my head, encouraging her to express herself.

She responds, "Let's just say it's comfortable and familiar, like the holidays and a home-cooked meal."

CHAPTER FIFTEEN

Catherine
December 1992

The savory smell of pot roast hangs in the air. I add a few more spices and seasonings before stirring. There's a knock. Prompt as always. Knowing it's Hunter, I yell out, "Come in. I'm in the kitchen."

I watch as he cracks open the door and sheepishly sticks his head into the room.

"Wow, what smells so delicious?" He makes his way into the kitchen. "Pot roast? Right?" He leans over my shoulder, peeking into the slow cooker. "With potatoes, carrots, and onions. Yum, my favorites."

"Mine too. I'm a big meat eater. I love protein, and if I were a dinosaur, I'd definitely be a predator, not one of those veggie eater dino-types."

"It smells great." He turns, looking into the dining area. "The table looks so nice."

He noticed.

"Shall I open some wine?" He pulls out a bottle from the large brown paper bag he's carrying. I also see a package tucked inside.

"Yes, please do." My curiosity is always getting the best of me. I eye the shiny Christmas wrapping and question, "What else do I see in the bag?"

Hunter's smile spans cheek to cheek. He wags his finger. "Now, that's for later, Catherine."

Dinner goes down smoothly, followed by the rich chocolates. The wine and our conversation flow.

Following the meal, we decorate the tree while talking about our likes and dislikes. Neither of us are fans of riding horses or Halloween, which makes me happy.

The Christmas tree shines with its many decorations, and festive carols play in the background. Our evening draws to a close. Hunter stands to retrieve the package from the brown bag sitting on the counter. He walks over, moving in close. His eyes meet mine as he hands me the wrapped package.

"Catherine, I would like to present you with this gift for your *first* Christmas in Denver."

We take a seat on the antique settee, where I eagerly accept the box and begin carefully removing the wrapping paper. I hold back my excitement and desire to rip into the surprise. To my delight, it's a beautiful and pristine, fluffy, white bear with a huge shiny brass bell for its body.

Hunter explains, "She's an Angel Christmas Snow Bear tree topper. And a bell."

How romantic. It's so beautiful and thoughtful.

"Awww. Wow. I'm at a loss for words, which isn't usual for me." I stare down at the bear. She jingles as I lift her.

"Would you like me to attach her to the top of the tree?" Hunter asks.

"Yes, but not yet. I want to admire the bear a while longer." I lean back, making myself more comfortable.

"So, Hunter, what exactly is an Angel Christmas Snow Bear?"

His whole face smiles. He blushes and shrugs his shoulders. "I don't know, I just made it up, but it sounds good—doesn't it?" Before I can reply, he reassures me, "It is a real tree topper and a huge bell."

His honesty melts my heart. "You're right. Angel Snow Bear. That will be her official name. It sounds perfect, and the name rings a bell."

I snicker at my pun, then pass him the bear and go to fetch the stepladder from the closet. Hunter busts out in a loud chuckle as I'm walking away.

Together, we fasten her to the tip-top of the tree. Hunter secures a white light at the base of the bell, highlighting the beauty of the brass, a perfect topper for the Christmas tree, and the evening.

On the way to the front door, the narrow width of the foyer guides our shoulders to touch as we walk side by side. I hand Hunter a sack of neatly packed leftovers. I place my hand on the doorknob. Before opening it, I look up. Hunter leans in, catching me off guard. His face moves closer to mine. I feel his breath on my face. His lips so near—too near.

I turn my cheek. Too much. Too fast. I gently push him away.

"I'm sorry, Hunter, I'm just not ready. I like you a lot, but I don't want to cross that boundary. I know if it doesn't work out, I'll lose you as a friend. I don't want to risk it at this point." I take his hand and squeeze his fingers. "I hope you understand."

Hunter stands tall, his back upright, making space between us.

"That's fine, Catherine. I understand. You're just not ready. I have stronger feelings for you than you do me. That's fine. No problem."

His eyebrows arch. "So, I'll make you a deal. I promise I will NEVER try to kiss you again. Never. But when and if you ever feel more for me and want to cross your boundary, then you will have to kiss me."

He maintains deep eye contact, challenging me.

I sustain his stare. "Okay, Hunter; I'll accept your promise; with the understanding, IF I ever kiss you, it will mean much more than a kiss. It will be an offering—an offering of my heart in return for yours. A serious commitment."

I watch his face, looking for any signs of faltering. He looks back, not rattled by my words. He appears at ease, staring comfortably into my eyes.

I return his challenge. "Is it a deal?"

"Yes. Catherine, it's a deal. And that will be the day…"

He purposely pauses to bait my curiosity.

"That will be the day I tell you my middle name." He winks, closes in, and then places a soft kiss on my cheek before he walks out, carrying the brown paper sack. He shuts the door quietly behind himself.

Catie
Spring 1963

The door opens. Anna sashays in carryin' a paper grocery bag filled with new games. Melinda and Shawnee follow, closing the door behind them.

First, Anna shows us a game called Magic 8 *Ball*. It's a black ball with the number "8" on top and a little glass window on the bottom. Anna says the ball is magic and can tell the future. All you have to do is ask a question and then flip it over. The answer appears in the glass window.

It knows everythin', 'cuz when Anna left the room for a quick moment I ask it if Anna is mean. When I turn it over, it spells the answer, yes.

Anna promises to teach us one of *her* new games every week. She never wants to play Candy Land, Old Maid, or any of our fun games. She says we already know those games and don't need her help.

This week Anna takes out another game called the *Ouija Board*. She says it's similar to the Magic 8 Ball we learned last week, but it will give more answers.

We huddle together as she explains the rules. It has a see-through hole on top with a black pointer. It's supposed to spell out the answer, letter by letter, on the alphabet game board. We each place one finger lightly on the teardrop-shaped thing-a-ma-bob and then ask it a question.

We start by askin', "What color are Charlotte's eyes?"

It spells out b-l-u-e. I wonder out loud if someone's pushin' it. Everyone swears they aren't.

It's spooky when Anna starts askin' questions 'bout Mommy. She wants to know weird things like where she is, meanin' where she's livin', I guess? Everyone knows Mommy's livin' in heaven. Anna also asks if Mommy is happy. She seems too curious 'bout our mommy. Her questions make me nervous.

"YIKES!" I shriek. Everyone stares wide-eyed. The plastic teardrop begins to move all by itself. We're so afraid that no one pays attention to what it's spellin'.

"Melinda, you pushed it. Din't you?" I accuse her, sure that she had.

"No. I didn't push anything," she says. Her bullfrog-eyes bulge more than usual.

Everyone else says they din't move the game, shakin' their heads side to side. I shove my chair away from the table.

"This game is creepy. I don't want to play this anymore. Anyone want to play Old Maid with me?"

Melinda and Shawnee tease me, like always.

"Catie, you're just a chicken. Chicken. Chicken. You're nothing but a big-fat-chicken!"

Turnin' toward them, I rhyme back, "Sticks and stones can break my bones, but words can never hurt me."

I lie. It does hurt my feelin's; my stepsisters thinkin' I'm a chicken. Maybe I am. Somethin' 'bout this game doesn't feel right. Why don't my sisters say somethin' about this creepy game? And it's scary. Am I the only one who can tell this game feels wrong? I wish my Mommy were here. She'd tell me what to do.

Durin' the followin' weeks, we practice playin' levitation, Eight-ball, the Ouija Board, and also listenin' to ghost stories. This Friday Anna mentions she has some friends comin' over to teach us a new game called a séance.

A nna's friends arrive right around dusk, after the streetlights have come on. She introduces Greta, who comes with two men. She's the lady who's gonna lead the game. Her dark brown hair is extra-long, almost down to her butt crack. Silver threads grow in it. I've known ladies with real long hair, but they put it up in a neat bun, and not danglin' down all over everywhere. Her dress is different too. Instead of fitted and to her knees, it falls to the ground, all loose and flowy.

I whisper into Claudia's ear. "These people's eyes look crazy, same as Anna's family—they're a bunch of weirdos. What do ya think?" I stare at our guests.

She shrugs. "Not sure. Different looking, but they're grownups, so they're probably okay."

Typical Claudia; she likes everyone. I see somethin' in them— just like what I see in Grandpa Buck. In their eyes. Black. So black, you can't see the dark dot in the middle. But Buck's eyes are a little different. He has a creepy diamond shaped pupil. Kinda gold lookin'. Snake-ish. It gives me goosebumps, and not the happy kind.

I look, then gawk at this crazy woman's face. Yep, she has the same kind of eyes. Claudia doesn't seem to notice. My sisters are older, smarter, and they're supposed to watch over me. *Why don't they see what I see? I'm sure they'd tell me if they did. Why am I the only one who has the willies? Is somethin' wrong with me?*

Greta's two men friends never say a word. Just stand off to the side, stiff like wooden soldiers. I lean against the corner, out of the way. Watchin'.

Gretta covers the dinin' room table with a pretty tablecloth and bunches of beautiful candles. With all those candles, doesn't she worry 'bout all that hair of hers catchin' fire?

I'm hopin' we're gonna eat somethin' special, seein' the table done up so fancy, but my doubts set in. I don't see or smell any apple pie or treats comin' from the kitchen or out of the strange woman's big black bag.

Greta lights the candles. She tells Anna to turn off *all* the lights in the *whole house.* Yikes! The corner where I'm crouched goes instantly dark. The center of the table glows. I'm not sure 'bout this new game. The darkness doesn't feel right. No. It doesn't feel right at all.

The creepy lady slowly walks to the head of the table, pulls out Daddy's chair, and takes his seat. She hunkers down and gets real comfortable—like she owns the place.

"Will you all join me? Please, everyone, be seated," she says.

I walk toward my sisters, but Anna grabs me by the shoulders and pulls me over, makin' me sit with her. I'm stuck sittin' between Anna and Melinda. I want to be with my sisters, who are on the other side of the table.

My heart beats like a drum. I'm scared to death. But I'm too afraid to tell Anna, 'cuz she'll make fun of me. And I bet she'll let Melinda and Shawnee call me a chicken like they did before when we played the Ouija board.

Everyone settles into a chair. We all scoot in close to the table. Two men sit on each side of Greta. They're dressed in all black and almost disappear in the darkness 'cept for their pale faces and dark saggy eyes. It looks like they have the flu.

"Hello. My name is Greta. Anna has invited me here this evening to share with *all of you.*"

Her voice sounds like she has gravel stuck in her throat. She looks at each one of us. I don't like her beady eyes.

Greta speaks loudly. "My gift is the ability to talk with our dearly beloved who have had the honor and privilege to pass over into the next world before us. And yes," she takes a breath, "some of you here would refer to that world as Heaven."

Her voice is too phony. Too slow. Eerie. She speaks, then stares without blinkin'. I hate it when her eyes stop on me.

"Now, please let us all join hands."

I don't want to hold hands with these creepy people.

Greta goes on to say she has a special tele-somethin' gift that allows her to talk to heaven. I've never heard of a tele-path to heaven.

My hands sweat as I ask, "What does *tele-path* mean?"

Anna pinches my thigh under the table. Hard.

"Ouch," I whine.

"Catie, shhh. Be quiet. Don't be asking any more questions."

Melinda chimes in. "Stupid questions." She sticks out her tongue at me.

Greta interrupts in her gravelly voice. "Quiet, everyone. Please. Quiet. I want to be able to hear. Hear into the other side."

My sister's faces are hidden in the shadows behind the flames of the candles. I want to say somethin' to them, but they're clear across the table, too far for me to get their attention. I can't see them, much less talk to them. I don't like sittin' away from my sisters. I have to figure out what this strange lady is sayin' all by myself.

Hmmm, maybe Greta is talkin' 'bout some special telephone? Our phone has a party-line we share with another family, but we weren't given the choice of a tele-path to heaven. If so, I know Daddy would have gotten one of those fancy phones so we could talk to Mommy. And Teenage Granny has a three-family party line, and not one of them has a line to heaven, or she would've told me.

Greta spins on, "We invite you dearly beloved spirits who have passed on, please come back to us. Please speak. We want to hear from you. We invite you to gather with us."

I know what 'passed-on' means. *Greta is* tryin' to talk to dead people! Then I remembered what Grandpa, Mommy's daddy, said about people tryin' to speak to the dead. It's WRONG.

The candles flicker. The strange woman stands and throws back her hair. She raises her hands high and closes her eyes. "This is very good. The spirits are here. They want to talk to us."

"Yikes! Uh, oh!" My words slip out. I quickly cover my mouth.

Anna pinches me again. I hold my breath. This game isn't any fun. The room turns icy cold. I shiver, then blow air from my lips, expectin' to see my breath turn into white smoke, like in the winter. Nothin'. I shake harder, and my teeth chatter.

I look out into the inky black darkness of the livin' room. I blink my eyes several times to erase the spooky monsters I see leerin' around. Nope. They won't go away. My stomach hurts.

Can't anyone see them?

The spooky creatures act like they're playin' a different kind of hide-and-seek game. They slip in and out of the shadows. Their black eyes look like they're smilin' at me. They're ugly, dark, and wrinkled up, like old rotten potatoes.

Why doesn't someone say somethin' about them? Am I the only one who seems to see these ghosts?

I want to call out to my sisters, but I know I'll only get in trouble. I wish daddy were here. I try to hold back my tears.

Anna speaks. "Wouldn't it be nice for my stepchildren to be able to talk to their mother?"

I lean into the table, movin' my head side to side, tryin' to signal my sisters that I don't want to do this. They lean in, too. No one speaks. We're all wide-eyed.

What's wrong with Anna? Everyone knows it's wrong to pray or talk to the dead.

That's what Grandpa and Granny Grunt told me. I know they

always tell the truth, unlike Anna. They also said Mommy's in heaven and I wouldn't see her till I go there. Anna's wrong to try to talk with Mommy beforehand.

Although I would love to see my Mommy again, I'm afraid to call her on this séance telephone path, 'cuz she might get stuck here on earth if she answers. Then she would be kicked out of heaven, and I'd *never* see her again! I squirm in my seat and pull my sweaty hands free from Anna and Melinda. It feels like real worms are crawlin' all over me.

I used to love Friday nights stayin' up late playin' games, but this isn't the same. This game isn't fun.

I stand and tell Anna, "I'm tired. I'm goin' to my room."

I start walkin' without waitin' for her permission. I stop where Charley sits and grab his hand, tuggin' him to come with me. Anna's distracted by Greta and doesn't see me whisper to Charley. We tiptoe out of the room. No one seems to notice, not even the creepy spirits or monsters or whatever they are.

The next mornin', the sun shines through my bedroom window and wakes me. Carolyn's bed is empty. I shake Charley. He stirs, stretches, and lets out a big yawn.

"Carolyn's not in her bed."

"Where's she at?" Charley asks.

We throw back the covers and run into my older sisters' bedroom. Charlotte, Claudia, and Carolyn are all sittin' in the bed. They tell Charley and me that the spirits showed up last night.

Carolyn says, "Last night books flew off the shelves all by themselves and Charlotte fainted."

Anna pokes her head into the bedroom. "Hey kids, I was just on my way to put away a stack of towels…"

She goes on talkin' tellin' us that a spirit talked through Charlotte at the séance, that is before she woke up from her faint. No one says a single word. It's like our mouths are buttoned shut.

We sit still, waitin' to make sure Anna is gone. After we hear Anna traipse down the stairs, Carolyn is the first to speak. "I'm not too sure about what all Anna said. It sounded more like mumbo-jumbo. I couldn't make out what the spirit said."

Claudia adds, "Catie, I wished I'd gone upstairs with you and Charley. I was so afraid, I bee-lined myself to the opposite end of the table, away from Greta. I kept my eyes closed durin' the séance and sang songs to myself while I played with Shawnee's hair till I got her to sleep. I didn't like all the commotion and creepy stuff going on with that lady talking about spirits and all."

I ask, "Charlotte, did you guys talk to Mommy?"

"No."

"I'm so glad." Relief fills my heart. "Mommy's extra clever. She probably knew that Anna and her creepy friends were up to no good. She musta known that what we were doin' was wrong."

Charlotte answers. "Yeah, I know. But another spirit talked after I woke up. It said someone had died in our house. Down in the basement."

I look at Carolyn and Claudia. They nod, agreein' with Charlotte.

"You believe that?" My tummy rumbles.

Charlotte and Carolyn say, "yes."

Claudia adds, "Kinda," she squints her eyes and scrunches her nose, "but I'm not sure."

"Were you guys afraid?" I scoot in closer to my sisters.

Claudia's the first to answer. "Yes. I was so a-scared, I almost peed in my pants."

Later in the day, Anna tells us that there was a suicide in our basement. I ask her what suicide means. She says it's self-murder. It's when someone kills themselves. And that's what happened in *our house*. And the person's spirit still lives here and is trapped in our basement!

I hate our basement. It's all cement, but it's damp and smells like dirt. Lots of creepy-crawlers and sticky spider webs too. Yuck! I knew I was right about that séance. God must've told my heart, 'cuz I sensed it was bad. Real bad!

Charley and me are scared to death knowin' a ghost lives in our house. We know without askin'—*this ghost* is nothin' like one of our favorite cartoons, Casper, the friendly ghost.

Marion
December 1992

While sitting in my cushy chair, I listen to Catherine describe her ghostly experiences with the dark games and séances. The Friday afternoon light paints the office gold, yet I am edgy. Prickly. I cannot seem to get comfortable. My heart intuitively knows where Catherine's story is going. I have heard of similar cases.

How do I prepare her? I absolutely must not lead or put anything in her mind that is not a part of her memories. I am guarded and determine to allow her memories to flow as God leads, without pushing anything forward before it is time. I record several notes into her file.

- Ouija board, levitation, and séances—not children's games.
- A deceiving and desensitizing approach or introduction into black magic?
- Knowing or unknowing involvement with the occult? —Anna and her family.

I take the time to think through my next question. "I imagine the séances were frightening. Amazing, even as a child, you were able to discern it was off—wrong. Did your father know about these games?"

Catherine flips her hair off her shoulder. "He knew about some, like the Eight ball and Ouija board. He didn't seem to think it was a problem. I asked him about it years—no decades later. He said, 'It never crossed my mind that the games were evil. After all, they were advertised on the television and made by Mattel and Hasbro.'" She bobs her shoulders. "Ironically, the same manufacturers sold Candyland and Matchbox cars. No wonder my dad didn't understand or suspect any wickedness."

"What about the levitation or séances?" I ask.

"Yes, he knew about the so-called games, but Anna, being cunning and deceptive, would change the subject or make light of the activities. It was her way of keeping it undercover—a secret. I don't think my dad realized the effects Anna's choices would have on us."

"Thank you, Catherine, this gives me greater insight. Based on what we discussed in our last session, and the fact that Satan is real and waging a spiritual war, how would you describe the effects Anna's decisions had on your life—then and now?

She immediately answers. "There's a total battle for my mind, spiritually speaking. I sense the enemy is behind the darkness in this world and is fighting to pollute my beliefs with lies, just like Anna."

She reaches for a tissue, dabbing at her nose. "Not just me. I'm not saying I'm all that important. I'm referring to everyone. I believe the enemy wants to keep us from knowing God's love, truth, and his purpose in our lives."

I watch her fold the tissue into a small square.

"Yes, I agree. However, God gave each of us a free will, which means the freedom to make our own choices. Unfortunately, some decisions, like Anna's, can offend, hurt, and even devastate others at the deepest levels. Nevertheless, those decisions are the responsibility of the individual…and not the responsibility of God.

"Same with Edward, cheating on me, right?" She crumbles the tissue tightly in her right hand. "He broke my heart."

"Yes. I realize Edward hurt you, and these words may not soothe your pain. Still, God has used your heartbreak, and turned it into good, by teaching you about love, forgiveness, commitment, and the importance of integrity and honesty in relationships."

The room has warmed up. I dab the perspiration from my upper lip.

"The truth is, we live in a fallen world. Natural consequences follow our choices. More seriously, someday we will all stand before the Lord and give an account for what we have done and have not done. My point is, we are accountable and responsible before God for our decisions, regardless of our reasons, justifications, and our many influences. No one gets away with anything. God knows everything."

I click on the fan to invite a soft breeze to flow through the room. Last week was cold, and now the weather feels like a warm summer day—typical Colorado weather.

Sweat pools on my back. *If I would only lose more weight, I would not be so hot. Choices? I need to heed my advice.*

I jot down two scriptural references on a sticky-note pad, Romans 14:12 and 2 Corinthians 5:10. "The verses say that everyone shall give an account of himself to God. All believers will appear before the judgment seat of Christ, and each person will face the things they have done, good and bad." I hand it to Catherine.

"Later this week, take some time to look up these passages and see what you think."

I set aside a second sticky note with the same scripture references for myself. Catherine attaches the small paper to the front of her journal without breaking eye contact.

I like that about her. "Of course, God could intervene, but he allows us to work through life's challenges, so we learn how to love, forgive, resolve conflict, and seek reconciliation. The list is endless. Some of the most painful offenses will bring us closer to God—if we allow it to happen."

Catherine fiddles with a paper clip, twirling it between her fingers. "I must admit, my pain was what drove me to seek your help...and my fears."

Her gaze focuses on something far away and she begins to bend the wire back and forth.

My attention is on the thin paper clip, wondering how much it can take before it breaks.

CHAPTER SIXTEEN

Catherine
December 1992

I paperclip several loose papers into my journal. My quiet time has brought me to the conclusion that Marion's right. I've chosen to live in fear—fear of everything. Afraid to remember. Afraid of pain. Afraid to trust. Even reluctant and fearful of taking a chance on love. It's difficult to admit, but I've had a choice in all that's happened. Maybe not an option in the events, but I did have a choice in how I handled the situations.

I skim through my journal notes and recall a conversation with Marion.

"Catherine," Marion said that day. "Do you remember sharing the emotions you felt toward your ex-husband, Edward, when we first met?"

I nodded.

"I have observed in recent days you have mentioned similar emotions are surfacing toward Hunter."

"Yes, kinda...I'm not sure. Why?" I sent Marion a side glimpse. My brows furrowed in skepticism. "Now what?"

Marion glanced down and referred to her notes, reading them aloud. "You described your emotions as fearful. You said you were consumed with uncertainty and felt inadequate to make wise choices."

Marion paused to form an explanation. "I am referring to choices concerning men. You were embarrassed, with a strong desire to run away." She looked up. Her glasses rested low on her nose. "Correct?"

"Uh-huh." I thumped my pen against my journal. My nerves prickled. "Where are we going with this, Marion?"

"You tell me." Marion challenged me. "In the past with Edward and even this week with Hunter, fear arose. How did you respond after feeling those familiar emotions of alarm?"

"Well...umm...I...I moved away. Kind of shut down. Tried to hide, maybe?"

"Catherine, in both cases, you were afraid, afraid of being hurt. In your fear, you fled. When the tender, romantic feelings stirred for Hunter, did you call upon the Lord? Did you ask God what you were to do?"

I lowered my head to avoid eye contact and mumbled, "No." Heat rose to my face burning with conviction.

Marion kept talking. "Catherine, please do not misunderstand my intentions. I am not scolding you. I am simply pointing out your patterns, meaning how you react, hoping that you will be able to recognize your tendencies in the future. Once you can identify how you cope, you will be able to stop, turn, and ask."

"Meaning?"

Marion purposely didn't answer me, which allowed me time to think.

I questioned her. "Do you mean asking God for direction and guidance in figuring out my problems?"

"Yes. Otherwise, self-sufficiency can become a stronghold in your life. Do you recall when we discussed strongholds? I described them as being anything we go to for comfort, security, and dependence—other than God. The more cognizant you are of your poor habits, the less vulnerable and less likely you are to act upon them."

Marion sat erect in her chair. She leaned forward, then raised her voice and spoke slowly with clarity. "This is a spiritual war. The battles are real, and it is of vital importance that you are aware—that you have your eyes wide open to recognize your coping mechanisms."

I glanced up. "It's hard for me to divulge my fears. I've spent too many years feeling afraid, especially with Anna. I avoid showing fear and pain. It's because my emotions were used against me. Anna and her entire family knew how to twist and turn anyone's worst fears into a painful punishment. They were like a pack of wolves looking to use anyone's weakness as a way to climb higher in the pecking order. To show your fear or pain made you vulnerable, like a young pup. They would leverage my fears or weaknesses to knock me down even further. Of course, it always seemed to involve pain.

"I understand, Catherine. I am so sorry about your past." Marion gently reached out and squeezed my hand. "But today is different. You are not alone. You are a child of the Almighty God. The Lord will see you through this. And I will do all I can to help you."

My mind comes back to the present. Marion's encouraging and soothing words jump off the pages of my journal. She's right. I know she's spot-on about my problems. I recognize, she's also correct about the solution. Feeling hopeful and confident, I slap my journal shut, determined to war against my fears—head-on.

Catie
Spring 1963

Anna yells at the top of her lungs from the front porch. "You kids come inside the house—NOW!" She stomps her foot on the front step.

I jump in fear.

I don't want to leave the front yard and go inside 'cuz my team is winnin' in a game of Red-Rover. I used to be the last kid picked, but now I'm one of the first, 'cuz I'm quick and have a special secret on how to break through the Red-Rover line. And I burst through almost every time.

Claudia, Carolyn, and Charley all go into the house. Charlotte and me stay behind to say goodbye to our friends.

Charlotte has a boyfriend. She's flirtin' with Tony. She denies it, but I can tell the way she turns her head, smiles, and bats her long eyelashes. Plus, I can see she's blushin', but Charlotte fibs and says her red color comes from the sun.

Carolyn runs out from the house and down the porch stairs, chargin' right at us.

"Catie, Charlotte." Her breath comes fast. "Anna says we have to go to her creepy parents' house." She leans in close, whisperin'. "To see...you know who."

My guts jerk. My tummy feels sick.

"Not those crazy people!" I pout. "Is Daddy goin'?"

"Yeah, Dad says he's going. But he won't be around all the time." Carolyn's quick to answer.

"What if one of them corners me in the house or the barn? Alone—all by myself? Like the last time when GG Dean tricked me into goin' into the barn. He din't want to play jacks. The creepy old man just wanted to stick his slimy tongue down my throat. Anna made excuses sayin' he was only a sloppy kisser, but she din't say anythin' about why GG Dean was tryin' to kiss me in the first place. She told Daddy I was nothin' more than a troublemaker."

I drop my head and give the grass a hard kick.

"I mentioned his icky kiss to Granny Grunt. She laughed and said sometimes old men are sloppy kissers."

Claudia giggles. "Well, I have to admit that is kinda true of Grandpa, but his kisses are nothing like GG Deans. Granny Grunt probably didn't understand what you were trying to tell her."

Carolyn eyeballs me, and then Charlotte says, "Claudia's right. Granny Grunt didn't understand, but we do. We believe you, Catie. We know, 'cuz the jerk tried the same thing with us. And Anna said the same lie about him being a sloppy kisser. That's bull! We need to make a pact to stay together."

Carolyn grips my shoulders and looks directly into my eyes. "Catie, you'll have to yell. Just holler, NO! Real loud. Then run. Come and get one of us older girls. And don't leave Charley alone either." She turns to Charlotte for her agreement. "Right? We have to promise to stick together. No one alone with any of them!"

Charlotte nods.

"I promise to yell." Tears sting my eyes. I sweep my hand under my runny nose. "But...but, what if it causes us to get a spankin'?"

Charlotte wipes a tear from my cheek. "It'll be okay, Catie. You can stop crying. I'll let Dad know that you're afraid. We'll stay with you. He'll understand."

"Okay," I sniffle, "but don't say anythin' in front of Anna. She'll get mad and say I'm tryin' to make trouble again."

Daddy and Anna traipse down the stairs with the rest of the kids. "Come on, you girls, pile into the car."

They motion us over to the driveway. I stand back, fightin'

tears. I swallow hard and wipe my eyes.

Maybe I am a crybaby. I haven't cried this much my whole life. And it's all been since Mommy left.

Carolyn takes my hand and walks me toward the car. Charley and Shawnee nestle up in the front seat between Daddy and Anna. Melinda's standin' outside the car door waitin' on Claudia to slide across the back seat and make room.

Melinda steps back. "You get in first, Catie, then you, Carolyn, because it's my turn to be next to the window."

Melinda always says it's her turn, even when it's not.

I slide by Melinda and tuck my head to get into the car. She pinches me—real hard. I jerk around and give her a dirty look.

Carolyn catches Melinda right in the act. Before I have a chance to speak up, I hear a loud whine and "OUCH," followed by, "Mommy, Carolyn pinched me!"

Carolyn's already scootin' across the seat when she fires back at Melinda. "Only because you pinched Catie first. I'll do it again, too."

Carolyn's mad and fed up. She leans toward Melinda, darin' her—no, double dog darin' her to touch me. She rambles on, "Everyone knows you're a big fat frog-eyed troublemaker. You started it. You're always sneaking around trying to pick on Catie and Charley because they're smaller than you. But you keep your distance from us older girls. So, frog eyes, how do ya like it? Huh? How do you like getting pinched?"

Anna glares at Carolyn with slitted eyes, then thrashes her arm back to slap her. Carolyn moves out of her reach. Anna makes another attempt. Again, she misses. Carolyn's quick to dart out of Anna's way.

Daddy jumps in. "Stop it. All of you!"

He stares at Anna. She pulls her arm back into her lap, shootin' daggers at Daddy.

We finish gettin' into the car. Daddy says Claudia has to sit between Carolyn and Melinda to keep the peace. Charlotte slides in next takin' Melinda's window seat. She flashes a quick wink at me 'cuz I'm sittin' next to the other window. No one says a word, but on the inside, I'm singin' Ha, Ha, Ha-ha, Ha. I got the window seat.

We arrive at Poison Ivy's house. Daddy pulls up and parks the car. Anna jumps out of the door, not waitin' for anyone. She yells over her shoulder, "You kids stay outside and play."

We're glad to hear it. We prance up the driveway. It's a beautiful day, and playin' outside is all I want to do anyway.

Melinda and Shawnee march themselves right into the house behind Daddy. I guess they think Anna's order isn't for them.

We find a stick and make hopscotch squares in the dirt, and then we collect different rocks for our placeholders. It's Claudia's turn. She loves actin' silly, like the clown, Red Skelton. With each hop, she wiggles and swoops to the right, then to the left, pretendin' to lose her balance. Charley chuckles with each sway. His laughter grows louder. We all join in gigglin'.

We notice a boy peekin' his head out of the front door of the bunkhouse. It's a small room attached to the barn. Granny Ivy says the bunkhouse is where the hired-hands sleep. The dark-headed kid stands hidden in the shadows of the doorway watchin' us. He looks too young to be a hired-hand and the way he's actin' he's probably shy.

I wave. "Hey, you. Ya wanna play?"

He looks around searchin' for someone, but I don't know who.

Charley hollers, "What's your name? I'm Charley, and these are my sisters. You like hopscotch?"

He slowly shuffles over, jerkin' his head back and forth, lookin' around. He peers at the house and then to the pasture. Seems nervous as he walks over. We gather around him, sittin' down makin' a big circle.

"Hi, I'm Charlotte. I'm the oldest." She points to each of us. "This is Claudia; that's Carolyn; she's Catie, and you already met Charley. Kinda."

We all giggle.

The boy wipes his nose with the back of his hand. "My name's Gilbert."

Charley's excited to have a boy to play with him. He turns into a chatterbox askin' more questions than I've ever heard him speak.

"Gilbert, you live here?"

"Uh, huh," the boy says, noddin' his head.

"Are you Anna's brother?"

"Nope, she ain't got no brothers. Miss Ivy and Mr. Buck are my foster parents."

"What's a foster parent?"

"They're people who act like your parents till you get to go back home."

"You like it here?"

He shakes his head. "Not really."

Charley fires another question at him. "Where's your folks?"

The boy shrugs. "At home, I guess?"

"You miss em?"

"Yeah. Real bad, but it don't matter. I ain't got no choice. I'm stuck here." Gilbert digs a small stick into the dirt, carvin' a deep line.

"How come?" Charley bends his head to look under the boy's long bangs, searchin' for his eyes.

"Court says I can't stay at home—for now." Gilbert keeps his head low.

"What'd you do?"

The hinges on the back screen door squeak. Gilbert's head shoots up. His face turns white. He jumps up and flies as fast as a yellow jacket into the bunkhouse.

Buck and Ivy come strollin' out of the house, motionin' for Daddy to follow them. "Come on, Forest. Let me show you some of our fine saddles we have in the barn."

Gilbert peeks his head out of the bunkhouse, but only for a second till he sees Granny Ivy. She tucks her arm around Anna, and the four of them head straight toward him. Gilbert disappears as quick as lightenin'.

It's then I remember seein' Gilbert, for the first time. He's the dark-haired boy I had seen through the window in the barn. He had waved at me from the bunkhouse when GG Dean was lookin' for the jacks under the workbench. He had the same scared look on his face then. I don't blame Gilbert for not likin' it here. I wonder if he saw what GG Dean did to me?

Granny Ivy turns and yells back over her shoulder. "You kids go on in the house. There are fresh cookies on the kitchen counter. Help yourself. If you want, you can turn on the television. You should be able to find some cartoons or a program to your liking."

We all jump to our feet, headin' for the back door, at the sound of the word *cookies*.

A few hours later, Anna stomps across the yard, steamin' mad. I think Daddy's mad too, 'cuz he shouts, "Get into the same seats you were in when we came here. I don't want to hear any if's, and's, or but's about it."

We do as we're told.

It's quiet in the car except for the swishy sound of the wind blowin' through the windows. Anna hasn't said much since gettin' into the car. I think she's mad, 'cuz we din't stay for dinner. But there's a good reason. GG Dean did it again. He tried to give me one of those icky kisses. He did the same with all the girls. He snuck up from behind and tried to pin them up against the wall. I know, 'cuz they told me.

I hid under the bed after GG Dean cornered me in the back bedroom. Snoopin' around lookin' at all of Granny Ivy's pretty things was a bad idea. But I did what Carolyn said. I started yellin'. Real loud, too. It wasn't too long before my sisters and Charley rushed in from watchin' the television.

GG Dean ran out real fast. I could see his shiny black shoes skedaddle from where I was lyin' low under the bed. Claudia stayed back with Charley and me, while Charlotte and Carolyn went to tell Daddy 'bout what happened.

Right after that, we're loadin' up in the car, headin' home for dinner.

187

Daddy turns on the car radio to listen to the ballgame. He says, "My favorite team is playing today, so you kids keep your chatter down to a low roar so that I can hear the game." He smiles at us in the rearview mirror.

Charley's the first to speak. "Anna, who's that boy that stays in the bunkhouse? He said Granny Ivy and Buck are his *faster* parents now."

Shawnee answers, "You mean Gilbert? He's fun. I like him."

"Yah. That's the boy's name. Why's he there?"

Anna stiffens. "Charley, you saw Gilbert today? What did he say to you?"

Charlotte whispers to Carolyn and me. "Anna looks way too interested."

Charley answers, "Nothing much, just he has to live there 'cuz someone said so."

Claudia taps Anna on her shoulder. "We met him this morning. He seems lonely and misses his mom and dad. He said your folks were his foster parents. Foster, not faster, Charley." She looks over the seat at Charley and then Anna.

Charley quickly asks, "So, what's a foster parent?"

Anna shifts her weight so she can face all us kids. "My parents have such big caring hearts; they take in children who don't have anywhere to live."

"How come they don't have a place to live?" Charley asks, shadin' his eyes from the sun with his hand.

"Sometimes it's because their parents have done something wrong and are in jail. Or the kids have done something wrong and are too young to be in jail. All of the many unfortunate tales I've heard would curl your hair." Anna reaches for a tissue from her pocketbook, tappin' the corner of her dry eyes.

"Some of the saddest stories are of sick or poor people who are unable to look after their own children. The court takes the kids away, and my folks help raise them until they can be adopted or placed in an orphanage. And sometimes when a parent dies…" She pauses, glarin' into each one of our eyes. "It's just too much. And so heartbreaking." She stops talkin'.

My tummy feels jumpy again. I ask, "Why do the courts take the kids away?"

"It's complicated, Catie."

Charley stares at Anna. "What did Gilbert do?"

"Nothing. The boy's parents are in trouble with the law for drinking too much. Your Granny Ivy said he told his teacher about some of the things that happened at home, and well, here he is, living with my parents."

Charlotte and Carolyn roll their eyes at each other. Anna goes on, not noticin' their looks.

"Gilbert would have been better off not to have said anything. You don't go around airing your dirty laundry. People are always gossiping, exaggerating, and making their story bigger than life. That's probably why the courts ripped Gilbert out of his home."

"Did his dad or the judge want to put him in an orphanage?" Claudia asks.

I sit quietly, rememberin' hearin' 'bout the old lady at Mommy's funeral. She asked Daddy if he was gonna put us in an orphanage.

"No. The boy's lucky to be at the farm. This place is much better than an orphanage. Because of my folks, he has a warm bed, food in his belly, and a beautiful place to live."

Claudia gulps. "Will he ever be able to go home?"

"I'm not sure. But whatever has happened to Gilbert, he is probably sad. So, you kids don't be asking him any questions. Besides, my parents prefer that you stay away from their foster children. They don't want them to be any more upset about their lives than what they already are. You stay clear of him unless Granny Ivy or Buck give their permission."

No one says a word.

I better not tell my teacher, Teenage Granny, not even Grandpa, and Granny Grunt. I best not tell anybody 'bout icky GG Dean tryin' to kiss me 'cuz that's airin' dirty laundry. I don't want them yankin' me away from Daddy and my family—like they did poor Gilbert.

My tummy churns.

Marion
December 1992

My belly growls, enticed by the sweet aroma of popcorn. Catherine brought a bag of warm popcorn for her dinner. I gather two bowls for us to enjoy the treat. I am doing quite well on my new diet. I think my stomach has shrunk because I am not as hungry as usual. Unfortunately, my waistline is slow to follow. I toss a kernel into my mouth. We settle into our usual spots, me in my wingback chair, and Catherine on the love seat.

"What did you think and feel after hearing Anna's version of Gilbert's circumstances?"

"Uncertainty, I was afraid of being taken away from my father. I believed Gilbert was taken away for telling what was going on at his home."

I watch her eyes. They barely blink.

"Share with me what you can remember, Catherine. Discussing these events will help recover the emotions behind your memories. Emotional recollection is a part of the retrieval process."

Catherine sets down her coffee cup. She is quiet at first as if profoundly considering my request.

"Marion, I believe it was in the summer of 1963. I was just about to turn seven years old. When I think about those years, although decades in the past, the memories feel close—too close, yet they also feel so far away. I know that sounds weird, but it's true." She shrugs. "As a child, I only knew how to depend upon adults or grown-ups, as I referred to them back then."

A brief smile drifts across her lips. She fiddles with her necklace as she talks.

"It never crossed my mind that I couldn't count on adults to protect me. You know, like family, neighbors, and especially my parents. I never questioned trusting family—until Anna and her relatives came into my life. Somehow, I sensed fear for Gilbert. It became apparent to Charley and myself who was trustworthy and who wasn't."

I roll my lips between my teeth, thinking. "You seemed to have a naturally sharp intuition, even at such a young age. Tell me about your siblings. Were they able to sense the same things as you?

"Yes and no. Charlotte and Carolyn were skeptical. Claudia always focused on everyone's best qualities. And Charley was too young; he followed my lead. I don't believe any of them could sense the evil like I could. They just knew it was different from what we had as a family when our real mom was alive."

"Did you ever see the dark-haired boy, Gilbert again?"

"Yes. Many times. He was there almost every time I went to the farm. He was a little shy, at first, but warmed up. We became best buds. He was a sweet kid with a big heart. I was six or seven when we first met. I think Gilbert was eight or nine. He was tall and lanky, with dark brown hair, longer compared to most boys who wore a Butch or a Princeton haircut. I liked Gilbert's long hair. At first, he was nervous. Twitchy. Afraid I suppose, because Ivy, Buck, Dean, and Anna always watched him—like hawks. I think they were worried he'd tell something. He never had to say a word. I figured things out on my own."

Catherine sets her empty popcorn bowl on the side table, poking through the unpopped kernels with a finger. "Anna and her family wouldn't allow us to ask Gilbert questions. Or inquire about any of the other foster kids for that matter. In the beginning, I never asked about his family, but I always wondered. Anna had *her story* about Gilbert. I learned fast, never to believe her.

She pauses, closing her eyes as a ghost of a smile tips her lips.

"Gilbert and I figured out how to talk in code. We used hand signals or whispers when they weren't watching or while we played hide and seek."

A tear began to swell. Catherine brushes it away, not allowing herself to cry. "I remember the first time Gilbert opened up to me. It was about Buck."

"What did he tell you?"

"He told me they were in the fields working on something. Gilbert had gone off to go to the bathroom. Buck came running up on him, causing him to lose his balance and fall back into his own pile. Buck laughed at him. The same devilish laugh that I'd heard. Gilbert said he could see the evil in him, just like me. Poor kid didn't have anything with which to clean himself. He said he scraped off what he could with a stick. The jerk made him wear those soiled clothes—all day. The smell was bad. And to make matters worse, Buck told everyone over at the farm. Gilbert said most of the men were kind and didn't have much to say. However, one guy who was afraid of Buck made fun of Gilbert. It was humiliating for him, especially being a kid."

Sadness lines Catherine's face. Even in her grief, she let out a small laugh.

"I remember my response to Gilly. That's what I called him. I told him…"

Catherine speaks in a little girl's voice as if she is with Gilbert, "I don't like Buck anyway. He's the real poopy butt."

Her face grows serious again. "Somehow, my words made Gilbert feel better. Afterward, he trusted me. I trusted him as well, regardless of what they did or made us do."

"What did they make you do with Gilbert?" I study her face for any reaction. "Do you remember?"

"I have memories of him, but I can only go so far. Then my mind goes black."

Catherine crosses her arms over her chest, pushing herself back into the corner of the love seat. "I sense darkness—something very dark. Feels like it wants to swallow me."

She grimaces and looks down, rolling the fabric of her sweater sleeves.

"I avoid going there. I'm not sure where *there* is, but it frightens me. Up until now, I've been okay with not remembering."

"Okay, Catherine. Let us continue with what you do remember and see where those memories take us."

Catherine settles back into the love seat, propping her stocking feet up onto the armrest. She closes her eyes, and her arms drop to her sides. After several deep breaths, she relaxes. The memories appear to come with ease. I watch as Catherine unwinds her stories with Gilbert. As she enters into a suppressed memory, her mannerisms and voice mimic a child—Catie.

"The weather is nice, the way I like it sunny. We don't go to Ivy's as much, but when we do visit, Daddy keeps a good watch on us. He's protective when he's around and not working. Maybe even a little more protecting around Anna's weird family, although he has never said anything. Even so, I shy away from Dean and his so-called, sloppy kisses. Anna's family only pretends to be nice so that we aren't so afraid. I know it's only pretend 'cuz eventually, their meanness always comes out. I like to stay outside and play—away from them."

She crosses and uncrosses her feet like a young girl playing. She goes on to describe a scene with her siblings at her step-grandparents home.

"Charlotte asks, 'Okay, who votes for hide and seek?' A raise of hands makes the decision. She lines up twigs in her fisted hand, keepin' the top of the small sticks even, and tells me it's my turn to pick.

"I study the twigs carefully, slidin' one out from her hand. 'It's long. I'm not it.'

"My sister moseys around the circle, givin' everyone a chance to draw. Gilbert touches several twigs before pullin' one out.

"'Aw man....the short twig!' he growls.

"We giggle and tease. 'Gilbert's the seeker. Gilbert's the seeker', we sing. Gatherin' around the safe zone, a telephone pole, at the far side of the backyard, Gilbert rests his face against the pole and starts the count. We all scram, runnin' to our hidin' places. I squat, waitin', as quiet as a church mouse. Gilbert calls out in the distance, 'Ninety-eight, ninety-nine, one hundred! Ready or not, here I come!'

"The shadows in the barn are good coverin'. Someone squeals in the distance. I make my way to the barn door. I peek out, makin' sure the coast is clear. Gilbert chases Claudia in the opposite direction.

"I dart out the door, movin' as fast as I can toward the free post. Gilbert stops. He turns on a dime. Yikes! He's headin' our way. Carolyn runs right behind me. He's on both our tails. Gilbert's a faster runner. There's no way I can out-run him.

"I make my move. I dive to the ground, scurry on my belly in an army crawl, wigglin' side to side, as fast as I can to get under the barbed wire fence. My excitement grows. My arms clear the wire. I rise when a sharp pain stings across my lower back. Barbed wire digs into my skin. Rippin'. I scream."

Catherine shakes her head. Her face twists from pain. She continues, "I keep runnin' and then reach out and touch the pole in the nick of time. 'Yay. I'm free. I'm free. I'm free.' I shout and dance around waitin' for the other kids to come flyin' up toward the free zone.

"A loud, shrill scream catches my attention. I stop my victory dance. I listen to the cry. It's Carolyn! I run back. One hand covers her eyebrow. Blood drips between her fingers onto her cheek. 'Uh, oh.' My guess is she was runnin' but lookin' backwards, and wham! She hit the barbed-wire fence."

Catherine's face twinges, sympathizing with her sister.

"After seein' Carolyn's blood, I feel my pain and reach back touchin' my lower back. A sharp twinge and the sticky blood on my fingers tell the story. *Uh oh, we're in big trouble now.*

"We start walkin' to make our way to the house, knowin' we need to clean up our blood. Claudia pulls me aside and whispers into my ear. 'Oh, Catie, I feel so bad. I yelled out to Carolyn to watch out for the horse. She turned around and didn't see the fence. She ran right into the barbed wire. It's all my fault.

"I wrinkle my forehead not understandin'. 'What do you

mean? How is it your fault? You were warnin' her about the horse.'

"Claudia lowers her eyes. 'Don't tell Dad but I lied; the horse was still in the barn and not in the pasture. She turned to see where the horse was, and it was then she ran into the fence. I wanted to distract her so Gilbert would catch her and not me.'

"'Uh oh! Does Carolyn know you were fibbin'?'

"'I don't think so. Once she hit the barbed wire and started screaming, she probably forgot what I said. Please promise not to tell on me.'

"'I won't tell Daddy.' I turn and lift my shirt to show her my back. "I ran under the fence and got cut too. Do you think we'll get in trouble?'

"'Ick! That doesn't look good, Catie. We better hurry and catch up with Carolyn and the kids and get Dad.'

Carolyn swings the back door open, and I follow her inside. I have my fingers crossed, on both hands, hopin' we won't get into trouble for not payin' better attention to the barbed wire.

"Ivy and Buck smooth it all over for us. Gilbert, too. Buck pats Daddy on the back, sayin', 'Don't let this worry you, Forest. These kids are just having a good old time. Living on a farm and playing hard comes with all sorts of scrapes, cuts, bruises, and wounds of all types. They'll heal, and besides, this kinda stuff will toughen 'em up.'

"My daddy agrees, then takes Carolyn and me outside and over to the hose to clean our cuts and to see if we'll need stitches.

"Buck examines Carolyn's eyebrow after he washes away the blood. The sun's bright and makes Carolyn squint, but the light makes it easy for Daddy and Buck to see the damage.

"'Forest, I think she might need a stitch, but tape will do the same thing and save you a lot of money at the doctor's office. Her eyebrow will cover most of it. I doubt she'll even have a scar.'

"Buck takes a second look at Daddy. 'Hey man, you might want to take a seat. You're looking pale. Feeling all right? You look like you might be feeling a little queasy.'

"'Huh?' I say, lookin' at my daddy. He's more interested in

seein' if Carolyn and me are okay. Daddy pays no mind to Buck's comment of him lookin' pukey. Besides, Daddy looks healthy and has color in his face. Buck's just tryin' to make Daddy look weak like he knows it all, and Daddy knows nothin'. Just when I was 'bout to say that, Buck says it's my turn.

"'Catie, girl, how 'bout you spring on over here and let me and your father take a look at your back?'

"I walk over. Buck inches up the back of my shirt. Ivy hurries over and presses a metal bucket against my lower back. He dips the sponge into the bucket of cold water and then squeezes water down my back to wash the blood away.

"'Well, Forest, looks like Catie lost the fight with the fence. She probably needs three-four stitches, but Ivy here has a nurse friend who taught her how to do butterfly stitches out of white tape. It might not look as good as a doc's work, but it won't cost you an arm and a leg either. Besides, it's on her back. No one is gonna see it.'

"Ivy fixes my cut and tells Anna to keep it dry for the next week, which means I have to scrub up at the sink instead of takin' baths."

Catherine opens her eyes and then shakes her head a little as if gathering her thoughts. "After the barbed wire accident, my dad didn't make us go to Ivy's as often, only when Anna would throw one of her many hissy fits.

"Shortly after that, the fun stopped for Charley and me. However, the scrapes, cuts, bruises, and all sorts of wounds continued, but they weren't accidents. They were intentional. All done in secret." She lowers her head, staring at the rug. "That's when the hush-hush night visits started."

Catherine's eyes widen. Her body jerks. She clamps her eyes tight as if she is hiding. Her breathing rises. Hyperventilation? What is frightening her? What does she see?

"What is it, Catherine?" I move to the edge of my chair.

Her eyes open. I watch as she calms herself. Her breathing slows. Color flows back into her once whitened cheeks. She remains seated and wipes her clammy hands on her lap.

Several moments pass before she speaks. "It's the same familiar feelings." Her body quivers. "Terror—immeasurable fear, like free-falling off a cliff into a dark abyss. It's hard to describe. I feel like I'm on the edge of remembering. I feel the emotions, but then my mind goes black—blank."

She wrings her hands. "Marion, do you mind if we take a break and come back to this subject another day? I don't have the energy to deal with this at the moment."

"Of course, we can stop. However, I want you to know you have more strength than you realize. In time, you will come to understand your resilience. As for now, shall we discuss your relationship with Hunter?"

Catherine jumps at the opportunity to change the subject.

"Yes. Actually, we're doing great." She twists a curl of her hair in her fingers. "I do care for him." She blushes. "He's working on stealing my heart. But I need to be sure. Right now, I have too much spinning around in my head. Most are fears, as you know." She smirks. "But I'm ready to overcome the anxiety and this nagging feeling in the pit of my stomach. That is with Hunter, at least." She bobs her shoulders.

"I am encouraged. Do you want to give yourself a serious chance with Hunter? You say he's a wonderful Christian man. If I recall correctly, you said he was kind, considerate, generous, sensitive…" I glance at my notes. "Let me repeat *your* words: fun, good sense of humor, actively working toward his goals and dreams. You also said he wants the same things in life you do. I believe that sounds like a good foundation." I smirk. "Shall I go on?"

"Marion, wait till you hear the latest. He has made a deal with me."

Catherine goes on to tell me how Hunter tried to kiss her and then left the ball in her court, so she said. I see this as an opportunity to stretch Catherine's ability to trust. This challenge will force her to face her fears and rely upon God as she moves forward in her affections for Hunter.

CHAPTER SEVENTEEN

Catherine
December 1992

I stretch across the floor to grab my flip-flops and shove them inside my already too-full suitcase. My long-weekend winter vacation visiting my sisters, Charlotte and Claudia, is coming to a close. Four days isn't long enough, but I'm grateful for the time I've had. With a quick slam, I force my reliable luggage shut before heading out into the kitchen.

"Wow, that smells delicious," I say, inhaling the smell of bacon, fried potatoes, buttered toast, and freshly brewed coffee. As I traipse into the kitchen, I notice Charlotte perched on the edge of her seat at the kitchen table, sipping on a hot cup of joe. Claudia's busy making breakfast for the three of us before we need to leave for the airport for my return flight to Colorado.

"Thanks for showing me such a nice time. Florida's always a nice break from the cold. And I love seeing my *see-stirs,*" I say, using our exaggerated pet-name for sisters. I give Claudia a big hug, then move on to embrace Charlotte.

"So, Catherine, tell me about these couple of guys you're dating. It's Patrick and Hunter, right?" Claudia chops the vegetables for our omelets.

"Which one do you like the best? You said both were nice-looking. Isn't one of them a big-time FBI agent? It amazes me the type of men you attract. How often do you hear of people dating agents?" She laughs. "That's what Charlotte told me. " Claudia gestures with her head toward Charlotte, who nods in agreement.

"That would be Patrick. He's nice but too pushy for me. I don't like men who are too presumptuous. On our first date, he wanted to hold hands. Yuck. I pulled away and let him know I take dating slow. He seemed taken aback."

"Well, maybe because it's 1992 and the twentieth century, Catherine." Claudia laughs. "You're so prim and proper. Do you think he is more assertive 'cuz he's a cop?"

"Maybe? But he's not solid in his faith, and besides, it looks like he may be getting transferred to LA to deal with the riots in their inner city. But he promised to let me fire a *Tommy* as soon as he could make the arrangements. If I'm honest, I'm more interested in firing a machine gun than I am in spending time with him."

"That's Catherine, all right, all prim and proper, except when it comes to guns. Charlotte points out. "She's like Honey West carrying a small gun in her garter belt, just in case any man gives her a hard time."

We all laugh at the truth in Charlotte's statement.

"So, what about Hunter? Is he the one who telephoned you this week? With the cost of long-distance calls, that conversation must've cost him a fortune. Claudia said you guys were on the phone for over an hour," Charlotte adds.

My stomach feels uneasy, nervous about having feelings for Hunter. I try to downplay my emotions.

"Yes, he called. He's a nice guy, but I'm just not sure."

"Not sure about what? What don't you like about him?" Claudia asks.

"Well,…umm…he's quite tall. And the man's a blonde." I furrow my brow, trying to come up with reasons for my uncertainty.

Charlotte adds a sarcastic, "Hmmm…let me get this right. You don't like the fact that this man is tall, handsome, and blonde?" Shaking her head, she looks at Claudia. "Sounds to me like you've already fallen for him if that's all you can find wrong with him. Or you've lost your mind." Charlotte crosses her eyes then bursts into laughter.

Claudia carries the steaming omelets to the table. "He called four days ago. Did you call him back?"

"No, I wouldn't feel right calling him collect, and I didn't want to make a long-distance phone call on your bill with money being so tight for you, Claudia."

"You could've paid me back. I know you're good for the money, Catie. I mean, Catherine. Sorry." Claudia makes a flat smile of apology.

"Thanks. You know, I prefer Catherine. I haven't gone by Catie for years. Ever since I was eighteen, I wanted, no, needed, to put my Catie name and those years behind me. Too many bad feelings associated with that nickname."

Charlotte takes a bite of toast. "Catherine, would you pass the jelly? How's the counseling going in regards to your *Catie* years?"

"Memories are coming back. They're pretty difficult to deal with…" I feel a lump building in my throat.

"All that stuff with Anna, huh? Do you recall those times when Anna and her family took you to visit that *special church*?" Charlotte raises her brows.

"Yes." My gaze goes unfocused as a rapid slideshow flits across my mind's eye.

"What are you remembering? Was I there?" Claudia asks. Charlotte leans toward me, listening."

I blink, realizing I'm holding my toast in midair. "Trust me.

You don't want to know. Besides, my counselor said, for the time being, it would be unwise for me to share my memories with anyone. She says it's best for each one of us to remember on our own. She emphasized the importance of not influencing one another's recall."

H ours later, after a long flight, I find my way to the baggage claim in Denver. Standing with the other passengers, I scan the numerous suitcases on the carousel, looking for mine. Out of the corner of my eye, I spot Hunter standing behind the roped-off area designated for guests. He's wearing the linen suit coat I love, and his blue dress shirt highlights his eyes. Eyes that are focused solely on me.

I turn and break into a huge grin, even before I see the beautiful bouquet of colorful mixed flowers.

"Hey, Hunter." I wave.

He slips around the cordoned off area to greet me with a big hug. I can't seem to wipe the smile off my face.

"Hi, Catherine. These flowers are for you." He extends the gorgeous bouquet in my direction.

"Wow, Thank you. They're beautiful." I inhale, smelling the variety of scents.

"I'm glad you like them. I wasn't sure if you still wanted me to pick you up at the airport since I didn't hear back from you." He raises his eyebrows. His smile is strained—a tad nervous.

My hearts melts. "Oh, my sister, Claudia, is tight for money, and I didn't want to add to her stress by making a long-distance phone call on her account."

His shoulders soften. I take another whiff of the flowers. Hunter and I stand engaged in conversation. We're so focused on one another that we didn't notice all the passengers collecting their baggage. When I finally look over at the carousel, there is no sign of my suitcase or any waiting passengers.

An hour later, I sit across from Hunter at a local brick oven pizza restaurant. The warm wood and brick décor feel cozy, and the smells wafting from the open oven at the back of the restaurant make my stomach growl. I hold up a menu, scanning the list of choices.

"Thank you for asking the customer service manager to retrieve my suitcase from the left luggage storage room. I can't believe we didn't see them take my bag away."

"I can." Hunter smiles and winks. The light from the candle on the red-checked tablecloth glints against his blond hair.

"I guess we were a little distracted." My face heats. I take another look at the menu to cover my embarrassment. "The selections look delicious. As long as it has garlic, I'll be satisfied." Just the thought of it makes me thirsty. I swallow a quick sip of iced tea.

"Sounds like I'll be eating garlic if we split a pizza."

"Hey, Hunter, please don't feel obligated to eat garlic. I can have them put it on half."

"Won't work," he grins. "Garlic is like onions. If we both eat it, it cancels the other out."

The waitress approaches and offers to take our food order. Before long, our salads and hot, cheesy, pepperoni pizza arrive.

Hunter seasons his salad with salt and pepper before taking a bite. Lowering his fork, without eating, he says, "Umm, Catherine. Do you realize we've been...umm...seeing each other...for a couple of months?" He furrows his brows, jutting his head forward. "Is it okay to say we're seeing each other? Or is it dating?"

"Sure. I'm okay with you saying whatever you'd like." I take a bite of pizza.

"Dating? Or seeing each other?" He probes.

I pause, pondering his words. He lets it go.

"You know what I find odd?" He wipes his mouth. "Unlike most girls, you've never asked me what I drive, where I live, or about my profession." He cocks his head, pressing me for an answer. "Why's that?"

My back straightens. I feel scolded and like I'm not measuring up. "Ah...I guess it's because I'm more interested in getting to know you. We've talked about a million things. Just not those."

I pick a piece of pepperoni off my slice to give myself a moment to think.

I explain, "I figured you worked. And you live in the same community as I do—somewhere near the church. And I've seen your Jeep Wagoneer. I...I'm sorry. I hope I didn't hurt your feelings by not asking?" My stomach stirs at the thought.

"Are you kidding?" His eyes widen. "No hurt feelings here. It's refreshing. I can't tell you how many first dates I've been on where the women asked those three questions in the first thirty minutes."

"Oh." I let out my breath and relax my shoulders. "I suppose I should have asked. After all, I've talked with you about my job, school, and of course, you know where I live and what I drive. Well, now that you've brought it up, I'm curious. Do tell."

Hunter wipes a drop of dressing from the corner of his mouth with his napkin. "I live in a gated community across from the local elementary school."

I nod, indicating I know the location.

"I work in finance. Guess I have several titles, depending on who you ask. There's stockbroker, financial planner, or wealth manager."

"Oh. Hmm. I see. And you drive the Jeep Wagoneer..."

"I have several cars. The wagon is my beater-car, but she runs great. It doesn't matter if it gets scratched. I used to collect cars. I've had several great cars, but now I'm down to only three."

"Oh, really?" I cut up the tomatoes in my salad into several bite-sized pieces. "I was raised in a city where the automotive business was big. I know a little about cars. What kind do you have?"

"Besides my Jeep, I have a classic red Ferrari."

"Chick bait, huh?" I wink.

He laughs, and his cheeks redden. "Well," he says, shrugging his shoulders, "what can I say?"

"And the other car?'

"You've probably never heard of it. It's an older car, a 1964. I bought it right after college. I've had it the longest, longer than any of my other cars."

"Give me a try. You never know." I reach for another piece of pizza.

"It's a 1964 AC Cobra." He says, one eyebrow raised as if expecting me to be unaware.

"Original or kit-car?" I pitch back.

"What?" Hunter's mouth drops open. "You know the car? And the difference between an original, the real deal and…"

"Sure. I said I know a bit about cars." I snicker, entertained by his amazement.

"Wow, Catherine, I am truly impressed. I have to admit, I'm shocked. You could have knocked me over with a feather. I don't think I've ever dated a woman who had a clue about cars, much less Cobras."

"Well, don't be fainting on me." I tease. "I don't think I could carry you to the car."

Catie
Spring 1963

Psst…psst. Anna shakes me, whisperin', "Come on, Catie. Get up." She slides her arms underneath my back and legs and carries me out of my room.

"Whatcha doin', Anna? It's still dark. School isn't till daylight."

"Shhh...shhh."

I'm groggy, half-asleep in her arms while she takes me down the stairs. Bright lights sting my eyes. I hide my face in the corner of my arm.

"Stand up, Catie." She orders and then lowers me to my feet.

I lean against the wall, wantin' to go back to sleep. Anna's fingers squeeze my cheeks.

"Open up." A metal spoon presses hard on my lips.

I squint. "What's that?"

"Cough syrup. You and Charley have been coughing your heads off."

"Huh? I wasn't coughin'. I ain't got no cold." I clamp my lips together.

Anna grabs my arm—hard.

"Don't sass me, young lady! Open your mouth. I won't have you and your brother waking up the whole house. Do as you're told. Now!"

I open, tastin' the sweet cherry liquid. It burns goin' down. She sits me against the wall and walks away. My eyes drift shut, but when I hear a noise, I turn my head to see Anna carryin' Charley into the room. He's sound asleep. No coughin' either. She lays Charley on the floor, so his head rests on my lap.

"Catie. Wake him up. He needs cough medicine."

She gives me the look that says, *do it or else!* I gently shake Charley. He whimpers.

Anna turns sharply. "Don't you make him cry, Catie."

"S-s-shh, Charley, don't cry, just wake up a little, and take this cough syrup."

I look at Anna then back to Charley.

His eyes flutter. "Why we up?" he mumbles and then covers his eyes in the crook of his elbow.

"Cuz, Anna says we've got colds and been coughin'."

Anna is swift. She moves in with the spoon of medicine. It's too big for his mouth.

206

"Here." She shoves me the spoon. She's mad, but I don't know why. "Catie, you better make sure he finishes it all."

I obey.

"It tastes sweet, Charley. It just stings a little on the way down." I ease the spoon into his tiny mouth. He slurps at it and swallows. A little bit dribbles down his chin. I wipe it away with my finger, then lick my finger clean before Anna returns.

May is 'pose to be spring, but it's freezin' in our house. We snuggle together to warm ourselves on the cold kitchen floor. Anna screws the cap onto the bottle before tossin' it and the spoon into her pocketbook. She buttons her coat, then again dashes out of the room.

When she comes back, she's carryin' our coats. Crackin' the back door, she orders, "Get in the car!" She yells in a whisper.

It's jet black outside and hard to see. We wobble to stand. Charley presses up against me for balance.

"Where we goin'?" I ask.

"To a friend's. I don't want you getting the rest of the kids sick. All I need is seven kids sick with colds. Hurry up. Get outside." She waves us toward the car.

We bundle into our jackets and load ourselves into the backseat. Charley falls fast asleep. My eyes struggle to stay open, waitin' on Anna to come to the car. Before long, my head feels dizzy. Everythin' moves in and out of focus—blurry.

The car door opens, causin' the light to flash on. Anna pushes Carolyn into the front seat. She's throwin' a fit.

"I told you, Anna, I don't have a cold. And I wasn't coughing! I don't care what you say. I'm telling my dad when he gets home from work in the morning," Carolyn shouts.

SMACK! Anna sends a backhanded slap across Carolyn's face. My sister's eyes narrow. If looks could kill, Anna would be dead. That's the last thing I remember till wakin' up to the night's cold air rushin' into the car.

The bright overhead light glares into my eyes. I can't see who's pullin' me out of the car. Once outside, someone smacks their hard fist into my back and pushes me toward a barn.

I squint to focus. I recognize this place. We're at Poison Ivy's. My legs feel rubbery, and my eyes blur. Everyone sounds like they're talkin' in slow motion.

Lanterns on the barn walls cast a glow on the old barnwood. Men dressed in hooded black bathrobes stand in a circle. Buck and Dean walk up to Carolyn and me. Charley's fast asleep on a bale of straw. I see some kids, but their faces look fuzzy. Not sure if I know any of them, except Gilbert. I wave.

Dean slaps my hand, sendin' it flyin' to my side. "No talking to the foster kids!" he growls.

"I wasn't talkin'…just wavin'," I explain.

Dean pinches my shoulder—hard. I can't move my neck or arm. Buck moves in beside him and grabs Carolyn and me by our hands, and pulls us toward the circle of men.

My sister pulls away from Buck. "Take your hands off me, you jerk! And leave Catie alone. What's wrong with you, and all these weirdos?" Carolyn's voice fades away.

My legs won't work. They feel soft like chewed bubblegum. I collapse onto the barn floor, fallin' on my belly. Dean walks up to help Buck. The old man heaves me onto my feet, yankin' me up by one arm.

The room spins. Dean laughs a devilish laugh. His eyes change. There's somethin' evil lookin' at me through his eyes. Same kind of wickedness I saw in Buck's eyes on the horse ride. I blink several times. *Am I seein' things?* Nope. The creature is still there. It must be hidin' inside of Dean, lookin' out at me. *Why?*

Sensin' danger, I search the darkness to find Charley, who's still fast asleep.

Again, someone pushes us closer to the other children who are standin' in the center of the barn surrounded by the men dressed in black. Each man, one by one, picks a kid and takes them back to their spots in the outer circle.

It's my turn. I stagger. I'm spinnin' and feel too dizzy to walk straight. Suddenly I'm bein' carried in the arms of a scruffy man whose whiskers scratch my cheek. After he lowers me, he holds me by my shoulders. I'm glad he's holdin' me up 'cuz I don't think I can stand on my own. I fall in and out of sleep.

Carolyn stands near me. She's wide awake. A strange man has her in a full bear hug. Her legs are kickin' to high heaven.

Buck and Dean talk and laugh. Can't make it out. Carolyn hollers. It seems like I'm seein' everythin' from underwater. Their voices are all mumbles. The shabby man turns me around. I fall into his stomach.

"This little one has the right idea." He laughs out his words.

He pushes me out, then steadies me with one hand and unzips his britches with his other hand. He takes out his pee-pee. I lean out of his way so that he can go to the bathroom. Again, laughter.

A man screams! I look toward Carolyn. The icky man has his pee-pee in her mouth. She bites him. Her teeth clenched so hard her head shakes. She has a hold of that pee-pee like a dog fightin' to hang onto a bone. *Why? None of this makes sense. Why would a grown-up man want to pee in someone's mouth? That's nasty.*

WHAM, WHAM...the man hits Carolyn. He slugs her in the head and calls her bad names.

"No...No...you're hurtin' my sister!" I lunge toward her—only to fall to the ground. "Stop! Stop! Stop!" I sob.

Carolyn falls down too. She lays still—there's no movement. They drag her away.

The raggedy-whiskered man grabs my face and tries to make me do what the other icky man was doin' to Carolyn. I choke, gag, and heave. He won't stop. I bite down.

SMACK.

Everythin' goes black.

I wake in what looks like a barber's chair. My arms and legs are roped. I can't move. Buck has a tight hold on my head. He presses his fingers hard into my cheeks to force my mouth open. Then he shoves some rubber thing between my teeth. It won't let my mouth close.

209

What is goin' on? The room spins.

Buck fastens pliers on my back tooth and slowly pulls, then releases, pulls again, releases. I moan a scream. Pain. Awful pain, unlike anythin' I've ever felt before. Tears pour from my eyes, fallin' into my mouth, tastin' of salt.

"You do that again, Catie, I'll do more than a little pulling, I'll rip every tooth out of your head. You hear me?" Buck yells close to my ear. I feel his hot breath on my cheek.

Old mean Dean stands in front of me, arms crossed. Watchin'. Glarin'. He makes an evil smile. He orders Buck. "Turn them pliers onto the inside of her cheek."

The pliers squeeze. I taste blood.

"Wake up." I hear Claudia's voice. I peek open one eye. It's mornin', 'cuz the sun is bright.

"Wake up, Catie. Come on, wake up. You're gonna get in trouble. Anna told you to get up nearly half an hour ago."

I stretch. Rub my eyes. My whole body aches. I moan as Anna comes around the corner.

"Claudia, get moving. I'll get Catie up." She sits on the corner of my bed. "Hey, sleepyhead, you're going to be late for school if you don't hurry."

"What happened last night?" I squeeze my head. "It hurts. Everythin' hurts."

Anna pulls the covers back. "What do you mean? You were as snug as a bug in a rug all night asleep to your little heart's content."

"Huh?" I turn, lookin' right into her eyes. "What about goin' to Granny Ivy's barn? And all those men in bathrobes sayin' the pledge to the allegiance to *Luci*—somebody? They hurt Carolyn and..."

I look over at Carolyn's bed. She's gone.

"Where's my sister?" I demand.

"What are you talking about, silly girl? Carolyn is downstairs having her breakfast."

Anna pets the top of my head like she is pettin' a puppy.

"Sweetheart, you must have had a bad dream. Aww, I'm sorry." Her voice is soft, and her eyes are gentle. "Sometimes, bad dreams cause you to thrash, which can make your body sore. Have you ever had a nightmare before?"

"Don't know. Do nightmares make things sound like they're in slow motion and blurry?"

"I think so. What was your dream about, Catie?"

"Umm…not sure. Kinda…hard to remember. It's fuzzy, and I can't think."

"Well, enough of that, you can tell me later, if you remember. Now hurry and get up. I'll go make you a bowl of cereal." She stands to leave.

I rub my tongue on the inside of my cheek—it stings. I taste blood.

"Hey, what 'bout my cheek?

"What about your cheek?"

I open my mouth and slur my words. "It hurts."

Anna bends down and takes a peek. "Oh my. You must've bitten your cheek during your nightmare. Don't play with it. Keep your tongue off it, and it will be better in a few days."

She walks away toward the bedroom door. Right before she leaves the room, she turns and asks, "Wheaties or Raisin Bran?"

Marion
December 1992

211

C atherine shares her recent memory of having been drugged and abused in a barn. Her hands shred a tissue, and one of her feet taps incessantly. I ask a few questions to pull some loose ends together.

"How old was your sister at that time, and what happened to her? Did she ever say anything about the incident to you?"

"Carolyn's two and a half years older than me, making her about eight, going on nine. And I don't remember ever asking her what happened. Anna convinced me it was a dream. She had an answer for everything—even for me biting the inside of my mouth. I'm not sure what happened to Carolyn. I know they knocked her out, but who knows what they did to keep her quiet? Maybe the same thing they did to me—or worse? We never discussed it as kids, as far as I can recall."

"Do you know what happened to Gilbert that night?"

"I can't say for sure. I remember seeing him when the scruffy man was carrying me to the outer circle. I looked back into the middle of the barn. Gilbert was still standing in the inner circle, waiting for his turn. Once they started hurting my sister, I lost sight of him."

I jot down her answer.

"However, I did call Carolyn last night."

"And?" My stomach growls from hunger. Those carrot sticks didn't last long.

Catherine opens her purse, taking out some mints. "Would you care for a mint? Sugar-free."

"Yes, please." I accept the mint. "Thank you. Were you able to speak with your sister?"

"Yes. I explained that I'm remembering things about Anna and her crazed family. I told her right away that you, my counselor," she points to me, "advised me not to describe any details about anything because it's vitally important for her and Charley to recall their own memories in their own time."

Catherine fiddles with the mint tin. "Carolyn said she understood, but her voice cracked, and I could hear she was... I'm not sure. It sounded like she was upset, maybe stressed. I can't say for sure, but right before we hung up, she asked me if it had anything to do with men in black hooded cloaks in a barn, making us perform oral sex?"

I squirm. "Oh,…and, what did you say?"

"I only said, yes, nothing more really. Except that I was sorry about what happened." Catherine's tears stream down her cheeks. "I wish I could've helped her."

Two days later, I open my office door to let in a new client, knowing it will be Hunter. I greet him with a smile and a handshake.

"Hello. Thank you so much for coming. I thought it was time for us to meet."

His grip is firm yet warm, the right balance. He carries a small briefcase.

"Nice to meet you, Marion." He offers a confident smile.

I motion him towards the love seat. "Please make yourself comfortable." I take my own chair behind the desk. "Hunter, I have a few concerns I would like to discuss with you today."

Hunter takes off his coat and hangs it on the coat rack, revealing a nice Italian wool suit. He settles onto the love seat. He removes a writing tablet and pen from his briefcase, resting them in his lap. I hand him my business card. He takes it, then removes a wallet from his front suit pocket, and offers me his card, which reads, Hunter Stone, Vice President of Investments, from a well known national investment advisement firm. He holds himself very professionally and appears at ease with our meeting.

"Catherine has given me permission to talk with you and is aware we have scheduled this appointment." I shift in my chair to angle my position.

"Although we are meeting for the first time, I feel as if I know you. Catherine has spoken so highly of you. I think you know, or should know, she is crazy about you." My eyes meet his.

His face lights up. I can see why Hunter turned Catherine's head.

He settles into the couch even more. "Well, that is encouraging to hear. I know Catherine thinks a lot of you as well, Marion."

"I have been counseling Catherine for several months. She tells me she has confided in you about some issues from her past involving her recurring nightmare, blocked memories, and her suspicions concerning a stepmother."

Hunter nods. "Yes, I'm very aware. Catherine shares some of what you discuss at her appointments. I find it sad and infuriating at the same time." He leans forward, resting his face in his hands, then looks up.

"I've never known anyone who has gone through such abuse. Well, any abuse for that matter. I come from an all-American family. My childhood was pretty great. Mom stayed home to raise us kids, and Dad worked hard to make a good living. There wasn't much going on in a town surrounded by cornfields."

I understand the picture Hunter is painting as he describes his upbringing—a big contrast to Catherine's childhood. I ease into the subject of the recent memory in the barn.

"Hunter, because of details of the hooded men as well as other surfacing memories with Anna and her family, I believe these experiences point to the occult, individuals who secretly serve and worship Satan. These followers perform and participate in satanic ritual abuse."

Hunter's face turns white. He wrings his hands and sighs deeply. He listens with concentrated focus, taking notes during our conversation.

"Marion, I appreciate you telling me this information. I have to admit; I know absolutely nothing about the occult. I do know I love Catherine very much. I've been single a long time and believe Catherine is the right woman for me. She doesn't fully understand my feelings for her, and I haven't told her yet. I don't want to scare her off. But I am committed to her. She's not ready to learn my true feelings, but I'm willing to wait."

"I appreciate your commitment, but…your dedication needs

to be an *informed* commitment." I pause, allowing the emphasized word *informed* to linger. "The occult is very real, Hunter. It is dark, evil, and ugly. Most people do not want to talk about this reality. This is true for Christians and non-Christians alike. The general public is not informed on the subject because this reality takes them out of their comfort zones." I observe Hunter for his reaction.

He rests his pen on his tablet and steeples his fingers. "I've never given much thought to the authenticity of the occult. It's because I have no experience with it firsthand. I've only heard about it in movies, and Hollywood isn't the best reference. I don't know what to think. Or what to do." He searches my face. "What do you suggest?"

"Hunter, I wish I could say specifically, but I cannot. It is going to take time. The mystery of Catherine's past will be revealed as her memories return. I have confidence in her dedication to the Lord and that she will prevail." I lean forward; my hands folded tightly in my lap. "She is a fighter, but only time will tell how to proceed. I want you to know upfront; this journey is going to be challenging. At times, it will be downright hard. It is going to require strength, courage, and a determination to see this through to its completion."

His eyes are focused, unrelenting, as I explain. "I cannot give you an exact time frame. This type of counseling and healing is difficult under any circumstance, much less a new and blooming relationship. Catherine will need your support. However, if you are unable to be there for her, she should know *now*. As we get deeper into these memories, the emotional fallout will become harder."

I lean back in my chair, wondering what he will decide.

"Please excuse my slang. I feel a need to be direct. So, in summary, here is my question for you, Hunter. *Are you in or are you out?*"

CHAPTER EIGHTEEN

Marion
December 1992

A blast of winter air gushes through the front door, making it challenging to step out into the harsh December conditions. My bare feet touch the cold cement for only seconds while I retrieve the newspaper off the stoop. I cannot scurry back inside fast enough. I place the Denver Post on the breakfast table next to my steeping cup of tea. I stare at the newspaper as if it is a dangerous object. I can barely believe what I am about to do. Search the personal ads?

My mind bats around the emotions of hope, mixed with dread, framed in embarrassment. *How else am I going to meet anyone?*

I have let my circle of friends and clients know I want to meet

Mr. Right, but I am tired of hinting, asking, and now, what seems like begging, for them to introduce me to their eligible bachelor friends. Good-hearted people do not want others to know they have a counselor no matter how fond they are of me.

The front-page index jumps off the newsprint. Personal ads—page 17. I cringe. *How desperate am I?* I answer myself with another question—the same question I had recently posed to a client. 'Are you in or are you out?' If I want to meet anyone, I have to invest in my future by making dating a real possibility. Sitting in my office all day behind four walls is not making myself available.

I open the crisp morning paper, folding it in half and then into quarters to read the want ads. My finger scans the columns as I look for Prince Charming. I circle several clever personal ads before hurrying off to my bedroom to get ready for work. I will follow up with phone calls later.

I suppose everyone tries to say something entertaining in their ads, to make themselves sound intriguing. *What would I say?* I shrug. *Christian counselor, recently lost 20 pounds, loves cats.* Umm. That is not too impressive. Something about my job makes people think I can read minds. They feel awkward and are convicted of every petty offense they have ever committed. A cat lover? Sounds desperate—like an elderly woman. I am going to have to work on my introduction. First impressions can go a long way.

Catherine
December 1992

'My impression of the last few months—is amazing.' I write the words into my burgundy and gold paisley notebook.

Journaling helps me sort through my beliefs and opinions, examining them for accuracy. Feeling somewhat poetic, I keep writing, narrating the truths I have come to know.

I pen, 'I finally understand how the battle for my mind plays out. My downward skid begins with entertaining critical thoughts, usually about myself. My Achilles heel or weakness is being overly self-conscious and thinking I'm not good enough. I'm actually quite tired of my negative self-talk: nevertheless, it has become my banner—raised high. I end up doing the very thing I don't want to do. I mistrust men for reasons that are no longer valid, which sabotage any potential relationships. I'm feeling like I'm my worst enemy.'

I shift my position on the comfy olive armchair, tapping the pen against my lips, before continuing to write.

'It's all too familiar, like a pair of worn-out shoes. My insecurities, coupled with a deceiving enemy, whom I may add, has it out for me. The deceiver is always whispering lies to trick me into acting without thinking. It's a self-destructive cycle: one that has been my dance of defeat over the years.'

The room has become chilly, and I tug the creme, fuzzy throw blanket over my legs.

'I've always been a fighter...when had I become distracted? Had I forgotten how to fight? Thankfully with God's help, I'm not afraid to remember anymore. In fact, I look forward to my appointments with Marion. I'm growing, learning, and experiencing so many things. One is regaining the familiar urge to fight. My battle cry is rising larger-than-life. I'm no longer going to give way to a life in bondage, be intimidated by fear, or accept lies as truth.

'Besides persevering to unearth my memories, I've decided I'm going to take Hunter up on his challenge. After these last several weeks of racking my brain, examining my self-doubts, and battling my fears, I've come to the realization—I am in love with him.'

I draw a small heart next to my last sentence. There—I said it. I admit it and even wrote in down...in ink. I can't hold my

219

smile back as I add one last thing. 'P.S. I'm ready to plant our first kiss!'

The days fly by with my normal routine of work, school, studies, and building a social life.

I laugh with a friend telling her about having to initiate an upcoming kiss with Hunter. The funny thing is, I've never kissed a man. I've always received kisses but never initiated such a forward gesture. This challenge is a new mountain to climb. I make fun with acting out moves of yawning and then wrapping my arm around his shoulder like a school kid. The truth of the matter is, there's a lot of stress and pressure involved with making the first move. Hunter's sly. I suspect he knew exactly what he was doing with his challenge.

He has invited me to a Christmas party at his home this weekend. I've decided that it will be the perfect night for our first kiss.

The evening of the party finally arrives. After an hour of trying on outfits, I decide on a pair of fitted, deep teal, stirrup slacks. I match them with a soft sweater accented with creme colored angora and a few scattered sequins. The outfit is elegant and festive, perfect for a Christmas party. I take extra time with my makeup and hair. My hand shakes while I apply my mascara. I deny my nervousness blaming it on too much caffeine.

I pull up to Hunter's community security gate and punch in the entrance code written on the invitation. The number code triggers the gate, and I'm permitted to enter his neighborhood.

My sweaty fingers press against the doorbell. I ring the bell a second time. Then several more times. No one answers the door.

Music blares, laughter rises, and the beat of a bass drum resonates in my chest. I knock on the door—more like pounding. No one can hear my arrival over all the festivities.

I try the door.

It's unlocked. I slowly open the door and peek inside.

Hunter is within my sight. He's wearing a black collarless dress shirt and his black Italian wool slacks that set off his trim waist and muscular shoulders. He turns, and our eyes meet. An expression of excitement beams across his face. He runs straight in my direction, greeting me with a big welcome hug. He lifts me off my feet and spins me in a twirl. The grin on his face tells me he's in good spirits, or perhaps he has had a few spirits.

As Hunter sets me down, out of the corner of my eye, I catch the sight of people watching us. He places his hand at the small of my back and guides me into the formal living room where his gawking friends await.

"Hey guys, I'd like for you to meet...uhh...my...Catherine." Hunter's introduction is more than enthusiastic, though amusingly awkward. He doesn't try to hide his excitement about me being at his party.

Suddenly feeling like a celebrity, I shake one hand after another. "So nice to meet all of you." One hand feels particularly chilly, but then it's a cold night, I tell myself.

I notice a pair of cute earrings on a blonde woman, the one with cold hands. She wears a form-fitting red dress that accentuates her figure.

I smile at her. "Oh my goodness, I love your earrings. Are they Christmas ornaments? I've never seen anything like those before."

I reach out to touch one. She rears back, making the perfect impersonation of a crazed cat rounding its back and hissing.

Hunter spins me around. "Hey, Catherine, let me take you on a tour of my home."

I gladly accept his invitation. I look back over my shoulder as we leave the room, still in disbelief at the blonde's rudeness. When we're a few feet away, I squeeze his hand and say, "Okay, Hunter, what's up with the blonde chick?"

He ushers me into another room and speaks in a hushed tone. "I'm so sorry, Catherine. I don't know her. The couple with matching sweaters you met are friends of mine. They asked if they could bring a guest. I've never seen her before tonight.

However, it wasn't clear to me until after they arrived that they were bringing me a blind date."

I clear my throat loudly. "And?"

"I told my buddy I wasn't interested. I let him know right away that I was expecting you, being that you and I are...umm, well, I hope we are exclusive. Uhh...right?" Nodding his head, he searches my face.

I purposely avoid eye contact while I sort through my unexpected emotions.

After Hunter's house tour, I make my way more comfortably around his home. I scan each room. Modern. Contemporary. Clean. I make a mental checklist confirming what I want in a man. His home—very clean. Check. His friends, except for one, are warm, friendly, and down-to-earth. My kind of people. Check.

I find myself lingering in front of the open refrigerator, pretending to look for a cold drink. I spot them...capers. A man who knows how to cook will always have capers in his fridge. Another check.

As the final guests say their goodbyes, my mind ricochets to my original plan for the evening. *The kiss.* My thoughts whirl. Questions fly. When? Where? How? Butterflies take flight in my stomach.

I spot the blonde slithering down the hallway, whom I decide to refer to as *Miss Kitty.* I move into action and make a pencil-sharp-point of walking her to the coat closet and the front door. Of course, I take it upon myself to escort her out of the house as Hunter's co-hostess.

Miss Kitty and I have an entire conversation, intense and firm, based on body language and facial expressions alone. No words are exchanged. None are needed. She leaves in a huff. She and her ornament earrings bounce all the way down the front brick stairs.

I don't need to break the silence, but I can't help myself. A quick wave and a syrupy sweet goodbye slip out of my mouth.

The blonde turns and sends a deep squinted glare, colder than the frigid night air. I didn't mean for her to hear me, but I don't regret that she did. But, I admit, exposing my big Cheshire cat smile as I shut the door might have been a bit over the top—too much.

CHAPTER NINETEEN

Catherine
December 1992

I'm thankful to see Miss Kitty leave, although she may not share
the same sentiment.

It isn't long before Hunter and I wave goodbye to the last
guests. We close the door and head toward the kitchen. I stop to
close the coat closet as Hunter goes ahead of me, carrying a few
empty glasses into the kitchen.

We're finally alone.

I spring around the corner, slipping on some spilled wine. My
arms flail, and my legs slide to the side and throw me up against
the wall where I clumsily regain my balance.

Hunter looks up, smiling. "Now that's an entry. Good recovery,
Catherine."

I immediately fake an Olympic gymnast stance; my arms high and back arched. We burst into laughter.

I help Hunter clean up the kitchen, then begin wiping down the counters while he sweeps the floor. He refreshes our wine, then leads me into the great room where we sit, making ourselves comfortable in front of the warm, cozy fireplace.

The threat of another woman and the resulting jealousy confirms my feelings. Regardless of the butterflies in my stomach, I'm determined to plant *the kiss*. My heart fights against my doubt. My nervousness stirs, but I push through my fears and focus on my hopeful excitement.

Hunter jabbers on about the party. It's hard to pay attention. I only hear half of what he's saying.

"I'm glad you came tonight. These...from my car club. I told...knew what a real cobra was...Guys are...impressed...winning points...should have seen...faces."

"Un-huh..."

After a brief pause in the conversation, we stare into the blazing fire's glow. I have to think fast. I take a quick breath.

To gain his attention, I gently put my hand on his chin. Turning his face towards mine, I lean in before I have a chance to rethink it. Or chicken out. I place a soft, lingering kiss against his lips. I pull back and look closely to read Hunter's expression.

His response is instant—a fiery kiss. One I accept.

Marion
January 1993

I embrace Catherine, wishing her a happy new year. I smile after hearing of her recent success stories of overcoming her fears, including her first kiss with Hunter. I am glad they are moving forward in their relationship. I wish I had a budding love story to share. The last few dates I have accepted from the personal ads have been more like a comic strip feature.

"That is great news about you and Hunter, but what about the other guy who works for the FBI?" I inquire.

"Oh, you mean Patrick. Even though the opportunity to fire a machine gun was tempting, I ended our dating a while ago. I wasn't interested in taking that relationship in any direction other than friendship. And who am I kidding? Friendship with Patrick would've never worked." She twists her bracelet several times.

"I mentioned him to Hunter. He made it clear he wasn't interested in getting involved in any dating triangle. He said, 'You need to decide if you want to be with the other guy or me.'

"I am serious about Hunter." Catherine curls up on the love seat. "Marion, I've made some regrettable choices in my past, and I don't want to make the same mistakes with Hunter." She stirs her coffee. "I want to learn from my mistakes without continuing to learn the hard way. You know, the way of the Two by Four Club."

"What is the Two by Four Club?" I inquire.

"It's a club for people who are hard-headed and have to be hit up the side of their head with a two-by-four piece of lumber before they learn the lesson. It's something my Teenage Granny use to say. She was a wise woman. I wish I had her wisdom."

A grin pulls at my lips. "I am entertained by your Grandmother's humor. If I recall correctly, she was not only wise; she was also a Christian. Correct? Was she a part of your life growing up, especially during the time with Anna?"

"Yes, all three of my grandparents were involved in our lives and they were believers. We didn't get to see them as much as we wanted. Anna made sure of that, but Dad tried. We would talk on the phone, sometimes, but Anna made sure to listen.

Not that they were perfect, but they sure were special. Even with my grandparents and my father's advice, who all raised me to understand right from wrong, I still made poor choices. It seems to me that each generation should become smarter. Tell me, Marion, why do you think people keep making the same mistakes over and over again?"

"That is a loaded theological question." I wink. "I suppose we all have regrets. Remember where the Bible refers to our flesh or flesh patterns, meaning self-life, self-sufficiency, or coping mechanisms? These terms all define how we manage or cope with life, making decisions *without* conferring with God."

"Yes. I remember. Teenage Granny would say that's a know-it-all-hard-learner. You might guess—she had occasions to call me that name." She smiles and bobs her head. "But where's God in all of this? I mean where is God when we reject his counsel or don't even bother to ask him and when we're just being a know-it-all?" Catherine takes a sip from her mug.

"God is always there. However, unbelievers are disconnected from him because their spirits are darkened and not in a relationship with God. Remember they are working out of an Adamic spirit."

I push my reading glasses up on my nose. "Romans 8:5 says it well, 'For those who live according to the flesh set their minds on the things of the flesh, but those who live according to the Spirit set their minds on the things of the Spirit.' You can be a Christian and still default to depending upon yourself, instead of God."

Catherine underlines the passage in her Bible. "I know about this subject all too well—totally guilty. I often act without thinking." Her nose crinkles. "I don't like that about myself. I'm making a point to stop, turn, and ask God for his response, versus my standard triggered reaction. This goal is a part of learning from my past and giving up my membership in the Two by Four Club." She snickers.

"Oh, I see, Catherine, this sounds like a reality check." I laugh. "Everyone, if they are honest, is searching for acceptance and significance and security. These foundational needs are fulfilled and built upon in our identity in Christ as children of God. We have free will to make our own choices. There are a lot of bad habits to break and lies to be replaced with truth. You have experienced this firsthand. Still, you are learning that trusting and depending on the Lord is a journey and a process."

CHAPTER TWENTY

Catherine
February 1993

M y relationship with Hunter continues to be an adventurous journey. For starters, finding out his middle name, Wiley, as in Wile E. Coyote, explains a lot about his fun-loving personality.

In light of all my fears and anxiety, Hunter hasn't given up the chase. Despite the obstacles surrounding my reluctance to trust, I'm finding a committed, energetic, and deep love between us. I never thought I'd fall in love again. I feel strengthened and willing to rise to the challenge of overcoming my fears.

It is Valentine's Day. Not exactly my favorite holiday, since it just so happens to mark my wedding anniversary with my first husband, Edward. It's supposed to be a day for sweethearts to celebrate their undying love. Unfortunately for me, I was robbed of those promises, and Valentine's Day has become a dreaded reminder of a failed marriage. My mind battles to overcome my foul mood. Words grapple within me, fighting to fall back into familiar, dysfunctional, and harmful patterns. I push them away.

I hear Marion's voice in my head reciting the words to Philippians 4:8. *Finally, brethren, whatever things are true, whatever things are noble, whatever things are just, whatever things are pure, whatever things are lovely, whatever things are of good report, if there is any virtue and if there is anything praiseworthy—meditate on these things.* I decide to take heed of the scriptures and focus on the good things in my life.

While attending the Sunday morning Bible study, I put forth my best effort with Hunter. He walks down the aisle, passing out a lesson sheet. I secretly slip him a red-foiled chocolate heart, and then when no one is watching, I discretely mouth, "Will you be my Valentine?"

He smiles, pats his heart, and slips the candy into his shirt pocket.

Good job, Catherine. I commend myself for choosing to make the best of the one day of the year I'd like to forget. Yet an undercurrent of emotion still swirls beneath the surface.

I don't remember much of Hunter's presentation or what the pastor preached afterwards. Still, for the most part, I'm doing much better than previous Valentine's Days.

Hunter drives me home and walks me to the door. I fake a half-smile before turning to let myself into my apartment.

He pulls me to his side, placing a lingering kiss on my lips. "I'll be back at six. Dress up—I've got something special planned." He saunters back to his car, and I walk into my apartment once I hear him start his engine.

My emotions burst like a broken dam. In tears, I run into my bedroom and close the door as if I am hiding. A full-fledge-pity-party breaks out with plenty of ranting and raving. Self-doubts. Past regrets. Guilt. Hunter. On and on I go—venting. Once having said my piece, I collapse into a chair, my shoulders sagging.

I call out to the Lord.

It's then I hear the Lord speak into my heart. He quietly answers my questions.

"Catherine, Edward was an old covenant. Hunter can be a new covenant."

"I'm not sure, Lord. I do love him, but my choices in men are not so good—more like rotten. I want the man *you* pick, so I know for sure that he's the right one."

Again, the Lord speaks to my heart. "Edward was an old covenant. Hunter can be a new covenant."

I realize the Lord is telling me that Edward was a past relationship where our covenant had been broken and is now void. And, Hunter could be my future.

"Are you sure, Lord? Did I hear you right?"

The story of Gideon setting out a fleece to confirm he was hearing from the Lord pops into my mind.

"Okay, Lord, *if* this is truly you…" I plead, feeling self-doubt pushing against my mind, "*if* you are giving me the go-ahead with Hunter, then he will ask me to marry him."

I'm shocked by my boldness. I walk to my jewelry box and take out my old wedding band, a row of diamonds easily worn as a cocktail ring. I place it on my left middle finger.

"Lord, if Hunter is the man you are picking for me, and you have been in this all along, he will ask me to marry him."

Pausing, I take a big breath. I twirl the ring around my finger.

"I will take off this old covenant and will put on a new covenant."

Touching my bare left ring finger, my heart races as I wonder if it's okay to be so gutsy. Is it disrespectful to ask God for such a detailed answer? An edgy fear tries to creep into my thoughts. I remind myself God didn't give me a spirit of fear, but one of power, love, and a sound mind.

H unter arrives at 6 pm sharp. He walks with confidence sporting a nice suit, and looks incredibly handsome.

I dressed in formal attire per Hunter's request. I'm wearing an elegant, black lace dress that hugs my silhouette. My hair is styled in long soft curls, cascading off to one side, accessorized with sparkling earrings and a necklace to match.

"Wow, Catherine. You look lovely." His stare fixes upon me. "Do you mind if we take some pictures before we go?"

We take several photos using the camera's timer feature. Hunter presses the button and runs into position. We pose with what I believe to be the perfect smiles.

I feel relaxed and hungry as we drive to Boulder, heading toward The Flagstaff House, a restaurant Hunter promises will be unforgettable.

We arrive and are immediately escorted to our table. Hunter, suggests we order the Chateaubriand for two having dined here before.

The thick tenderloin of beef with a side of béarnaise sauce is fabulous. Tender, juicy, and delicious. With every bite, I close my eyes, savoring each and every morsel."

Hunter smiles. "Catherine, I am amused and amazed at how much you enjoy food. You transform the act of eating a meal into an event. Very special."

He gazes down at my empty plate. The savory beef, garlic mashed potatoes, and a roasted selection of vegetables are gone. Even the au-jus has been wiped clean with a piece of bread.

"Hmm, I think you are even more amazed at how much I can put away."

We laugh.

The waiter approaches. "Would you care for dessert this evening?"

"I called in earlier requesting a special dessert to be prepared for this evening," Hunter informs the waiter.

"Yes, sir, I will check on that right away. Would you care for some coffee to accompany the special sweet you've ordered?"

"Yes, please, black for me, and cream and sugar for her."

The waiter returns with a silver decanter of piping hot coffee, two cups, and a cream dispenser with a matching sugar bowl. He places it on the table, then pours our first steaming cups.

Hunter glances around nervously as if he's looking for the waiter, perhaps hungry for our dessert. I try to reel in his attention by pointing toward the large window.

"Look, Hunter, what a beautiful night sky. There are so many city lights in the distance. I love watching them twinkle."

He briefly looks with a distracted half nod, then turns back. The waiter approaches, carrying a large, elegant, silver platter with a mounded decorative top. He places it on the table directly in front of me. He removes the lid with a sweeping motion, exposing a small gift-wrapped box encircled with roses, red on the one side and yellow on the other.

I'm surprised and bewildered without words.

The waiter backs away, leaving us alone.

"Catherine, I remembered what you said once about the meaning of flowers. Yellow for friendship. Red for love." He smiles. His upper lip twitches slightly.

My heart pounds. *Is this you, Lord?* A large painful lump grows in my throat. I can't speak.

"Catherine, why don't you open the box?" He offers with a strained smile and nervous eyes. Hunter searches my face, attempting to read my expression. I feel frozen. I look at the box. I rub the satin lining of my lace dress under the table, trying to calm myself.

Then it hits me: the gift is shaped more like a watch box. Too large for a ring. My shoulders relax, gently easing the tension around my neck. I remove the gift wrap ever so gently.

Yes, it's a watch. Is it a watch? Why on earth would he buy me a watch? He knows I've lived in Switzerland and have way too many watches.

My nerves ramp back up. My back stiffens. Rubbing my hands together, I pause to smile at Hunter before lifting off the lid.

Puzzled by the unveiling, I tilt my head. "A box inside a box?"

"I know how much you like surprises." Hunter winks.

I begin unwrapping the smaller box.

What is it? A necklace? Earrings? The lingering question—*a ring?* Suddenly, it feels like someone has turned up the heat. The pleasant room temperature closes in, clinging to me. I slowly push open the velvet hinged jewelry container.

CHAPTER TWENTY-ONE

Catherine
February 1993

I peer at the velvet case. Nestled inside the velvet/satin lining, a diamond ring sparkles in the candlelight.

My mouth drops open. Taking in a quick breath, I lift my gaze to meet Hunter's.

His stare is focused, and his jaw tense. He clenches his teeth into a hesitant, hopeful smile.

I'm so surprised, yet not at all surprised. My mind swirls back to my conversation with God.

This is it? This well-planned proposal is my confirmation? Are you saying Hunter is the man I will marry?

Pulling his chair closer, Hunter takes my hand. "If it's too soon, I understand. I can wait. Pleeease don't feel pressured." He fumbles with his words.

My own words catch on the walnut-size lump in my throat. After a few seconds, I choke out, "It's fine. I'm fine. Everything is great. Please—just give me a minute. I don't want to say anything that will take away from the moment."

My mind races. I'm having a major conversation with God.

God, is this the sign? Did you truly change the once-dreaded Valentine's Day into my engagement day? Lord, you are so great!

He leans in close. I know he is seeking an answer.

My eyes flutter closed. "I just need a minute."

Swallowing is still difficult. My thoughts continue to explode like fireworks.

How can I tell him about my conversation with you, God? Do I tell him about Valentine's Day and the past connection to Edward? Surely not now. When? Will he love how you changed this day for me? For us?

Hunter watches my every move, searching, surely uncertain of what I'm thinking or going to say. My heart aches for him as he patiently waits for my response.

"So sorry, Hunter, I'm trying to compose myself." I turn to him, drawing near. I take a deep breath. "I love you."

Hunter smiles and reaches for my hand in his damp hands. He arches his brow as if asking for an answer.

My focus drops to the velvet ring box. A beautiful, dazzling, diamond ring sparkles back—at least a full carat. *Yes*—the word is poised on the tip of my tongue. I want to respond, but realize he hasn't actually asked the question—will you marry me? He continues to stare, waiting for my answer.

"Hunter, I see there's a card."

I release his hand and reach to take hold of the envelope. The back fold shows a rose matching the wrapping paper now laying on top of the table.

"This is beautiful. Shall I read it?"

"Oh, no...that's...that's my proposal." His shakes his head and his brow is furrowed.

Hunter looks down, seeming like he's trying to hide his embarrassment. His face lacks color.

"Well, sweetheart, perhaps *you* should read the card?"

"Catherine, I don't think you understand. That's where I'd written my proposal."

Lifting his chin with my finger, aligning his eyes with mine, I arch my brows, and then smile.

"I know. Why don't you read it to me?"

His face brightens, as if a light just came on. He snaps up straight.

"Oh, man..." He looks at the card and then back to me. "I had this memorized, and now...I can't remember a word I've written." He nervously chuckles. "Okay, Catherine, I'm going to have to read this to you."

Yes, this is it! Lord, you are unbelievable. Oh my goodness—this is it!

His hands tremble as he unseals the envelope.

Hearing his words brings back memories of my friends in the Midwest. We had coined our friendship group as the "Laser Lane" because we were always doing fun and exciting things. Hunter wanted us to have a motto or a saying, yet something more profound, intimate, and more spiritual. Previously, we had played around with a few sayings. Still, as he read his proposal, the words, our motto, came together—promising a bright, shining future.

Taking my hand into his moist palm, he reads his penned words at a slow pace. Glancing up occasionally, he studies my facial expression, looking for agreement and affirmation.

Catherine,

I believe you are God's gracious gift to me, to cherish, to hold, to love, and to protect.

I have humbly accepted His gift and have vowed to serve you all the days of my life.

I believe: "As husband and wife, together, we will soar to heavenly heights, on the wings of the wind, in a chariot of fire."

So on this day, Catherine Kay, I propose to you! Will you marry me?

Hunter

2-14-1993

I dare not keep him waiting a minute longer.

"Yes, yes, Hunter! I will marry you!"

I take his face into my hands and place a prolonged kiss on his lips. Hunter pulls back—beaming. He quickly turns, addressing the tables behind us.

"She said, yes! HA!"

The room breaks into applause.

The entire dining room has been watching us?

Two waiters prance up to our table, both carrying a huge silver platter covered with a variety of desserts. Displayed in the middle is a 'Congratulations' sign, made of golden caramelized sugar.

"Did they all know?" I blush as I scan the room.

"Yah, man."

Like brush strokes on a canvas, Hunter paints a picture of the comedy of errors that were happening behind me.

"We were all sweating bullets. The waiters would stick out their heads from the kitchen, signaling me, Yes or No? I was a nervous wreck. I felt like I was on the worst rollercoaster ride. Every time you'd say, 'just give me a minute', my heart panicked and plummeted. Then, you'd smile or say you loved me and up I'd go again. I believe the whole room was watching and rooting for us. I had prepared to get down on my knee but blew that plan. I was shaking so bad. I was afraid I'd fall over, so I decided to stay in my chair."

We both burst into laughter. Hunter turns, showing me the side of his head, the side not facing me—and it's soaking wet. I cock my head in confusion and amazement.

"How can you only sweat on one side of your head?"

"Who knows, but I think this other side is the *only part* of me that isn't sweating."

The evening continues, a whirlwind of excitement—our conversation laced with joy, and the sweetness of love and desserts. We nibble on several selections. The waiter wraps up the remaining sweets.

While waiting for our car in the restaurant's beautiful foyer, I slip my hand under Hunter's suit jacket to pat his chest. As I pull my hand out, I notice something brown and sticky on my fingers.

"What's this?"

We both examine my hand.

Squinting to focus, he suggests, "Smell it."

"No..." I crinkle my nose in uncertainty. "I don't like the color."

Hunter raises my hand to his nose.

"Hmm...smells like chocolate."

I pull back his coat. A puddle of chocolate has melted down the front of his white dress shirt.

"Is that the red foiled chocolate heart I gave you this morning?"

He tugs on the fabric pulling out the shirt pocket for a better look.

"Must be. What's left of it," he says in laughter. "I told you I was sweating. Big time, like a furnace!"

We laugh with huge smiles permanently pinned in place.

Our car arrives. Hunter hurries to open my door. Once seated and on our way back to Denver, he turns to me. "So, Catherine, what did you think of our motto? 'Together, we will soar to heavenly heights, on the wings of the wind, in a chariot of fire.'"

"I love it. It's perfect."

I shift in my seat for a better angle to see his smiling face. I can't take my eyes off him—or the ring!

Catie
Spring 1963

I'm learnin' not to take my eyes off Anna. Livin' with her is always surprisin', but not the good kind. Charlotte says it's like walkin' on eggshells. Claudia doesn't say much, but always prays. Carolyn says it's a guessin' game 'bout when she'll explode again. Charley and me watch, ready to hide or get out of her way. Daddy says he's gonna make things right with Anna and her kids, but it's gonna take a lot of time and lovin'. But I'm not sure you can love the prickers off a cactus, like Anna and her brats—not to forget her crazy family.

The smell of yummy food fills the house. It smells almost as good as last week's Easter dinner. I love ham and cheesy potatoes.

Anna calls out, "Dinner's ready." My tummy gurgles.

Melinda already sits at the table when I skip into the dinin' room. She eats like a pig, faster than everyone, makin' sure she *always* gets second helpin's. Anna gives her bigger portions too. It seems like when I leave the table, I'm still hungry, except for when I go to Grandpa's and Granny Grunt's house. They let me eat as much as I want. I love goin' to visit them. Daddy says we can visit them every other week, but Anna seems to always come up with an excuse not to go, so we're lucky to see them once a month. The same is true with visitin' Teenage Granny. I keep my lips buttoned about Anna and her weird family. I don't want to be airin' our dirty laundry. I'm scared that Anna will do to me what happened to Gilbert. I don't want to have to go into one of those foster homes or the orphanage.

Daddy bows his head, and after he says grace Anna fills our plates. Charley and me listen to one of Claudia's riddles. She says, "It's May, but what does April bring?" I raise my hand, thinkin' the answer is Memorial Day, the day we get to go see Mommy's grave. Claudia doesn't call on me. She just tells us the answer. "April showers bring May flowers. So what does Mayflowers bring? Pilgrims." I don't get it. It's not funny to me, but the other kids laugh, except for me, Charley, and Shawnee.

Carolyn elbows me. She gives me a heads-up look. Anna's sourpuss face says she's mad 'bout somethin'. I take a bite of my mashed potatoes. Daddy's quiet and distracted. He's not listenin' to Claudia's silly tale. Charley and I laugh and have a pretend sword fight with our forks when Anna gets up from the table to go into the kitchen.

"Hey, Mom," Shawnee calls out. "Can I have some milk?"

Anna comes back, carryin' a small glass of milk in one hand and the salt and peppershaker in the other. She stands at the end of the table as Shawnee reaches for her milk. We go back to eatin' and our chatter.

In a split second, the table flies into the air and flips over. Everythin' flies; food, plates, glasses, and silverware sprawled all over the floor. And all over us.

Is it the ghost from the basement? Has somebody levitated the table?

My guesses are wrong.

Anna stands at the end of the table. Her eyes narrowed into slits. *Uh, oh.* She's havin' another one of her temper tantrums.

I hold my fork in midair, stacked with meatloaf, potatoes, and a couple kernels of corn. I gobble my last bite, knowin' we'll go hungry tonight.

The table rests on top of Claudia's new cat-eye glasses. We all stare.

Anna screams, "Get the hell out of the room!"

Daddy jumps up in disbelief. His eyes flash to each of us kids to see if we're all right. He even nods at Melinda and Shawnee to make sure they're okay. Daddy moves in between Anna and us, then looks to the floor and all the wasted food. He shakes his head and rolls his eyes. I wonder how he's gonna soften all her prickliness with love. Maybe some folks like Anna aren't able to be lovable. I'm thinkin' it's hopeless.

I'd be okay with scoopin' me up some dinner off the floor, but I know that ain't gonna happen. We remain sittin'. Silent. We watch and wait.

Daddy glares at Anna. His eyes narrow. "Good God, Anna, why in the hell did you do that?

Anna screams again with her ragin' eyes focused on Daddy, "You'd better get these kids out of this room before I...." She bends to grab the saltshaker and a big fork. Her hands shake with anger. Salt sprinkles the carpet.

Daddy pushes his hair back with both hands lookin' *bewildered*. That's what Charlotte calls it. I say he looks plum scared. He spreads his arms out in front of all of us kids, includin' Anna's girls. The back of his neck looks wet with sweat. Poor Daddy.

"Come on you kids, why don't you all head upstairs so I can deal with Anna and this mess."

Anna tries to move in closer to us. Daddy blocks her and then motions for us to get movin'.

We dare not disobey, or we'll end up with Anna's fork somewhere we don't want it. Even though Charley is the youngest, four, almost five, he is the first to push his chair out, away from the up-side-down table.

"Come on, Catie, let's go play with my Matchbox Cars."

Like ants marchin' to a picnic, we all head upstairs wantin' to get ahead of the fight stirin' in the air. But unlike the ants, there's no food for us.

Melinda and Shawnee go into a different bedroom to color.

We pounce on Charlotte's and Claudia's bed, except for Charley, who plays with his little cars on the floor. "Rum-m-m-m," he revs the engine, tearin' his car around a make-believe race track. "Errrrr!" He squeals the Matchbox Corvette to a quick stop.

"Great job, Charley," Claudia says.

Glad to have somethin' to distract us, we all laugh.

I turn to Claudia. "It looks like your glasses got busted. Are you sad?"

"Naw, Catie, I only pretended I couldn't see with the school nurse. I thought it'd be cool to have some cat-eyes." She shrugs and crinkles up her nose, kinda sneaky-like, bein' she fibbed about needin' the glasses in the first place. "I can't see out of them anyway. They give me a headache."

The screamin' and yellin' begin downstairs.

CRASH. Somethin' hits the wall and breaks.

Charlotte raises her voice above the fight sounds. "We're gonna run out of dishes if Anna doesn't stop breaking them."

Carolyn makes a funny. "I'd like to break a plate over her head. Maybe knock some sense into her. She's a crazy mess."

We're gettin' used to the fightin'. We talk louder to drown out the racket. Eventually, we fall asleep. We cuddle up in Charlotte's and Claudia's bed, all five of us. No baths, no tooth brushin', no goodnight, sleep tight, and don't let the bed bugs bite wishes, but most of all—no dinner.

The next mornin' we tip-toe down the stairs, lookin' to see if the Anna-tornado has passed. She seems to be in a good mood. Daddy's drinkin' his coffee. They talk 'bout him workin' an extra shift tonight. He says he needs the extra overtime for the holidays.

I waste no time eatin' my pancakes. I have a good appetite this mornin'. Now I understand why Melinda eats so fast. Around this house, you have to eat before the fireworks erupt, and the food gets blown away.

Everyone pretends everythin' is fine, and that the night before never happened. It's just like Teenage Granny said when she taught me 'bout the silly games adults play, the one called, *the elephant in the room*. We ignore the obvious and are happy to have breakfast.

After Daddy leaves for work, Anna comes upstairs holdin' Shawnee's beautiful satin and chiffon layered yellow dress. It's her princess dress. The one I've always wanted to wear.

"Hey, Catie girl, I have a big surprise for you."

"What's that, Anna?" I goggle-eye the pretty dress.

"I'm going to a wedding tonight, and you will be my special guest. And...."

She wiggles the hanger, holdin' the gorgeous dress.

"Do I get to wear Shawnee's princess dress?"

I jump up and wait for her answer. I stare at the pretty yellow dress. It is the most beautiful dress in the whole wide world. I've never worn a dress like that in my entire life. Anna must feel better now, and Daddy says I need to love all the meanness out of her. Maybe this is Anna's way of sayin' she was sorry for her hissy-fit last night?

"If you're good, I told you I'd let you wear it for a special occasion."

My eyes grow wide with surprise, and I reach out to touch the soft-lookin' cloth.

"But first…" Anna pulls the dress away from me. "Do you promise to be a good girl?"

"Yes. I promise. I'll be a good girl."

"That means minding me, doing what you're told. Right?" She pauses, waitin' for my answer. "Well? What do you say, Catie?"

I run and wrap my arms around her waist, squeezin'. "Oh yes, Anna. I'll mind. I'll be a good girl. Thank you, Anna, thank you, thank you, thank you." I dance with excitement, imaginin' how pretty I will look in a real-life princess dress. "Can I go take my bath now and get ready?"

"We don't have to leave for a few more hours. You can wait a bit. I'm going to curl your hair, too."

"Oh, today is gonna be my best day ever." I beam.

Charlotte questions, "What about the rest of us kids? Whose wedding is it?"

"Oh, an extraordinary friend of my family. No one you know. Only Catie will be going. Charlotte, you will be babysitting," she informs her. "Maybe you kids can have a game night?"

It's startin' to get dark. Anna drives into the parkin' lot of a big, beautiful, white church on top of a hill. But we pass right by the church and follow a small dirt road to the bottom of the hill that leads to a small gravel parkin' lot.

A group of people have gathered: older men, pretty women,

and a few kids, all dressed in fancy suits and cute dresses, but none as special as mine.

I feel like a real princess. I gaze down at my shiny patent leather shoes. Even though they belong to Shawnee, they're mine tonight. Shawnee's feet are a little bigger than mine, but Anna stuffed the toes with toilet paper, so they fit just fine. I twist my waist back and forth to make the silky yellow dress swirl.

Anna taps my shoulder and motions with her hand for us to begin walkin'.

I wish my real mommy were here to see how pretty I look. I carefully touch my curls, makin' sure they're still in place.

Anna nudges my arm toward a set of steps. They lead down a hill and around to the side at the bottom of the church. As we approach the end of the sidewalk, we head toward a second set of steps, leadin' into an underground area, like a creepy cellar.

Somethin' doesn't feel right.

"Why are we goin' into these doors and not into the church up there?" I point to the beautiful white church on the hill.

No answer. Anna stretches her neck, lookin' for someone or somethin'. My tummy starts to hurt. It feels like grasshoppers are flyin' around inside. I grab hold of the end of the dress, rollin' the silky hem between my fingers.

CHAPTER TWENTY-TWO

Catherine
October 1993

I slide my hands down the silky fabric of my gown hanging on the door in the bridal preparation room. It is hard to believe our wedding day is finally here. After eight months of making arrangements, I couldn't ask for a more beautiful autumn day. The sun shines brightly, a mirror image of my excitement.

And my wedding dress is a dream come true: satin, lace, and a beautiful form-fitting pencil gown with a train that swirls around to fasten in the front, making two dresses into one. With the train attached, it looks like a traditional wedding dress. A few unbuttoned pearls transform the dress into an elegant evening gown.

Every detail has fallen into place. There's even the bonus of a couple of mule deer munching on the autumn foliage through the chapel's glassed wall. Our photographer captures the moment.

Charlotte, my maid of honor, scurries into the bridal room.

"Hunter and his family have just arrived. He looks incredibly handsome and is excited beyond words," she says, her hands on each side of her cheeks. "I met his parents, Jefferson and Marie. They seem very sweet. His two sisters walked up right as I was leaving. Lee and Harriet are their names? Right?"

"Yes." Is all I muster as I try to sit still.

My dear friend, Diane, is finishing my hair, styling it with cascading soft curls. She bobby pins my headpiece and removable veil into place. "Oh, Catherine, you look stunning. Hunter will be mesmerized by your beauty." She winks and looks to my sister for her approval.

Charlotte beams. "Just gorgeous!" She's so helpful. She notices every little detail and holds no punches as she hustles around making sure everything is to my liking.

Claudia isn't able to attend, but she will sing three songs during our ceremony, which have been prerecorded.

Charley and Carolyn couldn't afford to attend. They said they weren't big on weddings anyway, but they wished us the best.

And poor Jeannine, who I consider my sister, must also deal with my onset of emotions. She's very much a real sister to all of my family, and I'm so grateful she's here. I confide in her that I'm feeling overwhelmed and confused.

"Jeannine, it's not the normal skittish bride sentiment. These emotions are something different. Agitation? Irritation? Annoyance?" I shake my head, feeling uncertain. "And all these negative feelings are toward Dad. But I don't understand why."

At that very moment, my father barges into the room. He irritates me by asking too many questions as if he's my self-appointed, last-minute wedding planner. I know I should be able to deal with his nervous chatter, even if it feels more like an interrogation.

I offer him a few uh-huh's and a couple of umm's, followed by, "Dad, you should probably ask Alice; she's the wedding coordinator. I can't think straight right now," I say with gritted teeth as my stress builds.

Something flashes out of the corner of my eye: a shadow, a silhouette, a…umm…I'm not sure. What is it? The hair on the back of my neck prickles. There's an eerie feeling of someone or something staring at me. I quickly scan the room, expecting to see someone bearing their eyes down upon me. The room is bright; nothing out of the ordinary is present other than my father and sisters scurrying around the room making preparations.

The bridal room suddenly chills. Did someone turn up the air conditioner? I wrap my arms around myself, rubbing my silk bathrobe against my skin to stimulate some much-needed warmth.

A foul scent fills the air. Am I the only one who notices the sour stench? It smells like somebody has a bad case of gas. I turn and pinch my nose, then walk toward the dressing table to put on my white, button-up sweater.

I sense there's something more than my dad's nonstop questioning bothering me. I'm on edge. I can't pinpoint what it is, but the emotional sensations feel ragged. Sharp. And that smell, the stench, causes emotions from somewhere deep inside me to well up. But what are they? My nerves are unraveling.

Focus. Today out of all days is supposed to be the happiest day of my life. Why am I struggling?

My emotions heighten. My feelings are distinctly present, but the words to describe them are out of focus, yet on the tip of my tongue. Anger? Disappointment? No…no, it's more like a relentless rage invading my mind. Rage toward my father.

But why?

The onset of emotions doesn't match my circumstances. These emotions must be something more profound. They must because none of this makes sense.

Charlotte notices the beads of sweat on my upper lip and quickly powders them away.

"Catherine, breathe. I don't think I've ever seen you so edgy. Is everything okay?"

"I suppose it's all the excitement, Char." I lie.

I'm afraid of myself and the extreme outrage spewing from within me. My mind spins with confusion.

Lord, help me. Why's this happening? Cover me with your love, peace and presence.

I do my best to put on a smile. I steer clear of Dad, not trusting what I might say. I spot Jeannine as she comes around the corner carrying a tray with a pitcher of water and glasses. I wave her over to ask a favor, pulling her to the side of the dressing table as Dad walks out of the room.

He shouts over his shoulder, referring to the endearing nickname he gave me as a child. My emotions whirl. "Peanut, Charlotte, Jeannine, I'm going to go say hello to Hunter. I want to see how my future son-in-law is doing. I'll leave you girls to all your primping."

He lets out a chuckle as he passes through the door and out of sight. Charlotte closes the door behind him.

"Jeannine, please keep Dad away from me." Tears fill my eyes. My hands shake. "I feel like I'm going crazy. I don't want to hurt his feelings, but I want to kill him," I say dramatically, though I don't really mean it.

Her eyes widen. "Really? What's he doing?"

"Nothing really, just asking too many questions. I think it's more about me. I'm on the brink of losing it. I don't understand why I'm feeling this way, but there's such a righteous indignation rising within me, insisting Dad should have nothing to do or say about this wedding."

Righteous indignation. That's it, I find the words to describe my emotions, but I haven't a clue as to what is fueling the rage.

Jeannine listens intently and goes to work at fulfilling my request. She does an excellent job of buffering and keeping distance between Dad and myself.

I make excuses to go off by myself for a few moments to gather my thoughts.

"Charlotte, I think I'll take a few minutes to go to the bathroom before I put on my wedding dress."

"Good idea, Catherine. It will be much easier without having to be bothered lifting your dress and train."

Within about five minutes, I pray and pull myself together. Without difficulty and with decades of practice, I'm able to suppress my explosive emotions and keep my thoughts from igniting.

I make a mental note to take this matter up with Marion. I need to get to the bottom of this surge of rage. In the meantime, I'm not going to allow these feelings to spoil this moment. I'm determined to become an excited and elated bride.

My sisters gather around and help me dress, fluff my train, and add a last-minute spritz of perfume before we head upstairs to the chapel.

The music begins. Claudia's voice echoes from the speakers, a song she wrote for Hunter and me. Jeanine starts the procession, followed by Charlotte. Their steps are beautifully paced to the music. They saunter down the aisle to where the preacher, Hunter, and the groomsmen are awaiting.

When the music changes to play my song, *Here Comes the Bride*, I beam with anticipation, then grasp my father's arm. With each step, I float down the aisle where Dad passes me into the arms of Hunter.

Hunter's face lights up, his smile is huge, stretching ear to ear. He squeezes my hands, and when I thought he couldn't look happier, his smile grows.

After the introduction of Mr. and Mrs. Hunter and Catherine Stone, the music 'It's Only the Beginning' by Chicago, penetrates the air, capturing the intent of my heart. A new beginning.

Catie
Spring 1963

"But I want to go in the front entrance of the church on the top of the hill. Why do we have to use these icky cellar steps?" I ask Anna for a second time.

"Catie, this is where they perform the weddings. This is a special room for these types of ceremonies. Besides, we are the honored guests. Through these doors are how they present the *special* people."

I smile, admirin' my princess dress. "I don't know much 'bout all this weddin' stuff, 'cuz it's my very first weddin'. But I sure feel pretty wearin' this dress. I've never worn anythin' this fancy or beautiful in my entire life!" I squeal in excitement and prance my feet in place.

Anna looks pretty too in her form-fittin' lavender dress and matchin' hat. She likes to wear dresses that shows off her figure. That's what my sister Charlotte says.

Anna opens the white doors that smell like fresh paint. We enter the dark, dingy room, and the smell changes. I plug my nose. No one but me seems to notice the horrible stink. And even though it's warm outside, this dark room feels more like a dungeon and feels as cold as winter. I continue to roll the hem of my dress.

Somethin's not right.

Two policemen stand guard, just inside the doors. I recognize the blonde-haired one. I've seen him at the 'Little Store' around the corner from our house. I remember him bein' there the day we bought bug spray. We had a bunch of flyin' ants swarmin' on our front porch. Anna was too friendly with him—then and now.

She smiles at both men. I do the same, wonderin' if they see my pretty yellow dress. They nod at me as we walk down the hallway. It's icky and dark with creepy cobwebs. The room looks like a yucky, unfinished, cellar-like basement with oiled dirt floors. It smells of dampness and dirt, the kind filled with worms.

It takes a few minutes for my eyes to adjust. I see Poison Ivy walkin' toward us at the end of the hallway. She's all dressed up, like Anna. She looks like she has on her Easter clothes with a pretty matchin' light green bonnet.

Torches light up the walls of this big room. Chairs fill both sides of the aisle, also lit by torches on tall poles in the ground. In front of this weddin' cellar church, millions of candles flicker in their holders.

"It's s-o-o-o-o pretty. I can't wait to see the bride." I whisper, but I'm not sure why.

"Catie, we have a surprise for you. Guess what it is?" Anna and Granny Ivy ask.

"What? What is it? I love surprises!" I bounce in place.

"You're going to be in the wedding. You will be the virgin princess!" Granny Ivy starts clappin' her hands, and so does Anna. I join in, 'cuz they're so excited for me.

Granny Ivy pulls me in tight to her side at the same time as she hugs her daughter. "Anna, you have done an excellent job. Catie is perfect for the virgin princess."

Granny Ivy strokes my hair as she winks at Anna. "Darling, your stepdaughter, Catie, reminds me of *you*, on *your special day*."

Anna stiffens and pulls away from her mother. I wonder why Anna's givin' her mother the stink eye. I stare at them.

Anna turns my face towards her and pinches my cheeks. "So Catie, dear, are you excited?"

"Charlotte told me all about the weddin' she attended. She'll be so thrilled to hear I get to be in this weddin'. Is the virgin princess like a flower girl or bridesmaid?"

They both smile and nod. "Yes, but even better," Granny Ivy says.

Now I know why Anna let me wear this princess dress. I start dancin' on the spot. "I'm in the weddin'... I'm in the weddin'!" I sing. "Are you gonna take pictures so Daddy can see me in this beautiful princess dress? I wish he could be here."

"Catie, your daddy couldn't come because he had to work, but he said he's so proud of you. He didn't say anything about the wedding because he didn't want to ruin your big surprise."

"Daddy knew? Daddy knew I was going to be in the weddin? And that I was gonna get to wear the princess dress?" I dance, swishin' the yellow satin and chiffon side to side.

Yes, but you must keep this a secret, so your sisters don't get jealous.

Marion
December 1993

I'm jealous that I cannot be outside enjoying the fresh, crisp air like the students who walk by my office window. I let out a big yawn and stretch side to side to alleviate the stiffness in my back. The day has taken its toll on my muscles. I pour myself a cup of coffee before sitting at my desk. I go through the client files from the last week or so and make additional notes and observations that I did not have time to elaborate on during our sessions. I also fulfill my commitment of doing a year-end summary and assessment.

Catherine Williams-Stone: December 1, 1993
  • Adjusting quite well to married life.
  • Spouse, Hunter, is transitioning well to dealing with her nightmares and associated screams. He is understanding and willing to wake her if she cries out, thrashes, or sleeps later than

usual; often an indication of being caught in a terror dream-mind loop.

• Catherine continues with a full-time job at the dental office. Part-time college classes. Last few months, she has been attending an intensive Biblical counseling program at a local ministry counseling center.

• Maintaining her bi-weekly sessions with an occasional monthly appointment.

• Very open and willing to look into her past. Making promising progress.

• Still a block with her nightmare. Feels stuck, struggles with numbness. Other memories are flowing. Hopeful.

Upon finishing my notes, I sign and date the entry. Closing Catherine's file, I set it to the side, pick up another file, then again stretch the ache in my back.

The phone rings.

"Hi, Marion. It's Catherine. I know I don't have an appointment, but I need to come by and talk to you." Her voice sounds broken and stressed. "I wouldn't ask if it wasn't important. I need to see you."

"I am finishing up some paperwork. If you would like, come by in the next half hour or so."

"Thanks, Marion. You're a lifesaver. I owe you. I'm on my way."

The receiver clicks, leaving a buzz in my ear.

The door abruptly opens. No knock. Catherine sprints into my office. She heads to the love seat and plops down. Her body trembles. Bent at the waist, she crumples over and grips the seat cushion so hard her knuckles turn white. She rocks uncontrollably. I cannot make out her words. She sobs. Groans. Stutters.

Something significant and of great concern must have

happened. Catherine is usually quite composed, often pushing back her emotions, fearful of looking weak. Not today. I stand from my chair.

"Catherine, I am going to sit next to you. What has happened? I want you to know, you are safe. I am right here."

I gently place my hand on her back, patting her with an occasional small sweep. "You allow the pain to come out. Cry as hard as you need. Releasing your emotions is good. It is cleansing."

It takes her about ten minutes of wailing before she slows her sobs, blows her nose, and wipes her swollen red eyes.

"I'm sorry, Marion. I've had the most horrible breakthrough. I can't believe it, yet I do because I kn-know, kn-know it's true."

She takes deep, interrupted breaths. Wadding up her used tissues, she tosses them into the wastebasket. Catherine presses her hands straight out against her thighs several times like she is ironing out wrinkles in her slacks.

"Do you remember me telling you about the counseling course—the internship?

"Yes. You said it was going great. What has happened?"

"A lady from out of town, also taking the course, was teaching on a fairly new method of prayer ministry. It addresses people with suppressed memories. They say it's the latest rave in the counseling world—having miraculous results." She rubs her eyes in between words.

"Yesterday, two facilitators demonstrated a session with a classmate. They asked her to close her eyes and focus on her emotions. You know, the feelings that are triggering her at the moment. Kind of like what you do with me. Well, anyway," she sniffles, "once she was able to connect with her feelings, the instructor asked her to follow those very same emotions back to the *first time* she had ever felt that way."

Looking up at me, she adds, "Of course the Holy Spirit was invited to be present, with her permission. And the second facilitator was taking notes while praying silently during the entire session."

Catherine is now calm. She is focused on telling me about the counseling techniques. I suspect avoidance, delay, and distancing herself from her pain. I do not question her. She needs more time. I continue to listen, watching her description unfold.

"The whole session went well. My classmates and I were amazed at the results. The facilitators explained that the emotions provide a pathway to the memories. While she was in the memory, they questioned what she believed about herself and others. The focus was on identifying the lies. As the false beliefs were identified, they asked the Holy Spirit to reveal the truth. They reworded the question a few times, asking things like, 'what does so-and-so need to know about what she's believing? What is the truth? What is important for her to understand?' Stuff like that."

Catherine's eyes brighten and now look hopeful. "Wow, it was amazing. As the Holy Spirit spoke to the lady, she repeated back his words. The simple truth in her words came pouring out of her mouth. It was like hearing a direct line to God. I witnessed her being healed."

She presses her hand to her chest. "This woman's entire countenance changed. Her body language softened. Her fears disappeared and were replaced with joy. Her facial expressions reflected relief. It was wonderful. The woman said she had struggled with those lies her entire life. Now she could see the truth. She looked stunned but happy."

I try to follow the conversation. "Yes, and…?" I tilt my head gesturing for Catherine to continue.

"It reminded me of the lies I've believed all those years about my mom's death. After the revelation of truth, it changed my life, my heart, and my beliefs about God."

Her shoulders slump, and her eyes brim with tears. Yet, again she manages to calm herself right away.

"Later in the day, a director who was unable to see the demonstration asked if I'd be willing to volunteer as the client. She was aware of my issues with blocked memories and my unsolved nightmare.

"I was thrilled. I jumped at the opportunity in the hope of

259

having another revelation like the one I'd had in Switzerland."

I cock my head, trying to figure out where this conversation is going.

"And did you have a memory surface?"

Catherine stiffens as if someone has knocked the air out of her. She holds up her hand.

"Oh, Marion, this is extremely hard to share. Give me a minute. Just give me a minute."

Her hands shake. She squeezes a tissue, which eases her trembling, followed by several deep breaths. She straightens her back, then stretches over to her book bag and pulls out a sheet of paper.

"These are the notes from my session. You're welcome to take a look so you can follow along."

I take hold of the paper. "Please, continue; what has happened?"

Catherine chokes back a sob.

"I prayed and trusted God and the Holy Spirit to be with me. I gave myself permission to connect with the repetitive emotions I feel during my nightmare. The anxiety. The dread. Then, suddenly I- I- saw myself skipping up a walkway going into some cellar-like church—to attend a wedding."

Her tears pour down her cheeks. She doesn't bother to wipe them away.

"And...Anna kept her word. She let me wear Shawnee's dress, the beautiful, yellow, satin, and chiffon one. It was my favorite. She let me wear it just like she promised. I was so proud."

The tears continue to pour, and her speech stutters through her painful cries. "But right after...the memory went dark. Black. Evil. I had an instant revelation. I-I-I realized, I just knew. I-I-I knew."

Catherine's deep moans fill the room. Grabbing hold of me, she shakes and cries out, "I feel so ashamed. So dirty, so filthy. NO —defiled! Anna and her family deceived me."

She buries her face in my shoulder. "I was in the wedding, Marion. Oh. My. God. I was in the wedding!"

CHAPTER TWENTY-THREE

Catherine
December 1993

I'm still in shock, fighting denial—yet trudging forward after remembering glimpses of my past.

Marion remains diligent in working on my memory recovery. She, like myself, is eager to solve the mystery of my nightmare and lost years. However, it has been a much slower process than I'd hoped.

I appreciate her wisdom. Our friendship has grown as she counsels me. She's intrigued by my recent recall at the counseling center and the new method of transformational counseling.

Marion placed phone calls to the right people in Kentucky, inquiring about this counseling technique of dealing with the recovery of suppressed memories. The founder of the ministry referred my case to his female assistant, Bethany Taylor, who has agreed to meet with Marion and myself.

We've scheduled a four-day, eight hours per day, intensive session in Kentucky, although it will be a month before we can go. We're scheduled for the new year in January. However, on the upside, Marion and I will have time to prepare.

The ministry shipped her the training program, a large box full of tapes, workbooks, and worksheets. I'm thrilled that Marion is willing to take on this continuing education, with me in mind.

I t has been over a week since the counseling incident. I find myself still searching for the courage to talk to Hunter. To tell him what I've remembered. *How will he react?* I don't know how to tell him. It's an awkward conversation, no matter how many times I've rehearsed the horrific description.

Negative self-talk screams inside my mind; *He'll leave you. Who wants to deal with such a crazy past? If he knew what lies ahead…he'd run like a bat out of hell. Save the man the heartache. He didn't sign up for this.*

"Yes, Hunter, I know I said I'd tell you more about…umm… what I remembered, umm…"

Fear overwhelms me as jolts of adrenaline stab through my body. My mind rages, unable to think, unable to form the perfect words.

I mumble what seems like hundreds of "umm's" and "uhh's" before I make an excuse to leave and get myself together.

"Sorry, Hunter, I need to go to the bathroom. I'll only be a minute."

I jet around the corner into the powder room to quietly speak out loud the way Marion had instructed me.

"God did not give me a spirit of fear, but of power, love, and of a sound mind. No weapon formed against me will prosper. I am more than a conqueror in Christ. I can do all things in Christ who strengthens me. So any evil speaking outside my head, you shut up now, in the name of Jesus Christ!"

Having regained control over my mind, I walk back into the living room to share my memory with my husband—at least the part I remember.

Hunter, being sometimes stoic, isn't saying much; he only listens. His lack of conversation suggests that he might be afraid or stressed. I continue describing the details.

To ease the tension, I point out a hopeful resource. "There are people trained in dealing with this type of abuse. Even though I'm unaware of anyone offering this type of counseling in the Denver area, Marion's willing to take the training course."

He pinches the bridge of his nose in thought, taking a deep breath. "I'm fine with that. You need to know before we were married, I talked with Marion about this possibility. I told her then that I was all in and one hundred percent committed." He squeezes my forearm. "And, I'm telling you now, I'm still committed.

He waits until I make eye contact. "I knew from the beginning that something from your past haunted you. You've always been upfront about your struggle. It has never been a secret between us."

I pick at the fringe on a throw pillow. I focus on my fingers, too nervous to look him in the eyes again.

Hunter lifts my chin. "The fact that you are actively receiving counseling and growing in your spiritual knowledge and faith encourages me. I saw from the beginning that you're a fighter and not one to cower before challenges. You never give up in hard times."

Hunter squeezes my hand, then kisses my cheek, and he blinks away his brimful eyes. "You're the best thing in my life, and I know a good thing when I see it."

He winks and offers a smile of encouragement.

"Thank you, sweetie. Before we met, I couldn't imagine marrying again, but the Lord blessed me with you. And the fact that you asked me to marry you on Valentine's Day is a demonstration of God's restoration. He took what was once a sad day for me and turned it into a day of celebration. Valentine's

Day will always be our engagement day and a day reflecting new beginnings."

Hunter pipes in, "Hold on a minute."

He points his finger to the stereo as he walks over. After the click of a few buttons, music flows out from the speakers and fills the room. And it isn't just any song. It's the song that was played at our wedding as we walked down the aisle. A song by Chicago called 'It's Only the Beginning.'

My husband takes me in his arms, and we sway to the music. He guides me into several twirls, my favorite part of dancing ever since I was a little girl. He hums the chorus in my ear. We dance, cheek to cheek, singing, "It's only the beginning."

Hunter reminds me. "We are both truth-seekers and a great team for what lies ahead. Remember our vows? For better, for worse, for richer or poorer, in sickness and in health, till death do us part."

He pulls back slightly to look into my eyes. "And not to forget our motto: Together, we will soar to heavenly heights, on the wings of the wind, in a chariot of fire." He smiles, proud of our battle cry. "The key, Catherine, is that we will be doing this *together*. We'll have a lifetime of new chapters and new beginnings...*together*."

Hunter pulls me close. "I admit I'm entering new territory, so I will need you and Marion to instruct me on what to do and what *not* to do. I want to be there for you, Catherine. We can do this."

We dance to the music, holding tightly onto each other's embrace. In the back of my mind, I know Marion and I will soon depart for Kentucky.

I hold on to the hope of remembering.

EXCERPT FROM BOOK 2
THE UNSPOKEN—SCREAMS HAVOC

Don't miss book two of the Unraveled-Rewoven Trilogy, Ripped: Lies Exposed. Available for preorder now. Keep reading for an exclusive sneak peek.

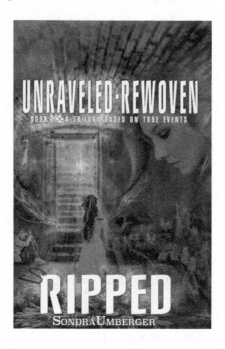

A novel based on true events. Catherine knows all too well that the unspoken-screams havoc. As her life unravels and her past rips at her heart, she chooses to fight once again. This suspenseful story takes you into the depths of an evil realm swirling with lies, abuse, and sheer terror. Yet faith rises and light battles against the darkness, finding perseverance, promises, and power.

Preorder the book now! www.Amazon.com/dp/B08H8TQ262

Catherine
January 1994

My hands tremble as I grab my Bible off the nightstand. My suitcase sits at the foot of our bed; my clothes neatly packed. Our flights are booked and ticketed. All I have left is to finish loading my book bag.

But what about me? Am I ready?

My husband, Hunter, walks into the room. He leans his muscular frame against the doorjamb; his hands tucked into the front pockets of his jeans. I'm going to miss him.

"Do you have everything?" He rakes his fingers through his blonde hair, pushing it off his forehead, exposing his bright blue eyes.

"I think so. Just a few last-minute things to do."

"Do you have your ID? Your plane ticket?"

I smile, knowing his questions hint at his anxiety about my trip. I know because my own anxiety keeps climbing up my throat. "Both my ID and ticket are in my purse."

"How about your camera and film? You'll want to take a few photos if you make it to Churchill Downs. Have you ever been to the Kentucky Derby?"

Hunter talks as if I'm going on a sightseeing vacation instead of traveling to receive serious memory retrieval counseling. It's his way of covering up his concerns. Perhaps fears?

We're both unnerved by the uncertainty of what will be

revealed in Kentucky. I need to know the truth about my past, about those lost years from six to almost nine years old. It's time to solve the mystery of my haunting recurring nightmare.

"Catherine." Hunter's voice pulls me back into the conversation.

"Huh?" I look up.

"I just asked if you've ever been to the Kentucky Derby."

"Nope," I say, stuffing a notepad in my book bag. "I've never been to the Derby. But it's on my to-do list, as well as trying out a Mint Julep."

"Good luck with that." He forces a chuckle. "It's made with 120 proof Kentucky bourbon." He crosses his arms over his chest. "Hard liquor and strong Southern booze don't quite sound like you." He shakes his head. "I don't think you'll like it—at all."

"Oh...bourbon?" I frown. "I thought it was a sweet, minty drink, like chocolate chip, mint ice cream."

"I'm afraid not. But when in Rome? Give it a shot. At least you can say you had a Mint Julep where they run the Kentucky Derby ."

The inane conversation centers me—and distracts me. I'm so grateful for a supportive husband.

The doorbell rings. We both look towards the front door. "It's probably Marion. Would you mind answering that while I finish getting my things together?" I check my watch. "We need to leave in about ten minutes. Let her know where you'd like her to park her car while we're gone."

"Sure thing." Hunter turns to walk out of the room.

"Thanks, sweetheart," I shout over my shoulder. My stomach grumbles with nerves.

I whisk my flight itinerary off the top of the dresser. I fold the paper in half, then quarters, and place it inside my purse. I quickly fasten my heavy suitcase and roll it out into the hallway along with my book bag, leaving both at the top of the stairs for Hunter to take to the car.

Marion's waiting in the foyer when I come traipsing down the stairs. A small suitcase, the size of a carryon bag, sits by her feet.

"Hey, I see you've packed light—unlike me."

"Yes, I am a light packer." She tilts her head and offers a small grin. "How are you feeling, Catherine? We will be in Kentucky by noon. Are you emotionally prepared for the day?" Her face lights up with encouragement.

"You mean, other than this early morning flight?" I roll my bloodshot eyes. "I'm doing fine. I've waited a lifetime for this opportunity. I'm ready to solve this mystery. And now...I'm more psyched up than you know." I say, trying to convince myself.

Hunter breezes by, going upstairs to retrieve my things from the hallway. Within seconds, he tromps back down the steps carrying my suitcase and book bag.

"Ready, ladies?" He offers a hopeful smile.

"Yes," we say in unison.

Marion pats Hunter's shoulder. "Thank you so much for making this trip possible. I appreciate the investment you are making into Catherine's life, as well as into my continuing education." Her smile is humble, her eyes compassionate.

"No, Marion, thank you for being Catherine's counselor and for being there to support her...and me. You are our Godsend." He lowers his head, his tone sincere. "Not many people know how to deal with this type of issue."

I turn to them both. "Thank you. I'm the one blessed to have the two of you in my life."

I lean into Hunter, giving him a big hug. "I'm sure you're ready for the middle-of-the-night screams to stop."

He nods a vigorous yes, and smiles, making light of the fact, but I know we're serious.

Second thoughts arise. Am I opening a Pandora's box? Will I dig up something I don't want to see? Or worse—maybe it's something that should be left buried—forever.

A cold shiver runs through me. I focus on the warmth of Hunter's hand instead of the fear of the unknown shadowing my thoughts.

Catie
Winter 1963

"You're just like your mother, Catie. You're hardheaded. You don't listen. She wouldn't listen either." Poison Ivy raises her voice. "Yes. That's right. We were there that night."

Poison Ivy is nothin' more than a creepy scar-faced, Frankenstein-looking hag. She leaves Charley with the two adults and slithers around her devil dad, Dean. She puts her face close to mine, nose to nose. Her hot breath reeks of icky cigarettes and stinky coffee.

"Yes, darling Catie, we were there. We came in through your mommy and daddy's bedroom window. We waited in their closet until *your mommy* came down the hallway toward her bedroom. She'd just finished serving you kids corned beef and hash for dinner ."

Ivy scrunches up her nose and gives me a straight-lipped smile, mockin' me. "We grabbed her just outside the bathroom."

She pauses to make a huge smile. "You heard her scream. Didn't you, Catie? One of *our* friends put chloroform over her mouth. It knocked her out cold. Then...."

Ivy lets out an evil laugh, just like the others. "Your stupid mother didn't even realize what we'd done. Real easy. Nothing to it. We quickly hid in the bedroom closet and waited."

She laughs her ugly laugh again. "And while the house was full of neighbors, we quietly snuck out through the window without anyone being the wiser."

ABOUT THE AUTHOR

Sondra Umberger, Christian counselor, an ordained minister, and President of Healing Hearts Ministry, Inc., and Connecting to Christ, offers faith-based materials and counsel on how to prevail through the challenges and struggles of life. Sondra instructs on a variety of topics, including confronting and overcoming abuse.

Sondra loves to laugh and enjoy outdoor activities and adventures with her husband in the vast playground of Colorado.

www.ConnectingToChrist.com

Facebook.com/SondraUmbergerAuthor

PRAYER

Prayer

Unraveled-Rewoven is a trilogy inspired by true events. I understand the accounts are challenging, having your eyes open to the darkness. Nevertheless, as you turn the pages, my desire and prayers are that you will find the truth, hope, and healing, as Catherine found through her faith and trust in Jesus Christ.

I am supplying a prayer for those who desire to invite the Lord into their lives.

Dear Father God,

I realize I have made many mistakes, knowingly and unknowingly. I admit my sins brought death and destruction into my life and into my relationship with others and with you, Lord. I do not have the answers on how to change my heart or my path in life. But I believe you do and that you are the answer.

Your word says in John 3:16 that you loved the world so much that you gave your son, Jesus Christ, to pay for our sins and that whoever believes in him would not perish but that you, Lord, would give them eternal life. As best as I can, I now place my trust in you. I am grateful that you have promised to receive me despite my many sins and failures. Father, I take you at your word.

Lord, I confess I have sinned and need your forgiveness. I believe you sent your Son, Jesus Christ, to die in my place, paying the penalty for my wrongdoings. I believe he died on a cross and rose from the dead. I ask you to please fill my emptiness with the Holy Spirit and make me whole. Teach me your ways and show me how to have an intimate and growing relationship with you. Thank you for all you have done. I surrender my life to you. Thank you for hearing this prayer. In Jesus' Name. Amen.

If you prayed this prayer and would like to know what steps to take next to grow in your faith or have questions, you may contact me at www.ConnectingToChrist.com

Blessings,
Sondra Umberger

AFTERWORD

Unraveled-Rewoven
Book One: ROBBED-Innocence Stolen
Book Two: RIPPED-Lies Exposed
Book Three: RESTORED-Truth Unfolds

Author: *Sondra Umberger*

Author's purpose:

This trilogy, based on actual events, is a story of survival and victory.

I have written Unraveled-Rewoven to motivate and inspire you, the reader, to understand that you can be an overcomer and victor in Christ. I encourage you to conquer your conflicts and challenges by examining and applying Biblical truths and Christian principles. Although your struggles may differ from the story's characters, the answer is the same, Jesus.

As you journey into your faith, seek the truth. Take hold of the promises, the power, and the authority given to you as a child of God, to bring victory into the battles you face.

Connecting
To Christ

Published by Connecting to Christ
www.ConnectingToChrist.com

ACKNOWLEDGEMENTS

My deepest gratitude to my husband, Thomas, whose loyal support and understanding helped me fulfill this goal. His continual encouragement made this trilogy come to fruition.

My sincere appreciation and gratitude for Debbi Wise and Gigi Gray for being my writing partners. Thank you for the many hours you spent reading and critiquing these books as the accounts came to life on paper. I love the laughter and time we spend together, giving input and hand-holding through times of fatigue and feeling overwhelmed. You are both such an inspiration to me. Thank you.

Thank you, Chris Richards, for believing in me and the story I had to tell. I appreciate your skillset and the time you invested with me from day one at the coffee shop. Expressed gratitude for sharing your expertise and insights into the world of writing and publishing.

Beta group: MaryJean Cipro, Nicole Adrain Cyler, Tracy King, Roy Richards, and Tom Umberger. Thank you for taking the time to read this trilogy. I appreciate your feedback, suggestions, and encouragement to have this story published. Your inspiring support motivated my completion of these books.

Thank you, Marlene Bagnull, for responding to my email and sending your book: Writing His Answer, as a gift. Your response and invitation to attend the CCWC (Colorado Christian Writers Conference) years ago was the beginning of my journey to becoming an author. Your continued support and encouragement to urge Christian writers to use their voices, via words, to tell a broken world of the good news of Jesus is making a difference.

Thank you, Bob Tamasey, for investing the time to proofread this trilogy. Your support, encouragement, and creative feedback are much appreciated.

My heartfelt thanks to book cover designer: Keno McCloskey. Your artistic and creative ability captured the essence of this trilogy. Your talent shines through each book's cover and reflects the story before the books are even opened. I can't thank you enough for your commitment and perseverance to create truly stunning works of art.

Thank you, MaryJo Gensemer, for the time and effort invested in editing the first draft of book one. I appreciate your expertise and talent and want to wish you success in your editing career—may your cup overflow.

My sincere gratitude and appreciation to Debbie Maxwell Allen, for your diligence, perseverance, and the efforts you invested in editing and formatting. Your encouragement, and hand-holding was a huge blessing to me. I can't thank you enough.

Made in the USA
Monee, IL
13 February 2021

60413714R00173